Terminal Chaos: Why U.S. Air Travel Is Broken and How to Fix It

Terminal Chaos: Why U.S. Air Travel Is Broken and How to Fix It

George L. Donohue, Ph.D.
and
Russell D. Shaver III, Ph.D.

with
Eric Edwards

LIBRARY OF FLIGHT

Ned Allen, Editor-in-Chief
Lockheed Martin Corporation
Palmdale, California

Published by
American Institute of Aeronautics and Astronautics, Inc.
1801 Alexander Bell Drive, Reston, VA 20191-4344

American Institute of Aeronautics and Astronautics, Inc., Reston, Virginia

1 2 3 4 5

Library of Congress Cataloging-in-Publication Data

Donohue, George L.
    Terminal chaos : why US air travel is broken and how to fix it / George L Donohue and Russell D. Shaver III with Eric Edwards.
        p. cm.
    Includes bibliographical references and index.
    ISBN 978-1-56347-949-6
    1.   Air travel--United States. 2.   Aeronautics, Commercial--United States--Passenger traffic. 3. Airlines--United States. 4.   Airports--United States.   I. Shaver, R. D. (Russell D.) II. Edwards, Eric, 1967- III. Title.

HE9787.5.U5D66 2008
387.70973--dc22

2008016644

Cover design by Gayle Machey

Foreword

This is a very disturbing book—and it was intended to be. The crisis in U.S. aviation is far more serious than most people imagine.

Airline deregulation, enacted in 1978, was a huge success in democratizing air travel. It unleashed competition that transformed air travel from a luxury good to an everyday phenomenon for the vast majority of people. But those benefits are now at risk, as the aviation system nears catastrophic overload.

Alfred Kahn, the father of airline deregulation, was one of those who warned at the outset that simply removing obstacles to airline competition would not be enough. Unless aviation infrastructure (airports and air traffic control) were also transformed by market forces, continued growth in affordable air travel would be put at risk. For the first two decades of deregulation, there was enough slack in the system to accommodate growth. But in the last 10 years, we have started bumping up against its capacity limits, both in air traffic control and, increasingly, at major airports.

George Donohue and Russell Shaver have done a masterful job of explaining how we got into this fix, why getting out of it will be very difficult, and how much is at stake if we don't make major changes. While I don't agree with every detail of their prescription, they have framed the debate and pointed to the directions we must go.

All of aviation—airline travel, business aviation, air cargo, and private flying—depends on airports and air traffic control that can accommodate ongoing growth. The status quo model for this vital infrastructure is broken. Donohue and Shaver have given us the best prescription I've seen for fixing it.

Robert W. Poole, Jr.
Director of Transportation Studies, Reason Foundation

Table of Contents

Preface

As this book goes to press, the administrative branch of the federal government is acknowledging the seriousness of an traffic management problem:

> Delays and customer complaints reached record levels in 2007. The President has made it clear that he will not tolerate a repeat of the travel nightmares passengers experienced last summer, and he is personally committed to rooting out the congestion and delays that are plaguing air travel today....

> All of us can agree, however, that we have got to do much more than just treat the symptoms of the problem. We need to address the long-term capacity issues facing our aviation system.... We are spending our time fighting over quick fixes, while Congress drags its feet on real solutions. That needs to change...

> The bill we sent them is a radical departure from the status quo of broken policies and taxes that have produced the current congestion crisis. It uses market forces more effectively at airports to address delays. It modernizes how we pay for airports and will allow us to overhaul the nation's air traffic control system...

> And quite honestly, I am a little tired of all the noise from Capitol Hill about how bad aviation delays are when they are sitting on the sidelines in Washington while passengers sit waiting in airports and on taxiways across the country.... How much longer is Congress going to keep critical aviation issues in a holding pattern? How much longer will their inaction force the American people to suffer unreliable schedules, missed connections, and lost opportunities?... How much longer will they ask Americans to pay the economic cost of congestion and delay – already estimated at $15 billion a year?...

> We have arrived at the cross-roads moment when it comes to the congestion that is clogging our airports and overwhelming our airways. Let's join

together to bring about real change in our aviation system. It is time to end the delays in Washington, and get travelers back on schedule. [Excerpts from "Remarks of the Honorable Mary Peters, Secretary of Transportation, to the Aero Club of Washington" January 22, 2008.]

While we share these sentiments, we do not believe that the administration's proposed policies go far enough. There is significant political opposition to even these proposals from Congress, the airlines, and the airport community.

Professor Paul Woodruff discusses one of the core issues of any democratic society in his book *First Democracy: The Challenge of an Ancient Idea:*

> In [the] First Democracy, ordinary people were asked to use their wisdom to pass judgment on their leaders. Expert voices could be drowned out by people with little training or education. The upper classes complained about decisions made in ignorance, but the heart of democracy is the idea that ordinary people have the wisdom they need to govern themselves. Where do ordinary people get their wisdom? Human nature is part of the story; so are personal experience, tradition, and education. Everyone has personal experience, and everyone soaks up tradition. Education is not so evenly distributed, however, and it may come in conflict with tradition.
>
> In democracy, every adult citizen is called upon to assist in managing public affairs. Therefore, the democracy should see that every citizen has the ability to do so. Citizen wisdom is common human wisdom, improved by education.
>
> The experience of Athens offers clues that should help us find our way...the value of holding leaders accountable, the importance of curbing the power of wealth, the vigor that grows in a state when every citizen feels part of it.

Terminal Chaos was written with the aim of informing the general public of the facts of the air transportation problem. The very nature of modern complex control systems makes this book both difficult to write and perhaps even more difficult to read. We would suggest that it be read on two different levels. The first level is aimed at the reader who is technically educated or has a natural curiosity regarding the details of how a modern air transportation system works. This reader is invited to read the book in its entirety. The second reader is one who is merely frustrated by the inability to have a predictable, comfortable, air transportation trip and would like to know what should be done without bothering to understand why we are making our policy change proposals. This reader may prefer to concentrate on the main chapters and forego the appendices.

At a January 2008 meeting of the National Academy of Sciences Transportation Research Board, we made a presentation to a collection of experts in air transportation and publicly stated that the much advertised space-based Next Generation Air Traffic Management System will add no significant increase in system capacity or, therefore, any decrease in flight delays or flight cancellations! With approximately 100 experts in attendance, no one challenged this statement. The new technology is good, but it will not address our key problems.

The Secretary of Transportation has now capped operations at all three major New York City airports and at Chicago O'Hare airport. We are back to where we were in 1968! These caps should be considered an inefficient "Band-Aid" solution to a deep and systemic problem. In addition, the courts have overturned the New York state Passenger's Bill of Rights on constitutional grounds. The recession of 2008 and the high cost of aviation fuel may provide some relief from summer 2008 delays, but they will return, unless major changes are made.

Air transportation played a significant role in 20th century economic growth, but the industry now is in crisis. No one individual, airport, airline, or government agency created what we are now experiencing, and none of these organizations can solve this problem individually. A collaborative effort among multiple levels of government and industry will be required.

The good news is that this system *can* be fixed. But it will only get fixed with the full pressure of an informed electorate in a democratic decision-making process. In the end, it is you, the traveling public, who will determine whether the vested interests of the few will dictate the future of our national economic growth and the possibility of safe and predictable U.S. air transport in the 21st century. Contact your congressional representatives and make your voices heard!

George L. Donohue
Russell D. Shaver III
April 2008

Acknowledgments

The authors would like to acknowledge the many people and organizations that have made this book possible.

First, we thank the faculty and graduate students conducting research in George Mason University's Center for Air Transportation Systems Research (CATSR). CATSR works closely with the Department of Systems Engineering and Operations Research in the Volgenau School of Information Technology and Engineering and the Federal Aviation Administration (FAA) National Center of Excellence in Operations Research university consortia (NEXTOR). The graduate students have done much of the hard work (which is cited throughout the text) to provide us with data and analysis that strongly influenced our understanding of these issues.

Second, we would like to thank Mike Wambsganss for providing a review of an earlier version of the manuscript and a valuable description of the history of the collaborative decision-making (CDM) process that is currently used by the FAA and the airlines. Michael Kennedy, a senior economist at the RAND Corporation, also helped with the lost consumer surplus calculations in Appendix G. In addition, RAND's Jerry Solenger made significant helpful suggestions regarding the book's organization and structure. Much of the research cited in this book was funded under multiple grants and contracts from the National Science Foundation, the National Aeronautics and Space Administration, and the FAA. The first author was granted a sabbatical leave by George Mason University (GMU) for a stay at the RAND Corporation in the spring and summer of 2007 to finish this book.

Finally, we would like to thank David Hinson, former administrator of the FAA (1993–1997), and Linda Hall Daschle, deputy administrator of the FAA (1993–1997), for providing the opportunity to work from 1994 through 1998 on a critical national problem. They were the best leadership team the FAA has had in over 20 years. Their support and encouragement were critical to the beginning of our campaign to improve the air transportation system for ourselves, for our children, and for our nation.

CHAPTER 1

Introduction: Frequent Flying, Frequent Frustration

When it comes to air travel today, everyone has a horror story.

In June 2007, a Federal Aviation Administration (FAA) computer malfunction in Atlanta, Georgia, led to an overload in the FAA backup computer in Salt Lake City, Utah, which disrupted many thousands of travelers' flight plans across the United States.

In March 2007, the University of California, Los Angeles (UCLA), was playing the University of Florida in the semifinals of the NCAA basketball championship tournament. Delta Airlines reportedly oversold 33 seats on one flight and 40 seats on the next flight from Los Angeles, California, to Atlanta, Georgia. In addition, a flight on the previous evening was cancelled for mechanical problems, and the passengers were rescheduled for the day of the NCAA game as well. The result? Many people who had purchased extremely expensive game tickets and hotel rooms were "bumped" with little compensation or legal recourse, and as a result they missed a critical game that they had hoped to attend for months.

In December 2006, American Airlines similarly inconvenienced passengers on a flight diverted to Austin, Texas, because of weather over its hub airport at Dallas. In February 2007, this happened again, at New York's Kennedy airport by JetBlue Airlines, one of the new breed of "passenger-friendly" airlines. Several years ago, 137 passengers sat cramped on a Northwest Airlines flight at the Detroit airport for nine hours only hundreds of feet from the gate, and they were not allowed to leave the plane. With no food or drink, fresh air, or operating bathrooms, passengers literally were held hostage. And no one would tell them why.

In 2005, a flight loaded with high school students changing planes in Chicago's O'Hare airport en route to San Diego was cancelled due to bad weather, yet there was not a single raindrop within 100 miles of the plane's flight path. Twenty-five students slept in the airport and missed most of the first day of a national academic contest.

And just recently, an American Airlines gate attendant refused boarding to a passenger, claiming he was already onboard and instructing him he would have to purchase another ticket. The passenger was then accused of stealing his ticket and was almost arrested for making a scene. After a stress-filled hour and a half, and a phone call to American's corporate headquarters, the passenger learned that another traveler with the same last name (but a different first name) was on the plane that had since landed in St. Louis. To make matters worse, passengers on that flight were held onboard for 45 minutes while Transportation Safety Administration (TSA) personnel grilled the passenger with the same last name about being a possible terrorist.

And the stories go on and on. For most passengers, air travel today has become one of the most stressful and frustrating experiences of modern life. Even seasoned travelers cringe when they proceed through security to board their flights, never knowing what will happen next. They cannot be sure if their flight will depart on time, will face delays while in the air, or will even occur at all. Flying often becomes a degrading and illogical set of random events in which grown people are treated like children. The traveler is not only subjected to arbitrary rules and regulations, but no one seems interested in providing him with a straight answer. He is purposely kept in the dark about a system to which he willingly gives over his personal rights, his hard-earned money, and even his life.

Unfortunately, these horror stories, and the many like them that occur almost daily, are not isolated incidents caused by random "bad luck" for which nobody is at fault. In short, we have reached a point of terminal chaos. In 2006, 22% of flights were delayed, the highest rate since 2000 (24%), and the average aircraft load factor (LF) (the fraction of aircraft seats occupied by a paying customer) was 80%, the highest in U.S. aviation history! And the trend is heading upward: 16% of flights were delayed in 2003, 20% in 2004, 21% in 2005, and 22% in 2006.

Actually, flight *cancellations* produce more delay time for the passengers than flight *delays*, and high LFs make the system extremely fragile to any disruption and barely able to recover when those disruptions come (and they always come). The year 2000 was the worst year for flight cancellations (3.3%) and, some say, the worst year for bad flying experiences. However, during that year, though flight cancellations were at 3.3%, the load factors were only at 72%. In subsequent years, the numbers show that the passenger experience has been getting increasingly worse, with yearly flight cancellations trending upward (for the most part) and with LFs surpassing the 2000 totals and reaching a historic high of 80%! Why do LFs matter in this case? Because higher LFs lessen the likelihood that the passengers from a cancelled flight will find another flight with available seats within a few hours.

Many people think that all of these delays and flight cancellations are inevitable in a modern industrialized society. If that were true, however, the same poor performance would be seen in the European air transportation system. And it is not. Table 1.1 compares the numbers of total aircraft movements and passengers and the delay averages for several major U.S. airports and comparable European airports [EC 2007 and FAA 2006].

Clearly, from the delay data shown in the table, something in the U.S. system has gone terribly wrong. Although the United States and Europe use almost identical air traffic control systems and almost identical safety standards, the delays in most major U.S. airports are over **ten times larger** than those of European airports. Note also that the transportation efficiency, as measured by the number of passengers moved through the airport, is over 30% higher in Amsterdam than in Newark, New Jersey, with an order of magnitude less delay, and about the same number of operations.

Not surprisingly, the cost to the U.S. public for all of these delays is enormous. Using government estimates of $30/hour per passenger, and new passenger delay metrics under development at the Center for Air Transportation Systems Research (CATSR) at George Mason University, over **108 million hours** of passenger time, or **$3.2 billion**, was lost in 2006 as a result of delays and cancellations. And this loss in U.S. travel time productivity is only the tip of the iceberg. It has been estimated that the U.S. tourism industry lost **200,000 jobs** and **$98 billion** in revenue in 2004 and 2005 because of the poor quality of our national transportation service [*Washington Examiner* 2007]. (The authors estimate that as much a $30 billion of this may be due to our poor air transportation system.) That's right, $98 billion!

On a more individual level, with all of the activities that are packed into people's busy lives today, a single airline flight should not be able to ruin a business trip or sour a vacation, but very often it does just that. And there is scarce redress. Although passengers can complain to the FAA or to the U.S. Department of Transportation (DOT), which oversees the FAA and keeps statistics of customer complaints, both organizations have kept their hands off the quality-of-service (QOS)

Table 1.1   Comparison of Major U.S. and European Airports

Airport	Total aircraft movements		Total passengers		Average delays, minutes
	2000	2005	2000	2005	2006
Frankfurt (FRA)	458,731	490,147	49,360,630	52,219,412	2.7
London (LHR)	466,815	477,884	64,606,826	67,915,403	3
Newark (EWR)	450,187	437,402	34,188,468	33,999,990	28.8
Amsterdam (AMS)	432,480	420,736	39,606,925	44,163,098	0.7
New York Laguardia (LGA)	384,554	404,853	<28,000,000	<29,000,000	23.4
Munich (MUC)	—	398,838	—	<29,000,000	1.8
New York Kennedy (JFK)	<384,000	<353,000	32,856,220	41,885,104	24.3
Madrid (MAD)	—	415,677	32,893,190	41,940,059	1.8

Source: FAA Aviation System Performance and Metrics Data and EUROCONTROL 2007 Performance Review.

aspects of the system since the airline deregulation in 1978. Quite frankly, since its founding in 1958, the FAA has never considered airline service quality to be its responsibility. One of the FAA's primary jobs is to make sure that the air traffic control network—which keeps planes from hitting each other in the air and on runways—is adequately operated and maintained. Despite what many people think, the FAA does not regulate airline schedules, pricing, or passenger satisfaction.

Even though the U.S. air transportation system is a vital part of the nation's economic infrastructure (tourism is the world's largest industry), it is woefully behind the times, is sometimes unsafe, and, worse yet, is largely shielded from public scrutiny. The government and industry have made it virtually impossible to understand why the public is subjected to procedures that make little sense. Even a simple query from a passenger about why a flight is being delayed or cancelled is often met with outright hostility from airline personnel. When offered, their responses are often vague and misleading. And when the going gets especially tough (and many have been in at least one airport line when this has happened), these people simply close ranks, close mouths, and close the door on the passengers—their customers.

And the government knows all about it. But despite all of the recent rhetoric and highly publicized hand waving from the executive and legislative branches, even the government seems unable to stop this almost fraudulent activity. The whole system simply seems to be caught in one big downward spiral.

By contrast, Europe, which faces a much less severe problem, has passed a Passenger's Bill of Rights (see Appendix E). Although the U.S. Congress has discussed passing a similar bill, it has not as yet followed suit. But even if it did, without fixing the underlying problems, the situation will not improve (and might even be made worse).

Sometimes it seems that no one involved in the flying experience—not the airlines, not the government, and not the overseeing agencies (the DOT, FAA, and TSA)—is willing to offer straight answers about flying. The public is simply expected to listen politely, never question, and then obey, much like sheep being led to be fleeced.

And there are no quick fixes for this chaos. The much-touted Next Generation Air Traffic Control System (NGATS), promised to appear sometime between 2015 and 2025, will not fix any of these problems (even if the FAA can actually afford or technically deliver this system). And none of the recently publicized initiatives from Congress or the White House seems likely to do it either.

But it need not be this way. There are solutions, real solutions, that can work. (In fact, there's one called the "30% solution" that the authors believe can quickly and significantly reduce the current congestion at most major U.S. airports.) Accordingly, this book is aimed at educating the traveling public on the U.S. air travel system. Chapters 1–3 provide an insider's look at the background and true nature of the current problem. Chapters 4 and 5 then detail how the situation grew to where it is and why the airlines and others will not (and cannot) simply fix it. Chapter 6 profiles the various winners and losers (aka villains and victims) involved. And finally, Chapter 7 provides numerous recommendations for reversing the trends and putting the air travel system back on the right flight path.

The book is also aimed at those individuals in government and industry who have it within their power to help effect change. Just as the system did not arrive in terminal chaos by the actions (or inactions) of a single individual or organization, it certainly will not be able to depart from it without multiple people and organizations working together.

The basic themes that occur throughout the text include the following:

1) Commercial flying in the United States is often an abysmal experience in which there is a de facto Bill of Rights for the airlines but not for the passengers.

2) The situation is quickly getting worse.

3) The most serious problem is an overscheduling of flights by airlines at key airports, producing delays and flight cancellations that degrade the traveling experience system-wide. (The phrase "overscheduling of flights by airlines at key airports" reappears frequently in this book. To avoid any misunderstanding, note that no single airline is scheduling more planes into an airport than the airport could accommodate. Rather, it is the collective schedules of all airlines flying to that airport that yield "overscheduling." Why this is happening is a major topic of this book.)

4) The United States arrived at this chaotic situation through a series of rational decisions, including deregulation in 1978. However, because no one has overall network control responsibility, decisions are made at the system component level, which often harms overall network performance.

5) Attempts to improve the problem have been hampered by an autocratic air traffic controller's union and legacy airlines that have vested interests in the status quo.

6) For things to change, Congress and the DOT must change some important laws and regulations.

7) Failure to fix the system will have severe economic effects on the overall U.S. economy and will ultimately harm our nation's competitiveness in the world community.

In addition, for those readers who desire more detailed or technical information, appendices have been provided for several topics, including major airline/airport codes (Appendix B), airport performance measures (Appendix C), mathematical support for slot utilization (Appendix D), market-based slot allocation (Appendix E), the European Passenger's Bill of Rights (Appendix F), travel tips for frequent flyers (Appendix G), and tradeoff between passenger delay costs and lost consumer surplus (Appendix H). The interested reader with a technical background might also be interested in the many publications that are available on our Web site: http://catsr.ite.gmu.edu.

Finally, note that the authors have had much personal and professional experience with the issues discussed herein. George Donohue is the current director of the Center for Air Transportation Systems Research and a professor of systems engineering in the Volgenau School of Information Technology and Engineering at George Mason University. Previously, he served as the associate administrator of the FAA for Research and Development, as a vice president and director of the RAND Corporation's PROJECT AIR FORCE, and as a director of the Office of Aerospace and Strategic Technology at the Defense Advanced Research Projects Agency (DARPA). Russell D. Shaver, III, is a visiting research fellow at GMU. He recently retired from the RAND Corporation after more than 35 years. From 1994 to 2000 he served as the chief policy analyst at the Center for Advanced Aviation Systems Development at the MITRE Corporation.

Even more important, having been fellow "road warriors" (or rather "air warriors") throughout their careers, the authors understand and have great personal sympathy for the plight of the frequent flyer and for the deteriorating quality of his/her traveling experience. In short, they feel the flying public's pain. However, they also recognize that a collective, stoic acceptance of the current situation has gotten the U.S. system nowhere. And thus it is the goal throughout the pages that follow to shed the necessary light on the subject to awaken "the sheep" (and maybe even some shepherds) and together demand change. And who knows, before long, perhaps everyone will be able to confidently utter those all-important words when someone heads off to the airport: "Have a good flight."

CHAPTER 2

Passengers Who Act Like Sheep Will Be Treated Like Sheep

Better aircraft have not produced better air transportation. A half-century ago, the Douglas DC-6 aircraft was first introduced. The aircraft (some of which are still in service) could fly at about 300 mph, could carry 100 passengers almost 3000 miles, and had a service ceiling of about 20,000 feet. Over 700 DC-6s were produced from 1947 to 1959, when jets began to replace piston aircraft for commercial service. The DC-6 was a direct relative of the famous DC-3, which was produced from 1935 to 1945, and used the same flight controls and navigation electronics that were developed in World War II and adopted by the FAA (except for flight controls, largely without change) from 1947 to the present.

A modern Boeing B737 aircraft can fly at about 530 mph and can carry up to 190 passengers over 3000 miles. The B737 has a service ceiling of about 40,000 feet. Over 5200 of the B737 family of aircraft have been produced since 1967 (B737-100) to the present day (B737-900). The B737-900 has fully modern flight and navigation computers that can precisely control both its position and time of arrival and has automatic aircraft collision-avoidance electronics onboard. All U.S. commercial aircraft that carry more than 19 passengers have had automatic collision-avoidance electronics since 1995.

Despite the vast differences between the old piston aircraft and the modern jets, scheduled flight times between some major airports have not significantly changed. For example, the distance from New York to Chicago is 635 nautical miles. When flown by DC-6s 50 years ago, the scheduled flight time was a little longer than two hours. **But scheduled airlines today book this as a three-hour flight!**

Both the DC-6 and the B737 can overfly most bad weather. (Of course, the higher operating altitude of the B737 makes it much better in this regard.) The reason that the extra speed, altitude, and flight control advantages of the modern jet aircraft do not provide the traveling passenger with shorter flight times, however, is because of the inefficiency of the FAA's air traffic control system. It simply fails to take advantage of the improvements in speed, efficiency, and flight-control computers that modern aircraft offer. What is worse, the airlines have been padding their published schedules since the early 1990s to mask the delays that the air traffic control system introduces. To their credit, the airlines do this to try to regain some level of predictability for the passengers, even though it reduces their aircraft utilization rate and, ultimately, profitability. But this does not change the simple fact: *the FAA's air traffic control system is basically an early 1960s design using 1980s and 1990s parts.*

Federal Aviation Administration: Shepherd or Shearer?

In June of 2004, Donohue briefed senior officials of the FAA on observed "loss-of-aircraft-separation" statistics that several of his GMU graduate students (Clint Haynie and Yue Xie) had uncovered in the course of their research on the relationship between safety and capacity. They found strong correlations between high delays and the occurrence of "loss of separation" [Haynie 2002; Xie 2005]. [There are international standards regarding the degree of safety that the world's civil aviation authorities will uphold. One of the primary metrics regarding the maintenance of safety is the distance between adjacent aircraft, often called *aircraft separation*. The International Civil Aviation Organization (ICAO), the international organization that oversees all civil aviation authorities in the world, has defined specific separation distances as "safe" for different circumstances. The FAA is obliged to consider these standards. Loss of separation between two aircraft means that safety standards have been violated. The 2005 FAA headquarters audit of the New York Terminal Air Traffic Control center largely confirmed their findings [FAA 2005c]. There were a number of issues raised in the presentation, but the main point was that the airline schedules were overloading the major hub airports and the controllers had great incentive to minimize delay by subconsciously relaxing the separation criteria. It was not clear whether the existing separation standards were correctly set or not, but what was clear was that the agency should not have bent its own rules, but rather changed or enforced them.

This meeting helped set up a follow-up meeting in August with the FAA's assistant administrator for policy, planning, and the environment;

her deputy; the deputy administrator of the FAA; and others. Donohue laid out the case for a proposed research project, to be carried out by the NEXTOR consortia of universities [The FAA's National Center of Excellence for Operations Research, consisting of Massachusetts Institute of Technology (MIT), the University of California (UC) at Berkley, the University of Maryland, Virginia Tech, and George Mason University, with the authors having proposed to also include Harvard University and an airline economics consulting firm, GRA.] to study how auctions could be used to relieve the overstressing of major airports, such as New York LaGuardia, Chicago O'Hare, and Atlanta Hartsfield. Unfortunately, none of the audience seemed very concerned about either the congestion problem or the safety implications of not dealing with high delays.

Instead, more concern was expressed about what the legacy airlines would think about auctions. All agreed that the legacy carriers would not be in favor of upsetting the dominant positions that they had acquired at most of these airports, and the opportunity to provide for more schedule predictability and new air carrier entrants was of little interest to them. When the issue of safety was raised, the response given was that everything the FAA did was safe by definition and that if the air traffic controllers were doing something wrong, that was their problem. In the end, however, with strong encouragement from the DOT, NEXTOR was funded to conduct the aforementioned research.

In November 2004, with research funding from the FAA and the U.S. DOT, GMU and the University of Maryland (with additional technical support from MIT, UC Berkley, Harvard, and GRA, Inc.) conducted a strategic simulation of congestion management at LaGuardia Airport (LGA) (Appendix E). This "human-in-the-loop game" used detailed computer simulations of airport operations to simulate the delays and flight cancellations that would occur under different airline schedule assumptions and U.S. government policies. The game lasted for four days and was conducted on the GMU campus. The participants were actual senior government officials and airline scheduling and policy executives.

This "game" included several major airline, airport, and government officials and specifically focused on the LGA congestion and slot control problem. When Congress relaxed the 33-year-old slot controls at LGA in 2000, massive delays resulted, and Congress allowed the FAA emergency powers to reduce the schedule using a lottery to allocate the slots. The lottery was always viewed as a stop-gap measure, and the agency was coming up to a congressionally set deadline to come up with a more permanent solution. It was clear that the assistant administrator for policy and her deputy favored going back to the old high-density-rule (HDR) slot allocations that were grandfathered to the legacy airlines in 1985.

In the process of running the games at GMU, it was discovered that the FAA had never had a formal policy that set any definition on what was an acceptable delay. When Donohue was in charge of air traffic control moderation at the FAA, it was assumed that delays should be less than 15 minutes, the level at which delay statistics are formally recorded. The FAA's assistant administrator for policy, planning, and the environment stated, however, that as a matter of policy, the 30- to 60-minute delays that were routinely experienced at LGA were acceptable. She also stated that she hoped that technology might help increase the capacity in the future, but as Donohue explained to her, there was no technology under investigation that could reduce delays of this magnitude without better schedule control.

To stress the game players, they were presented with a hypothetical Passenger's Bill of Rights. (And unknown to us at the time, a very similar law had just been implemented in Europe.) The FAA was uncomfortable with this scenario and wanted to make sure the airlines knew this was not its real proposal (but the FAA felt it was much better than the wake-vortex accident incident originally proposed at Chicago's O'Hare airport as a stressful incident to stimulate game play).

What was learned from this exercise was that the FAA acted as if the airlines (and not the passengers) had a de facto bill of rights, including the following provisions:

- Airlines can over schedule an airport's runway capacity to any level they choose, even if this is greatly in excess of the airport's safe operating capacity.
- The FAA will attempt to accommodate these schedules by initially generating excessive ground delay holds and then en-route miles-in-trail-restriction delays and eventually by relaxing the FAA separation standards in the terminal area to keep the resultant airborne delays as small as possible.
- The airlines can over schedule their flights to the point of routinely cancelling flights, so that they can maintain schedule integrity when the delays that they generated in the first place become unbearable to the airline operations centers.
- The airlines have no obligation to compensate passengers for tickets sold for a departure or arrival time that could never be met.
- The FAA has no policy on the level of delay that is acceptable and on an airlines routine flight cancellation policy. Travel predictability is not an FAA policy objective.

- For some unexplained reason, the FAA has a de facto preference for legacy network carriers over new entrants.

By stark contrast, the previously mentioned European Passenger's Bill of Rights (shown in Appendix F) contains some very different major provisions. They can be summarized as follows (http://news.bbc.co.uk/1/hi/business/4267095.stm):

- **Overbooked flights**—Passengers can now get roughly double the previous compensation if they are bumped off a flight. This compensation must be paid immediately. In addition, these passengers also must be offered the choice of a refund, a flight back to their original point of departure, or an alternative flight to continue their journey. They may also have rights to meals, refreshments, hotel accommodation if necessary, and even free e-mails, faxes, and telephone calls.
- **Cancelled flights**—Passengers must be offered a refund of their ticket, along with a free flight back to their initial point of departure, when relevant, or alternative transport to their final destination. They also have rights to meals, refreshments, hotel accommodation if necessary, and free e-mails and telephone calls. In addition, airlines can only offer a refund in the form of travel vouchers if the passenger agrees in writing. Refunds can also be paid in cash, by bank transfer or check, and if the flight's cancellation is "within the airline's control," the airline must pay compensation within seven days.
- **Delayed flights**—Airlines may be obliged to supply meals and refreshments, along with accommodation, if an overnight stay is required. If the delay is for five hours or more, passengers are also entitled to a refund of their ticket with a free flight back to their initial point of departure, if relevant.

Unfortunately, from the authors' experience, this concern for the flying public expressed in Europe's Passenger's Bill of Rights has been, and continues to be, seemingly absent at the FAA and other "responsible" organizations. And the U.S. public, like good sheep, simply continue to graze.

"And Now, an Important Safety Announcement" . . . or Not

While at the FAA, Donohue attended a set of research briefings in the United Kingdom, at the Cranfield University, regarding aircraft evacuation and fire safety. During those briefings, it was mentioned that the standard international onboard safety announcement—"In the unlikely event of a water landing, your seat cushion can be used as a flotation device"—actually concerns a highly unlikely occurrence. What is not announced is that modern planes with their thin skins will probably sink in water immediately after a high-velocity impact. Passengers would have little time to escape, let alone use their cushions for flotation. Thus, it was asked at these meetings why this façade is maintained when a much more hazardous, but frequently survivable, threat exists: fire on the ground. The researchers had no real answer other than that a potential swim in the ocean was less scary to most passengers than the prospects of dying from fire.

Although the fact is unknown to the majority of flyers, *toxic smoke inhalation from fire is the most likely cause of death from a survivable crash.* Thus, it is the hazard that is of most concern to many safety experts. Nevertheless, the airlines are not required to supply passengers with commercially available smoke hoods (even though they are routinely available to private pilots, occupy a space about the size of a frozen orange juice can, and cost less than $100 a piece). In addition, when Donohue asked why the airlines were not required to give fire briefings on how to use potentially mandated onboard smoke hoods, he was told that the airlines objected to this requirement because it would scare the passengers and could decrease demand for flying. Amazing! Obviously, a full review of the commercial airline safety procedures (and specifically those regarding smoke inhalation) is in order.

The absence of requiring child safety seats on aircraft, a common requirement for automobiles, is another example of undue airline influence on the leadership of the FAA. The airlines were concerned that they could not afford to give the seat away for a child safety seat and the requirement to pay for the seat would depress leisure passenger demand. The FAA analysis that justified not requiring these mandatory safety devices was that young couples would drive cars if they could not afford to fly and that driving was less safe than flying. If one uses the Royal Society of the United Kingdom's safety statistics (that base relative safety on exposure time instead of miles traveled), however, one finds that flying and driving are almost equally safe.

Another common safety misconception is that any able-bodied passenger should be able to open the over-the-wing evacuation door in the case of an emergency. Flight attendants make a big deal about ensuring that passengers sitting in these rows are willing to "open the hatch" if an incident occurs. However, the truth is that not only do many of these doors weigh 50 pounds, but most pull **inside** the plane. And tests at Cranfield University have shown that during a crisis passengers rush the emergency door, pinning the person who is trying to open the door against the fuselage, thereby making the door's opening impossible.

A final safety area in which passengers are treated like sheep is the use of electronic devices onboard aircraft. When asked, airline officials cite government regulations and say that cell phones and laptop computers cannot be used on planes because they interfere with navigation systems. This is not totally true. It is a myth that began when pilots experienced glitches in their instruments during the early days of cellular phones, and they blamed the phones. The FAA has never been able to confirm these fears, and thus private pilots routinely use their computers close to navigation equipment without any problem. (On the other hand, it is a good practice not to use cell phones when the airplane is at altitude because they can disrupt the telephone companies' switching software logic.) Likewise, CD players, iPods, PDAs, handheld video games, and laptop computers have never been proven (at least to the authors' knowledge) to interfere with the technical workings of an airplane—an airplane that is designed and built to withstand a direct lightning strike.

By the way, there is also no real reason why laptops must be removed from their cases to be scanned at the airport security checkpoint. X-rays easily can see through laptop carrying cases. However, the 1988 terrorist bomb that exploded on Pan Am Flight 103 over Lockerbie, Scotland, was planted in a radio, and officials consider laptop computers to be "radio-like." But the truth is that only chemical-detecting systems are designed to detect explosive chemicals, and frequently these machines are not being used to "check" exposed computers. The good news is that new technologies are becoming available that will be able to check for bulk explosives far better and faster than today's chemical trace systems. The question is, will the government invest in replacing the current time-consuming and costly to maintain security systems with these new technologies? Or will we continue to follow the flight path of the DC-6 and choose to remain behind the technology curve?

Transportation Security Administration: A Modern Maginot?

Prior to September 11, 2001, the FAA was in charge of airport security rules and regulations. Repeated attempts to penetrate our security system in the mid-1990s (while Donohue was in charge of security research) showed that Inspector General agents were able to slip guns and knives through the airline-owned and -operated security systems in place at that time. With the explosion of TWA Flight 800, Congress began appropriating $100 million/year to develop explosive detection systems for use by the airlines at our airports. For a while, many believed that the TWA explosion was a repeat of the previously mentioned Pan Am explosion several years earlier. It was subsequently determined, however, that the TWA incident was not a terrorist bomb but a center-fuel-tank explosion.

Nevertheless, the FAA did develop high-technology bulk and trace explosive detection systems, many of which are in use today. At one major acquisition review meeting held with the integrated product team (IPT) tasked with the research and development (R&D) of airport security systems, the results of the authors' prototype operational test and evaluation (OT&E) of a number of new security systems were presented. One IPT leader mentioned that the tests were proving to be successful and were providing the data on acquisition/maintenance cost and training requirements for the new systems that the airport and airline community had requested. He further stated, however, that he had been hearing concerns from the manufacturers that, after significant investment on their part (in addition to a significant investment by the government to partially fund the R&D required), they were getting no orders from the airlines, which owned and operated airport security prior to 9/11.

Bob Baker (meeting cochair and a senior vice president of a major airline) was asked why the airlines were not buying the equipment that the authors had developed, especially because the authors successfully answered all of the industry questions. He stated that now that the airlines clearly understood the higher costs of procuring and maintaining these new systems (in addition to the longer training time and higher salaries that would be required to operate them), they simply did not pass any rational cost-benefit-ratio investment criteria. Quite frankly, the old systems provided a basic level of deterrence, and if deterrence failed, it was anticipated that only a few aircraft would ever be blown up by terrorists. And the airlines could buy insurance for those rare cases at far less cost. Admiral Irish Flynn (another meeting cochair and a retired officer in charge of the Navy SEAL program) also added that there were many ways for a terrorist to circumvent any of these machines, and if the public wanted these machines for a sense of security, the government would have to assume the airport security responsibility. Ironically, this is exactly what happened after 9/11. (Baker was correct; the government quickly limited the airline responsibility to just the lives lost on the aircraft, and their insurance paid for those losses.)

Interestingly, a former inspector general of the Department of Homeland Security has written that the post-9/11 security system is not performing any better than the airline-operated/FAA-inspected systems tested prior to 9/11 [Ervin 2006]. And a recent study published by RAND [Jackson et al. 2007] elaborates on Admiral Flynn's observation already mentioned.

As long ago as 1830, German General von Clausewitz observed, *"If you entrench yourself behind strong fortifications, you compel the enemy to seek a solution elsewhere."* The French learned this lesson the hard way. After World War I, they spent nearly a decade and a considerable amount of their national wealth constructing the Maginot Line fortifications between France and Germany. This effort was supposed to prevent another German invasion and provide safety to the French population. But this was a false sense of security. The German army went around the Maginot Line in five days in June 1940.

Today, the U.S. airport security system is much like a new Maginot Line defense strategy. Not only is it still leaky (as all systems will always be), but it is extremely expensive for the airlines to pay for out of the passenger ticket tax. Even though this tax was sold as the passengers paying for their own security, this money subtracts from the airline's profit margins as the ticket price is carefully selected to extract the maximum that the market will bear (referred to by economists as the "market clearing price"). In short, this is lost profit for an industry that is defaulting on its union pensions and on other legitimate debts in bankruptcy courts. Many U.S. national air carriers live on the brink of bankruptcy or are in constant jeopardy of going out of business. The nation simply cannot afford to let a critical service provider pay for an inherently leaky defense system that is primarily in place to make a public statement about government resolve to counter international terrorism. It seems that the needed upgrades to the system should be both employed more rationally and be paid for out of the general tax fund (and not out of the airline/air passengers' pockets).

In addition, as passengers continue to stand in the airports' long security lines (which arguably offer little real security), it is easy to think of the many airports that have been bombed in Europe over the last 30 years. Ironically, the long security queues are not only adding to passengers' transit block time but are actually providing potential terrorists with a large collection of people as a "high-value, soft target" and in a place that has national target symbolism. Passengers have shown that they are willing to be lined up and treated like sheep.

CHAPTER 3

A Typical Flight and Why It Is Often Delayed

An Inside Look at "the Machine" Behind a Typical Flight

Welcome to Mutton Airlines! Although passengers probably never realize it, a typical flight starts with the airline's selection of the "equipment" (i.e., the type and model of the plane) to be used for travel. This choice is often predetermined by the airline at least five years prior to an aircraft's flight departure time, at the time that the airline placed orders for new aircraft. This acquisition decision is, of course, made in light of great economic and regulatory uncertainty, leading to fleet mixes that can be significantly off optimum for the current conditions. In any case, three to six months before a flight's departure the airlines must settle on a schedule, which will define the departure time a passenger ultimately selects. The airlines construct these schedules knowing that the shifting economic conditions, competition, government regulations, and fuel prices can alter significantly in the interim.

Within three weeks of a flight's departure, the airline route manager will be looking at the number of unsold seats on that flight and the fares that the competition is offering. And the manager will start changing the ticket prices up or down to both fill the plane and extract the highest price the market will bear. In addition, as that departure gets closer, this fare might change hourly, making it highly likely that passengers on the same flight will have paid a wide range of prices for the same ticket. Suckers!

Roughly six hours before the flight, the dispatcher at the airline air operations center (AOC) will look at the weather forecast for the nation and look at the effect of adjusted schedule changes of all of the other airlines. This will be done through the FAA Air Traffic Control System Command Center (ATCSSCC), located in Herndon, Virginia, close to Washington Dulles International Airport. The FAA will also be looking at both the weather and the expected airline-schedule-induced congestion at major airports and ATC sectors (i.e., the expected controller workload). The FAA will estimate what the actual airport arrival rate (AAR) might be over the next six hours and notify the airline AOCs of the daily ground delay program (GDP), if any, that will be put in place for that particular day. The airlines will then individually start delaying or cancelling flights to match the actual network capacity.

The overall approach with the FAA and the airlines is "collaborative"; each airline is, in effect, a player in a poker game where the flights to be delayed or cancelled are the chips. The FAA is the effective dealer. Any flight might be given a green light by the airline, or it might be "sacrificed" (i.e., cancelled) to make the rest of the network work as well as possible in a systemically overscheduled system. And when bad weather occurs, the delays and cancellations get worse. This is because the U.S. FAA, unlike the rest of the airline world, allows for smaller aircraft separation standards for good weather, and the airlines develop schedules with the same optimistic assumption. Although weather fronts are often blamed for delays, the top of most fronts is usually well beneath the altitude that modern jet aircraft routinely fly. And even if the tops do reach flying altitudes, there are almost always safe routes through the front.

However, the data show that the FAA frequently imposes GDPs whether or not there is bad weather ("congestion" GDPs). And even if the FAA does not, the airlines routinely use the excuse of FAA bad weather delays to justify their cancellations no matter what (as surely there is bad weather somewhere in the United States at any given time). This relieves them of any responsibility for the flight decisions that they actually made regarding a flight. But the FAA does not dictate to the airlines which flights to delay or cancel, and for good reason. The FAA has no information on the value of individual flights to the airlines or the consequences that would arise in terms of schedule integrity, availability of flight crews, etc. Thus, for the FAA to make these decisions without understanding these consequences would be the worst option available.

If a flight is lucky to get off the ground within 15 minutes of its schedule (and it has about a 75% chance of doing so, on average), it is considered to be an on-time departure. Most airline schedules have included a delay pad that has been getting larger each year to mask the effects of system overscheduling and the FAA's failure to increase its air traffic controller's productivity or the airport's maximum capacity (by mandating the use of new technology and aircraft separation procedures that allow aircraft to safely fly closer to each other under all weather conditions). In addition, limited radio-frequency spectrum assigned to the FAA for flight control also limits the number of sectors that the FAA can have, and antiquated aircraft separation techniques limit the number of aircraft that any one controller can cognitively deal with. Accordingly, there are a number of major airports in the United States that will give a flight only a 50% chance of an on-time departure in the evening hours.

The pilot will then communicate with a sequence of air traffic controllers as he/she guides his/her aircraft from taxi out, takeoff, climb, level flight, descend, land, taxi in, and park the aircraft. A large number of controllers whom the pilot will talk to are federal employees who typically earn higher salaries than many physicians, lawyers, engineers, and pilots. But to do that, they do have to put in a long five-hour day (approximately). The basic requirement for their job is a high school education, and they are using World War II technology AM radios to talk to the pilot (at their own insistence, by the way). And despite over a half-century of Civil Aeronautics Administration (CAA) FAA intent, there is almost no transfer of data between the FAA ATC system and the aircraft that is even closely comparable to that of only digital cell phone or the Internet [CAA 1956]. This knowledge ought to make passengers rest especially easy as they sit back in their undersized seats, feel the circulation begin to leave their cramped legs, and fly through the air at very high speed.

Finally, in the not-so-unlikely event that a flight is significantly delayed or cancelled, the passengers can take comfort in knowing that they have no legal rights to compensation for loss of time or missed business meetings, weddings, or family funerals. Instead, the airline will matter of factly explain to passengers that although it took and spent their money as soon as they booked the flight (maybe months in advance), the passengers did not actually purchase a contract for transportation at a certain time. Rather, they simply bought a *best effort* lottery ticket that the airline has few obligations to fill. Of course, to be fair, each airline's actual "conditions-of-carriage" is different. (Each airline's detailed passenger contract for carriage is on file with the DOT.) But, to be sure, all print them in very tiny type.

Well, thanks again for flying Mutton Airlines! Good luck finding the luggage. Bah-bye.

Delays and Cancellations: Just How Bad Are They?

Once a month, the Department of Transportation (DOT) publishes air transportation statistics on an interesting Web site: www.airconsumer. ost.dot.gov. Here one can find tables that list the percentage of flights that are on time by major airport, airline, and time of day. One can also find a list of scheduled flights that are substantially late over 80% of the time. Sometimes referred to as the "Hall of Shame," it makes one wonder why these are even called scheduled flights and why the DOT allows the airlines to continue selling tickets for these flights. Table 3.1 is a partial list of flights in August 2007 that were late more than 45 minutes over 80% of the time [using Bureau of Transportation Statistics (BTS) data]. Frequent flyers take heed and take evasive action as appropriate!

These flights are not the worst, however. Statistics show that as the delay levels increase at any given airport, so do the number of flight cancellations. These are often the result of the already mentioned FAA-imposed GDPs, attributed to some bad weather somewhere in the United States (or more likely the result of excessive congestion at major airports). These cancellations are frequently a stop-gap response for excessive flight delays and are initiated to regain airline schedule coherence. Furthermore, as discussed elsewhere, the authors' data show that these routine airline flight cancellations cause more loss of passenger time and travel predictability than do the delays themselves. Table 3.2 is the DOT August 2007 report for airline flight cancellation statistics. Note especially that five airlines cancelled more than 3% of their flights in that month, and the overall cancellation rate was 1.9%.

For several reasons, the delays that passengers experience as the result of flight cancellations are not part of the government's 15-minute On-Time-Performance (15-OTP) database. (DOT/FAA uses a 15-minute delay threshold for declaring a flight delayed. DOT's delay database is primarily derived from flight departure and arrival data. If a flight in cancelled, it has neither a departure time nor an arrival time. This might be satisfactory to assess air traffic control performance, but it is grossly deficient for assessing passenger delays.) To explain, several new metrics that have been developed by Danyi Wang at GMU are introduced here [Wang 2007].

Figure 3.1 shows that passenger complaints are far higher for those experiencing flight cancellations than for those whose flights were only delayed. Dividing the number of complaints by the number of disruptive activities, the ratio is approximately **ten times** as many complaints when flights were cancelled than when flights were simply delayed. Furthermore, by normalizing the passenger delay statistics for

Table 3.1   Selected August 2007 Flights That Were Almost Always Late (BTS Data)

Carrier	Flight number	Origin airport	Destination airport	Scheduled departure time	% Flights arriving late	Average minutes late
Atlantic Southeast	4361	AEX	ATL	1750	100	69
Atlantic Southeast	4530	ATL	HHH	2004	100	64
Express Jet	2185	ACK	EWR	1415	97	117
Atlantic Southeast	4178	ATL	TRI	1600	96	71
Atlantic Southeast	4410	HPN	ATL	1855	96	82
Air Tran	228	BWI	SEA	1950	95	67
Air Tran	229	SEA	BWI	2305	95	55
Atlantic Southeast	4340	ATL	MYR	1900	95	60
Comair	5680	JFK	SYR	1635	94	69
Atlantic Southeast	4816	ATL	EWR	1900	94	81
Comair	5077	PHL	ATL	1900	94	64
Atlantic Southeast	4536	ATL	CHA	1705	94	51
Atlantic Southeast	4731	EWR	ATL	1905	91	77
Atlantic Southeast	4312	PIA	ATL	1615	91	58
Delta	413	JFK	SEA	1900	90	90

(Continued)

Table 3.1   Selected August 2007 Flights That Were Almost Always Late (BTS Data) (*Continued*)

Carrier	Flight number	Origin airport	Destination airport	Scheduled departure time	% Flights arriving late	Average minutes late
AirTran	440	ATL	MKE	2125	90	72
Atlantic Southeast	4822	ATL	MYR	1452	90	58
AirTran	203	CAK	LGA	1912	90	57
Atlantic Southeast	4525	ATL	GNV	1524	90	53
Atlantic Southeast	411	ATL	GNV	1803	90	73
Delta	1251	ATL	SEA	2130	90	59
AirTran	372	ATL	LGA	1721	90	71
Atlantic Southeast	4339	SWF	ATL	1730	90	72
US Airways	672	PHL	SEA	2030	89	50
American	857	MSP	DFW	1710	87	70
Northwest	809	MSP	HNL	1130	87	45
American	357	LGA	ORD	2055	85	46
American	882	MIA	JFK	1755	84	97
Delta	1287	JFK	TPA	1905	84	76
Continental	486	EWR	SJU	2050	84	50
Delta	420	LAS	JFK	1050	84	53
Delta	425	JFK	PDX	1855	84	73
American	585	MIA	SJU	1950	84	69
Continental	1177	BOS	EWR	1320	83	80

Table 3.2   August 2007 Air Carrier Flight Cancellation Statistics
(BTS Data)

Carrier	Number airports reporting	Flight operations scheduled	Flight operations cancelled	% Operations cancelled
Atlantic Southeast	139	24,723	978	4
Mesa	117	24,941	977	3.9
Pinnacle	114	22,840	870	3.8
American Eagle	117	47,061	1,731	3.7
Comair	94	20,772	716	3.4
United	78	43,176	1,189	2.8
Express Jet	125	39,905	833	2.1
Skywest	143	53,955	994	1.8
American	78	53,800	971	1.8
US Airways	78	41,211	651	1.6
Alaska	46	14,722	227	1.5
Delta	98	41,736	544	1.3
AirTran	55	23,259	277	1.2
JetBlue Airways	48	16,655	156	0.9
Continental	68	28,483	251	0.9
Northwest	104	35,142	303	0.9
Hawaiian	14	5,036	40	0.8
Southwest	64	101,673	489	0.5
Aloha	11	4,069	7	0.2
Frontier	44	8,790	15	0.2
Total	——	651,976	12,219	1.9

occurrences of cancellations and delays, Wang was also able to compare the number of complaints with the estimated hours of delay to passengers by each event. On average, in the summer of 2004, passengers in delayed fights at Chicago's O'Hare International Airport (ORD) encountered 45 minutes of delay, and passengers in cancelled flights encountered 13.5 hours of delay. **Although flight cancellations accounted for only 2% of the total flights, they contributed more than 50% of the total passenger delay.**

Moreover, Figs. 3.1 and 3.2 illustrate that the disruptions to passengers are more severe than a delayed push-back or a taxi-out queuing delay. With this in mind, Wang manipulated the data from the Bureau of Transportation Statistics database and computed two passenger delay figures of merit (FOM): the expected value–passenger

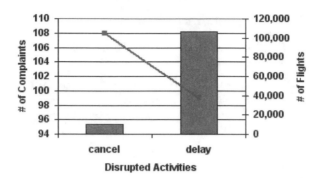

Fig. 3.1   Poor correlation between passenger complaints and flight delays [Wang 2006].

trip delay (EV-PTD) metric [Sherry et al. 2007] and the 45-minute passenger trip delay (45-PTD) metric. (See statistics for over 5,800 city pairs at the Web site: http://www.greenflights.info.) The authors have suggested that the FAA consider adopting these FOMs for its daily staff meetings, as this information relates directly to their customers—the passengers—and not the airlines; however, they have not done so.

For the year 2006, the top 35 U.S. airports [known to the FAA as the Operational Evolution Partnership (OEP) 35] experienced about three million flights between 1044 city pairs (see Fig. 3.3 for the location of these airports). Of all of these flights, 22% were delayed over 15 minutes, and 1.7% of these flights were cancelled. Additionally, 434 of these routes had an EV-PTD of 30 to 40 minutes, 157 routes had an

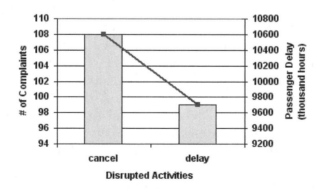

Fig. 3.2   Good correlation between passenger complaints and delays caused by flight cancellations [Wang 2006].

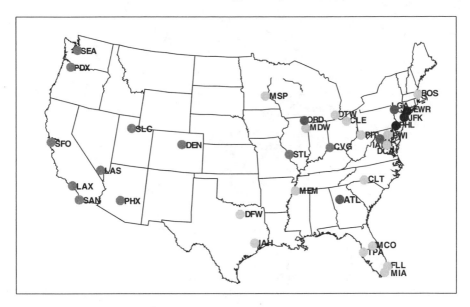

Fig. 3.3   FAA OEP 35 airports. Gray scale relates to congestion cluster, black being highest delay generation and light grey being lowest [Xu 2007].

EV-PTD of 40 to 50 minutes, and 82 routes had an EV-PTD of over 50 minutes! The authors' analysis indicates that the delayed flights generated 66 million hours of cumulative passenger delay and that the cancelled flights generated 42 million hours of passenger delay (which gives the 108 million hours of delay and $3.2 billion of lost passenger productivity noted in Chapter 1) [Wang et al. 2006].

Figure 3.4 shows the probability for a passenger at Chicago's O'Hare Airport (ORD) experiencing delays from 15 minutes to over 10 hours. Appendix B shows this new weighted metric for 18 congested airports in 2006. The units represent the total average delay experienced by passengers per month, including cancelled flights.

These delays and cancellations are largely caused by an overscheduling of the airport runway capacity and are not the fault of any one airport authority. Thus, they can be attributed to the airlines and to FAA/DOT/congressional policies (and even to the public, the sheep, to some extent) for tolerating this unpredictability in the U.S. air transportation system. Figure 3.5 shows that delays caused by flight cancellations were extremely high in 2000 and are approaching these extreme levels again. In 2000, the extreme passenger delay was the result of significant numbers of flight delays/cancellations (25/3.6%). In 2006, the number of flight delays/cancellations was down (23/1.4%), but the average LFs

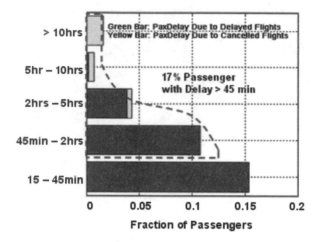

Fig. 3.4   Probability of a passenger experiencing a delay of a given magnitude for Chicago O'Hare. There was a 17% probability of a passenger experiencing a delay of over 45 minutes in 2006 (45-POTP) [Wang et al. 2006].

are now so high that the consequences of a long delay or a flight cancellation are catastrophic for the passengers.

The combination of the two is driving the average aircraft LF to unprecedented numbers that lead not only to uncomfortable flights but, more importantly, to a system that has no real ability to recover from either weather or aircraft mechanical disruptions (see Fig. 3.6).

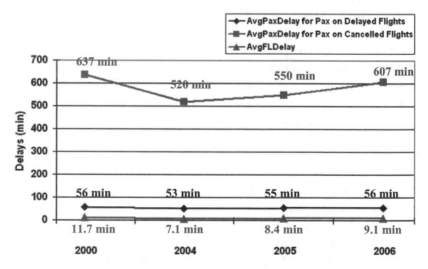

Fig. 3.5   Average passenger delay from a flight delay or a flight cancellation compared with FAA average flight delay statistics [Wang 2007].

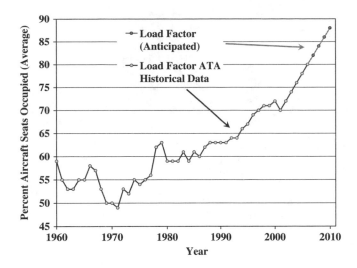

Fig. 3.6   Increased aircraft load factor and a transportation system vulnerable to disruption (Data from ATA and [Wang et al. 2006]).

Appendix C shows the aggregated probability of experiencing a passenger delay of greater than 45 minutes for the worst-performing airports from 2004 (a relatively slow year for airline operations because of 9/11 and the economic slump) to 2006 (in full recovery).

Because many of these airports have dominant airline carriers that generate these delays (by airlines that carry the majority of passengers through that airport), airline scheduling practices at hub airports create delays system-wide! Thus, there is really no place for the sheep to hide.

Delays at some airports impact on delays at others. Additional research is being undertaken in the center at GMU to analyze the statistical nature of delays throughout the entire U.S. air transportation network. The authors' work is investigating where and why some airports appear to generate delays, whereas others appear to either simply transmit or actually absorb them. The current state of authors' research is described in Xu [2007]. A few airports can be categorized as major *producers* of network-wide delays, others are primarily *transmitters* of these delays on to other airports, and still others exhibit a modest capability as *absorbers* of the delays. Unfortunately, the data also indicate that there is little capability by any airport to absorb a delay en route once that delay has been generated by a congested airport except through airline schedule padding. Figure 3.7 illustrates the balance between these three forces at New Jersey Newark Airport in 2006. This type of data for 18 OEP airports is also provided in Appendix C.

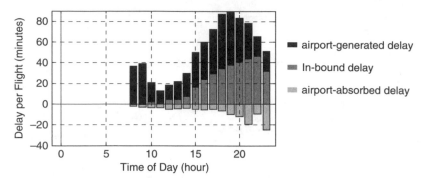

Fig. 3.7   The composition of delay vs time of day at New Jersey Newark Airport (EWR) 2006 [Xu 2007].

Table 3.3 shows a ranking of the airports that generate the most network-wide delays. The table lists the number of hours of aircraft delay produced at the *next* airport by the listed airport. The numbers are a monthly average for the summer of 2005 [Xu 2007].

A review of the official Department of Transportation delay and cancellation statistics reveals that almost all U.S. airports experience about 25% of their flights as delayed beyond 15 minutes. Moreover, this statistic (and Table 3.3) masks the fact that the *schedules* have already been stretched to compensate for systemic flight delays and that they do not reflect flight cancellations, which (as discussed) generate almost as much passenger delay as all of the delayed flights put together. Figure 3.7 and similar figures in Appendix C show that flights are most predictable from 10:00 a.m. to 2:00 p.m. Unfortunately, predictability deteriorates throughout the day as the delays spread and grow throughout the network. The worst predictability is in the evening between 3:00 p.m. to 10:00 p.m. when average delayed flights exceed 50% at the worst airports.

A detailed look at the data reveals that almost all of the airports in the country and most of the airlines have about the same on-time performance. Based upon this metric, there is not much to differentiate either airport or airline based upon QOS. Even Denver's new international airport, which was constructed in the early 1990s for over $5 billion and is perhaps the highest capacity airport in the world, is not much better than Atlanta or Chicago for most air carriers. This fact is caused by the network delay effect described earlier, and the situation cannot be fixed by simply addressing any one airport alone. **To properly work, policies to fix the system must address multiple airports.**

Table 3.3   Major U.S. Airports Producing Network-Wide Delays in
Summer 2005 [Xu 2007]

Rank	Airport	Network generated delay-aircraft hours/month
1	Atlanta Hartsfield	4,800
2	Chicago O'Hare	4,200
3	Dallas–Ft. Worth	3,200
4	Newark Liberty	2,200
5	Philadelphia International	2,200
6	Minneapolis St. Paul	2,200
7	Detroit Metro WC	2,100
8	Denver International	1,800
9	Boston Logan	1,700
10	New York John F. Kennedy	1,700
11	New York LaGuardia	1,700
12	Houston Bush International	1,500
13	Washington Dulles	1,500
14	Charlotte Douglas	1,500
15	Orlando International	1,400

Table 3.4 shows the ranking of the top 20 domestic airlines based on
the percentage of on-time performance in November 2006. The authors
have excluded two Hawaiian airlines (ranked 1 and 2) because they do
not fly in the national network and are thus not punished equally
by the systemic network problems. The shaded boxes indicate below-
average performance. Note that there is not much difference between
the best and the worst airlines. Also, if one looks at the other important
indicators of passenger QOS, one would rank them differently. United
Airlines had relatively few delays (21% of all flights delayed beyond 15
minutes) but had a relatively high flight cancellation rate. Table 3.2
showed that flight cancellation policy is constantly shifting and was
different in August 2007.

Real Delay Source

An airport's capacity is a direct function of the airport's runway
system, number of gates, and the FAA-imposed aircraft separation
rules. These separation rules are set based upon concern for aircraft
collisions on the runway or aircraft wake-vortex encounters that produce

Table 3.4   Airlines Ranked by DOT 15-Minute On-Time Performance Metrics[a] (other quality of service metrics are shown for comparison and completeness)

Airline	Rank	% On time	Involuntary bump per 10,000	% Cancelled	Lost bags per 1,000
Frontier	3	87	0.45	0.5	4.4
Southwest	4	84	1	0.9	5.5
United	5	79	0.5	1.2	6
AirTrans	6	77	0.1	0.7	3.6
Express Jet	7	77	—	2.1	7.9
Mesa	8	77	1.8	2.4	9.2
American	9	77	0.83	2.5	5.4
Sky West	10	77	1.1	2.7	5.5
Continental	11	76	1.9	0.3	4.3
Delta	12	76	1.8	1.2	6.7
US Airways	13	75	1.1	0.9	7.1
American Eagle	14	75	1.5	3.5	12.5
ATA	15	71	1.9	1.2	5.7
Alaska	16	71	1.2	2.3	3.7
JetBlue Airways	17	70	0.07	0.3	4.3
Northwest	18	70	0.9	0.6	4.8
Comair	19	67	2.8	3	12.7
Atlantic Southeast	20	66	4.6	2	15.8
Median	—	76	1.1	1.2	5.6
Mode	—	77	1.8	1.2	5.5

[a]BTS data for Nov. 2005 to Nov. 2006.

unacceptable, uncommanded roll maneuvers by an aircraft that is "captured" by the preceding aircraft's wake vortex.

The most dangerous part of any aircraft flight is in the landing. And this danger is greatly enhanced when there are other aircraft also trying to land at the airfield. Commercial aviation has addressed this problem by setting up landing queues at commercial airports, with each aircraft properly spaced one from another. These spacings have been codified in safety standards and should be carefully monitored by the air traffic controllers to ensure that the separations meet the standards. These spacings also determine the landing rate of the commercial aircraft at an airport and thus are of high interest to those who wish to "move metal" into and out of the airport in the most rapid rate possible.

There are three basic factors that go into determining the minimum safe spacing between arriving aircraft:

1) Will the leading aircraft, upon landing, have sufficient time to exit the runway before the trailing aircraft touches down?

2) Will the wake vortex generated by the leading aircraft have sufficiently diminished in intensity to be of no danger to the trailing aircraft?

3) Can the trailing aircraft be informed in time to take any necessary avoidance maneuvers in case the leading aircraft suddenly and unexpectedly maneuvers in a manner that could result in a collision?

Because the first two factors tend to dominate the separation distances, they are focus the in this book.

Figure 3.8 shows a simple deterministic relationship between a landing aircraft's speed, the distance behind the preceding aircraft, and the airport runway arrival capacity per hour. According to the relatively conservative separation rules (which have been adopted internationally), most aircraft are supposed to maintain about a three- to four-mile separation distance to provide a low probability of either encountering the preceding aircraft wake vortex or of simultaneously occupying the same runway as the preceding aircraft. Having two landing aircraft on the same runway simultaneously does not, of course, guarantee an accident, but it is a dangerous precursor to having a life-threatening collision on the runway.

The different speed curves allow for the divergence in aircraft approach speeds, higher for large aircraft and slower for smaller aircraft. These

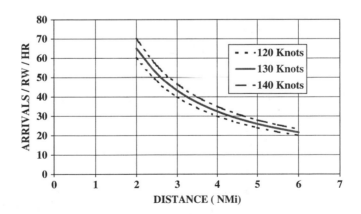

Fig. 3.8   Runway arrival rate per hour as a function of aircraft spacing. Decreasing arrival spacing from an average of four to three nautical miles could increase system maximum capacity by 34% if wake-vortex avoidance systems are deployed [Donohue 1999a].

speeds are related to the aircraft design and concern for aircraft loss of lift or stall. An arrival rate of 40 aircraft per runway per hour (or 90 seconds between aircraft) sets a maximum safe runway capacity. So an airport like LaGuardia should have a maximum safe arrival rate of 10 arrivals every 15 minutes. The 15-minute time period is a useful amount for analysis because it accounts for the airline practice of "banking" flights into tight arrival groups to facilitate hub operating schedules.

In reality, aircraft arrival rates at an airport are not deterministic; they are more closely characterized mathematically as "stochastic" (or random). There are several reasons for this: 1) Airlines select their schedules based on their business model (there is no law or rule that denies them the right to schedule any arrival time they desire); 2) airlines are not allowed by law (antitrust laws) to coordinate their schedules between each other and are thereby denied from synchronizing their arrival times; 3) each airline is free to schedule its aircraft arrivals at an airport without consideration of that airport's overall safe landing capacity or delay performance; 4) the resulting sum (from all airlines) of all scheduled flights into the busiest airports systemically exceeds that airport's capacity; and 5) airplanes are complex mechanical devices operating in uncertain weather conditions.

These facts (and others) led the authors therefore to characterize airport capacity using queuing theory, which takes into account the fact that real airport operational capacities are less than a maximum deterministic rate (shown in Fig. 3.8). Figure 3.9 shows how landing delays increase for airports as schedules approach the maximum safe operational rate. The figure plots expected values of average aircraft delay against a ratio of scheduled arrivals divided by the maximum safe schedule. So a value of 0.5 would represent a scheduled arrival rate of 20 arrivals per hour, and a ratio of 1.0 would represent an arrival rate of 40 arrivals per hour. (A more detailed discussion of this subject is provided in Appendix D.)

In practice, airports that are scheduled to about 80% of this maximum safe capacity can be expected to operate at about a 15-minute delay. As discussed earlier, flights that arrive within this 15-minute window of the scheduled arrival time are actually considered to be on time by the DOT. Even without any aircraft congestion, an aircraft can arrive 15 minutes late just because of bad headwinds. When scheduled arrivals at the airport approach the 90 to 100% range, however, delays go to extremely high levels, and flight cancellations become routine. In addition, the variability of delays increases, and aircraft separation standards can no longer be rigorously maintained by today's ATC procedures. (This can be illustrated by high-resolution data that have

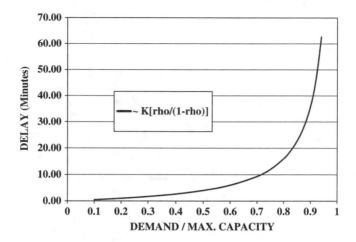

Fig. 3.9.   Average aircraft arrival or departure delay as a function of maximum runway capacity (see Appendix C).

been analyzed by several of the authors' graduate students [Xie et al. 2003; Jeddi et al. 2006].)

Future technologies offer some hope that airport capacities can be expanded. However, based on experience and research, the authors have found that technology enhancement alone will not be able to keep up with the anticipated growth in demand. And, based on previous observations, there is no real guarantee that the FAA will actually field and exploit new technologies in the foreseeable future.

Safety–Capacity Tradeoff

There is an implicit tradeoff between airport safety and capacity. The separation of aircraft by time or space is done to meet some internationally agreed to target level of safety (TLS). The authors' research shows [Xu et al. 2005; Jeddi et al. 2006] that high delays occur when an airport is operating near (or beyond) its arrival–departure Pareto frontier (shown in Figs. 3.12 and 3.13 and Appendix C). (The Pareto frontier represents the maximum feasible safe combination between aircraft arrivals and departures for the airport's runway and taxiway design. The boundary lines form an envelope within which ATC tries to maintain aircraft separation.) It is these times of high delay that aircraft get closest together.

Figure 3.10 shows a modern high-capacity hub airport, Detroit International Airport (DTW), which has a NASA-installed, FAA-certified high-resolution measurement system. Figure 3.11 shows

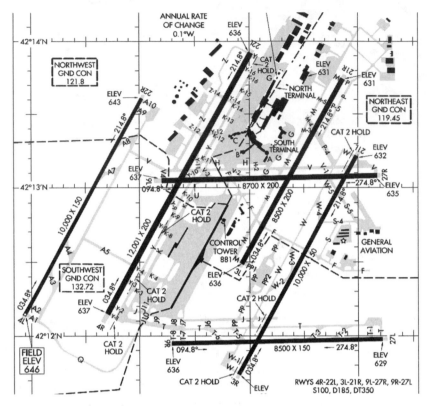

Fig. 3.10 Modern high-capacity hub airport (DTW) with six runways. Aircraft separation measurements were analyzed for Runway 21L.

time data taken with this system over a week of operations at this airport [under instrument meteorological conditions (IMC), for which the FAA has full legal responsibility for maintaining aircraft separation]. The vertical axis is a measure of the time it takes the leading aircraft to exit Runway 21 Left (21L) onto a high-speed exit taxiway. The horizontal axis shows the time between the leading aircraft and the following aircraft.

As discussed earlier, an average 90-second separation should be expected for a safe, deterministic arrival process. It takes a typical aircraft from 35 to 65 seconds to slow down enough to exit the active runway. The figure shows lines at 90 seconds (a safe separation limit) and 50 seconds (runway occupancy) for reference. Notice that there are a significant number of aircraft that land at less than 90 seconds apart, a characteristic common for airports that are operating close to maximum capacity. The diagonal line on the chart is simply those points where the trailing

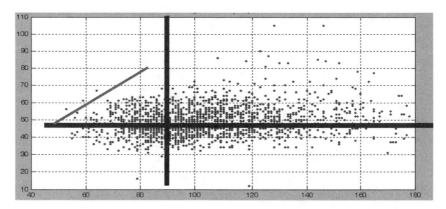

Fig. 3.11   High-resolution aircraft stopping times (vertical axis, seconds) and interarrival times (horizontal axis, seconds) for DTW under IMC high arrival bank conditions. A total of 1870 landings are shown for one week, with three cases of simultaneous runway occupancy observed [Jeddi et al. 2006].

aircraft's landing time exactly equals the leading aircraft's runway occupancy time. Dots above this line are incidents where the trailing aircraft landed prior to the leading aircraft exiting the runway. The figure shows three instances of simultaneous runway occupancy, which is **over 100 times higher than the FAA-reported rate**.

So, is this a serious safety issue? Some think yes; others think no. Admittedly, fatal accidents involving two aircraft on the same runway are rare, so that maybe no is the right answer. However, the safety standards suggest yes. They call for fewer occurrences of this separation violation in one year than these data showed in one week.

But why do these occurrences happen at all? The rules state that the controllers should have the trailing aircraft abort the landing if the leading aircraft is still on the runway when the trailing aircraft is near to the runway threshold. If the controller fails to call for this abort, the pilot is obliged to implement a "go-around" maneuver.

Nevertheless, one can only speculate as to the cause, but the authors believe that it stems from at least two factors: 1) the desire of both the controllers and the pilots to maximize the airport's landing rate and 2) their perception that the risk is low. The authors note, however, that neither controllers nor pilots really want to admit their actions, as write-ups of incidents of double occupancy on the runway are rarely recorded.

The FAA publishes this information in airport benchmark capacity reports [DOT 2004]. As shown in the arrival-departure Pareto frontier for DTW in Fig. 3.12, these airport capacity diagrams are analogous to

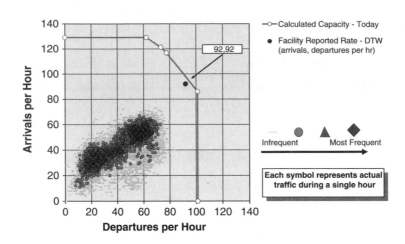

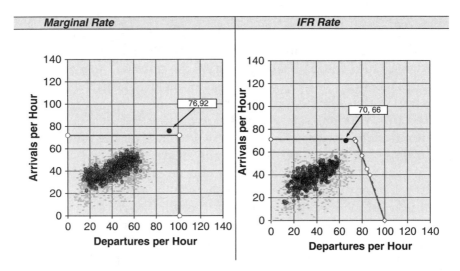

Fig. 3.12   Detroit International Airport (DTW) capacity diagrams [DOT 2004].

aircraft weight and balance operating envelopes. Just as the aircraft weight should be distributed so that the weight is within the FAA-certified allowable safe trim limits for an aircraft, airport aircraft arrival and departure rates should fall within the predetermined, FAA-certified "safe operating zone." Based on these criteria (and the boundary lines shown in Fig. 3.12), DTW is operating well within this envelope "on average."

Unfortunately, New York LaGuardia (LGA) is a different story. Figure 3.13 indicates numerous operations outside of the FAA-computed safe operating boundaries under both visual and instrument meteorological conditions. Technically, the operations outside of these boundaries under visual conditions are the responsibility of the pilots and the airlines involved, and the excursions outside of these boundaries under instrument conditions (which are associated with poor pilot visibility) are the responsibility of the FAA. Although the high-resolution aircraft

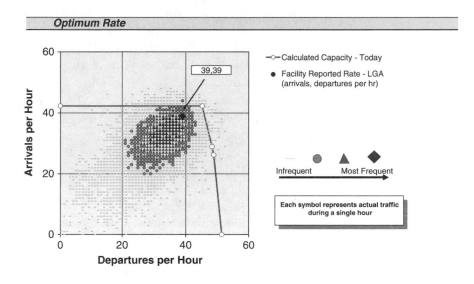

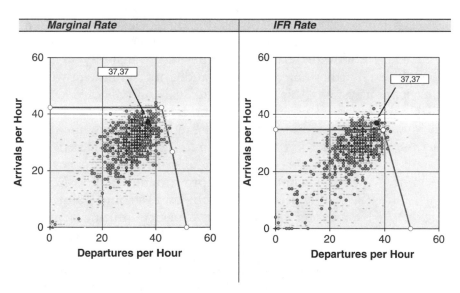

Fig. 3.13   New York LaGuardia Airport capacity diagrams. This is a highly regulated and congested airport [DOT 2004].

separation data shown for DTW in Fig. 3.11 are not available for LGA, detailed measurement by GMU graduate students (over several years) as well as radar tape reviews by FAA headquarters records numerous instances of lost safety separation at LGA. Moreover, similar diagrams are provided in Appendix C for selected U.S. airports to show that these are not isolated incidents.

These data are from official FAA/DOT reports and are known to be occurring (and are therefore officially sanctioned). Thus, it is critical that the FAA should either enforce its safety separation rules, conduct analysis to show why the rules should be changed, or mandate that the new technology be put in place throughout the network to allow these operational rates and rules to be maintained.

And new technology and procedures do exist to decrease the spread in aircraft separation times and increase both the safety and capacity at airports. Both NASA and other countries have made extensive investments in developing and proving this technology, but the FAA has been extremely reluctant to mandate aircraft equipage or to adopt the new procedures that will enable the technology.

An increased capacity of as much as 10% could be achieved by migrating from the use of radar surveillance to the use of aircraft-broadcast global-positioning-system (GPS) satellite navigation fixes over a wireless digital data link [referred to as Automatic Dependent Surveillance-Broadcast (ADS-B)]. The unaugmented GPS position accuracy is better than 15 meters (approximately 50 feet) with a one-second update rate. And using the FAA-developed wide-area augmentation system (WAAS), this accuracy is increased to closer than 7.5 meters. In addition, critical integrity and availability signals are now provided. Furthermore, as Europe and China add their own satellite navigation systems, this accuracy and availability is expected to be available worldwide. This technology and related new procedures will allow the average separation distance to be reduced because the *variance in separation* is reduced. Thus, arrival rate can be increased with a constant probability of aircraft simultaneous runway occupancy.

Admittedly, these technological improvements cannot, in themselves, solve the whole separation problem. At some point, wake-vortex (WV) encounter becomes the capacity-limiting separation based on WV residency time and strength. WV proximity warning systems have therefore been in development by the Europeans as well as by NASA (until budget cuts recently limited the scope of the program). Once again, the FAA has shown very little interest in developing a WV warning system. Instead, the FAA central flow control function is being increasingly used to institute the aforementioned GDPs to anticipate separation-related delays and to hold aircraft on the ground at the point of origin rather than in the air at the point of destination.

A final thought regarding delays has to do with why flights are so commonly overscheduled in the first place. As detailed in following chapters, one of the benefits of deregulation of the airlines in 1978 was unfettered access to almost all airports, with a strict rule of "first come, first served." Under this rule, each plane's scheduled arrival time was essentially irrelevant to the airport. The FAA would simply line them up to land, and the airport would accept them. So, a flight's scheduled arrival time was strictly the decision of the airline. There were no restrictions! None!

This situation was tolerable when the total number of planes scheduled into an airport was well within the airport's capacity (in units of planes per 15 minutes). But with the growth of hubbing at some of the largest metropolitan airports, the scheduled arrivals soon pushed up against the airport's safe landing capacity. In many cases, competing airlines accommodated the situation by having their aircraft "banks" arrive at different parts of the hour. This accommodation was done strictly without formal discussion, however, in part because the law strictly forbids any amount of airline collusion. But because of the continued growth in passenger volume, coupled with the growing need to fill aircraft seats in order to be profitable, the airlines started to increase their flights at those airports where they had a large stake, trying to gain passenger loyalty through scheduling frequency. And by the 1990s, large hub airports were experiencing what amounted to overscheduling at popular times in the day. This has persisted through today. Chapter 5 discusses why the airlines are trapped into a behavior pattern that they cannot escape by themselves.

In addition, subsequent chapters further discuss the five main actors that control the utilization of today's air transportation system (and that can most significantly affect the extent of delays). They include the following:

1) **Civil aviation authorities** (CAA) (the FAA in the United States)—The CAAs control regulations and aircraft separation flow control standards and services (i.e., radars, radios, navigation).

2) **Airlines**—The airlines control aircraft enplanement capacity/advanced avionics and the utilization of air traffic management information in their air operations centers.

3) **Airport operators**—The airport operators control airport infrastructure (i.e., gates, taxi-ways, runaways, etc.).

4) **Aircraft and avionics manufactures**—These manufacturers control the development of advanced technology required to improve both the safety and the capacity of the entire system.

5) **Operators of private aircraft**—These operators control the lobby to maintain substantial economic cross-subsidies to their operations by opposing a fee-for-service or a privatized ATM service provider.

The bottom line in all of this is simple. For the capacity and QOS to increase in the 21st century, each of these players will have to significantly revise operational procedures and/or make substantial capital investments in new equipment.

CHAPTER 4

Destination Chaos: How We Arrived and Who Were the Pilots

In the Air Transport Association's (ATA's) 2006 annual report, the U.S. airline industry reportedly had almost $40 billion in assets and $50 billion in liabilities. And the stockholders net equity was stated to be **–$14 billion**. (That's right, there is a negative sign as well as a "b" as in billion.) Thus, it does not take an economics professor to recognize that something terrible has gone wrong in the U.S. air travel system. And it is costing a whole lot of people a whole lot of money. But just how did we arrive at this condition?

The U.S. air transportation system is a complex interaction between public and private partners. Each depends on the other for survival, but each has quite different objectives. The public sector—represented by the Congress, various parts of the Executive Branch, and the regional airport authorities—values the following areas (in various degrees): 1) public safety, 2) the movement of commerce, and 3) the growth of the economy. [The Executive Branch includes a) the DOT and its agency, the FAA; b) the Department of Commerce; c) the National Aeronautics and Space Administration; d) the Department of Defense; e) the Department of Homeland Security and its agency, the TSA; and f) the Office of Management and Budget.]

The private service providers (i.e., the airlines) value making a profit for their stockholders. If the airlines cannot financially survive under our current regulatory framework, the United States will lose one of the vital arteries of economic viability in the 21st century. These inter-actions are further confounded by political pressures (both local and national) that seek to influence the outcomes. Both the unions and the various lobbying groups (representing airlines, cities, manufacturers, private aircraft owners, etc.) weigh in with both Congress and the Executive Branch for self-serving reasons. In short, there are a large number of players involved, frequently leading to less than desirable decisions (when and if they are actually made at all).

To make sense out of this situation, the authors have identified six primary layers of a complex adaptive system (CAS) that makes up the U.S. air transportation network. These layers, shown in Fig. 4.1, are mostly nonlinear, interacting networks. (A computer model of these networks exists and has been constructed by the NEXTOR universities.)

The following listing provides some context for each layer in the CAS (starting from the bottom layer and working up):

1) **Physical layer**—This layer represents the natural demographic distribution and clustering of our nation's population that uses air transportation. The cities and their regional airport authorities in this network decide how much money to borrow and request from the FAA Airport Improvement Program (AIP) fund to construct or expand airports.

2) **Weather layer**—This layer adds a stochastic (or random), and thus chaotic, perturbation to the daily flight schedule and occasionally severely disrupts travel predictability. Frequently, however, the common low-visibility or convective storm fronts have a reasonable degree of predictability, especially with today's advanced computer models (which, incidentally, could also be used to ease the management of air traffic flow and lessen the impact on airspace utilization). (See research underway by Lt. Col. David Smith, at GMU, forthcoming.)

3) **Government regulatory control layer**—This layer represents the network of federal laws and regulations. These regulations set airline competition/operations/maintenance and data reporting rules, air transportation safety standards, aircraft separation standards, airport access restrictions, federal government union work rules, technology acquisition rules, etc.

Passenger/Cargo Layer (Delays, Cancellations)

Airline Layer (Routes, Schedules, A/C size)

TSA/FAA Layer (ATC Radar, Radios, Ctr's, Unions)

Government Regulatory Control Layer

Weather Layer (Thunderstorms, Ice Storms)

Physical Layer (i.e. Cities, Airports, Demographics)

Fig. 4.1   Layers of the air transportation complex adaptive system.

4) **TSA/FAA layer**—This layer comprises the Transportation Security Administration (TSA), the organization that decides how much to increase passengers' travel block time at the airport and what level of missed weapons will be allowed to pass through the system, and the FAA, the organization that largely decides how safe a flight will be (i.e., how much separation space is required between aircraft, how many aircraft can occupy a runway at a given time, etc.), as well as what technology will be allowed for navigation, communications, and surveillance; when a scheduled flight will be allowed to depart; and how much flight delay will be tolerated in a trip.

5) **Airline layer**—The airlines schedule flights between airports in this transportation network and decide on the type of aircraft (i.e., the size or gauge of the aircraft), the acceptable aircraft LF (i.e., the fraction of aircraft seats occupied), and the frequency of service and city pairs to be serviced. The airlines also decide when to cancel a flight because of crew or maintenance problems or loss of schedule coherence as a result of excessive flight delays.

6) **Passenger/cargo layer**—In the end, it is the passengers who decide when to fly or drive (or not to travel at all), what cities to fly to, which airlines to fly on, how much to pay, and what travel QOS to tolerate. Thus, the passengers (and cargo) are the ultimate customers of this complex adaptive transportation system.

Another way of looking at this CAS is shown in Fig. 4.2. The following pages will more closely examine what has happened to three of the major actors in the system: the airlines, the airports, and the U.S.

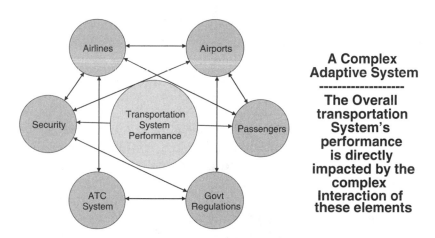

Fig. 4.2   Some of the nonlinear interactions between passengers, airlines, airports, and governmental agencies in this CAS.

government (i.e., the FAA). As for the other actors, passengers can do little to change the cities or the weather; the TSA delays are a national security and foreign policy question that should be addressed by the nation at large; and the rules and regulations that need to be changed (which, as it turns out, are really the foundation of our transportation problems) are discussed extensively in Chapters 6 and 7.

U.S. Airlines: Leading the World from the Back of the Pack

Air transportation is taken for granted these days. The regulations concerning air transportation in this country were largely established just prior to and shortly after World War II. And except for the introduction of the high-density-rule (HDR) slot controls at a few congested airports in 1968, these original rules remained in force until 1978. The Civil Aeronautics Board (CAB), established in 1940, tightly regulated most elements of aviation. The airlines had to obtain permission from the CAB to fly a city-pair.

The flights to and from the major airports were highly sought, and the airlines involved became extremely busy as a result. The Congress allowed the FAA to impose HDRs for those airports that were congested in 1968, restricting the usage by airlines already approved to serve those airports and essentially denying new entrants. As a result, many of the most profitable routes in the air traffic system were denied to potential new entrants, restricting competition and ensuring that the favorable conditions for the established (now-called "legacy") airlines were maintained. The aviation world dramatically changed in 1978 when the CAB was abolished and the regulations on airline route structures were abandoned.

Admittedly, some of today's flying hassles are the result of ever-changing and often capricious security measures enacted since 9/11; however, that is only a small part of the problem. The main reason why flying has become so arduous is that the air transportation system, as it is now structured in the United States, is untenable from a fundamental business point of view. To put it simply, as discussed in Chapter 5, the government-regulated aviation business model is unstable and irrational. Planes are purposely overbooked, flights are cancelled for no publicly explainable reason, and no one will offer the flyer a sound reason for why these events occur.

Though the seeds for the current failure were planted many decades ago, they did not find full germination until the industry was deregulated in 1978. Make no mistake, there were winners from deregulation. The public gained much greater access to air travel, and the nation's economy got a resulting boost from it. In addition, access to significantly lower prices (engendered by the resulting competition between the airlines) spawned a rapid growth in air travel, setting the stage for the emergence of new airlines that competed for passengers mainly on the basis of ticket price. And as part of the focus on cost, the larger airlines expanded the "hub-and-spoke" system at selected major airports. This scheduling approach is inherently efficient at serving a large and thinly dispersed network of airports, such as found in the United States, and the benefits were that many more city-pairs could be connected for a given aircraft fleet size at lower average air fares. Not surprisingly, this approach allowed airlines to profitably serve a large number of smaller cities that had previously had little or no service. (Without question, deregulation definitely spawned many new airlines. Many flew from airports that were not particularly busy. But many others did fly to the larger airports, where they interacted with the major carriers in one way or another. Without deregulation, an airline such as Southwest might never have flourished.)

But with the good also came the bad. And the attractive results of deregulation introduced a new set of problems that continue to confront the system today. The most noteworthy problem first arose around 1990. Because of the growth in airline flights, the hub airports started to experience operational rates (i.e., landings and takeoffs over an hour) that were causing severe congestion at some of the largest airports, with growing flight delays and cancellation the result. This growing congestion also affected the entire nation's air transportation network, resulting in flight delays and cancellations at many noncongested airports. Moreover, some of the hub airports became dominated by one or two airlines, which resulted in limited competition and barriers to new airline entrants (primarily because of long-term airport gate leases with the legacy airlines).

It can be argued, and the authors would agree, that deregulation of the airlines schedules and prices in 1978 was one of the best things that could have happened to the U.S. air travel industry. Unfortunately, because of the large growth in air travel that deregulation spawned, coupled with the inability of some notable major airports to accommodate the increased airline traffic, this has also led to today's crisis.

Consider the following domino effect of deregulation:

- Deregulation led to lower airfares and increased flight frequency.
- This led to increased use of hub-and-spoke network schedules by the airlines to provide the efficiency needed to offer the increased services at competitive and profitable prices.
- This led to increasing numbers of flights into the hub airports, creating congestion delays at these airports.

- This led to the propagation of these hub-caused delays system-wide, thereby decreasing travel predictability for all U.S. airports and air travelers.
- This led (and still leads) to 1) a rapid growth in some low-cost airlines (e.g., Southwest) that found the means to serve the high-volume routes between major metropolitan areas while avoiding most of the congested airports, and 2) the loss to the legacy airlines of the most desired passengers (i.e., buyers of first-class and business-class tickets) to the use of business jets, which provide better dispatch reliability, comfort, and productivity, albeit at a higher price.
- This led to loss of high marginal profits for the airlines, thus the need for the legacy airlines (those mainly flying hub-and-spoke routes) to fill up their aircraft to make money [which led to an increase in average aircraft LFs (economy passenger discomfort), increases in schedule frequency (to capture more market fraction), and an increase in air traffic congestion in major city airspace]. (The vast majority of business-class airplanes 1) carry fewer passengers than the commercial alternative, actually increasing the number of airframes that must be handled by the air traffic system; 2) either leave from or fly to major metropolitan areas, where the airspace is already crowded with commercial airliners; and 3) in some cases seek access to airports that are already crowded with commercial traffic.)
- This led to increasing airspace congestion delays.
- This led to increasing loss of travel predictability and viability (manifested through delays and flight cancellations), coupled with limits on access to airline flights at major metropolitan airports (e.g., New York and Chicago airports).
- This leads to a growing inability to meet the demands for airline travel (both for business and pleasure), with the inevitable constraint on an airline's ability to meet the anticipated growth in air travel. Even successful airlines such as Southwest are impacted. No airline or passenger is exempt. And even the nation is suffering, as these constraints on air travel are costing our economy tens of billions of dollars annually.

However, as has been said before, it does not need to be this way!

To address these problems, one must understand the causes. And one of the major causes of this unstable and unsustainable cycle is the lack of a rational pricing policy for allocating aircraft arrival or departure times at major congested airports. The cost of operating in the U.S. air transportation system has no relationship to the cost of providing the air traffic control services or to the scarcity of critical public resources (e.g., landing slots at major airports). Most economists agree that for an industry or even a single company in a free market to be viable it must have clear pricing signals so that supply and demand can find an equilibrium point. (This is somewhat of a problem with the U.S. air transportation system because the supply of adequate runway capacity in large metropolitan regions is limited. As the system operates at the maximum supply point, the prices go up substantially until demand is met, which would be bad for the tourism and aircraft manufacturing industrial sectors.) The law of supply and demand should determine the pricing of goods and services, and these pricing signals must feed back to the system so that the pricing experts know that the costs are set correctly and the closed-loop universe is in balance. However, the U.S. policy of using a passenger ticket tax and fuel tax (both unrelated factors for either the cost of an operation or the value of the airport arrival or departure time slot) to fund the air traffic control and airport improvements largely disconnects the true value of an airport arrival time slot from the rational assignment of aircraft size and flight frequency by airlines.

Airline marketing departments frequently sell tickets on aircraft that are too small and fly too frequently to be economically efficient, safely separated, or able to operate on a predictable time schedule. FAA officials know this but choose to do nothing about it. With the airlines charging widely varying prices for the same-class seats on the same flight, they are, in effect, running a commodity futures auction for ticket price (which is only a lottery ticket for the flight) while providing no guarantee of providing the service. This technique is called "yield management," which is a method to extract the most amount of money from passengers for any given flight. (An economist would call this reducing consumer surplus; see Doganis [2002] for a good discussion of yield management pricing theory.) Appendix G gives examples of the "ask" commodity prices vs advanced booking times for a few markets. There is nothing wrong with airlines doing this; it is their job to maximize their profits (or minimize the consumer surplus) for their stockholders. However, it is the government's job to ensure that a viable private sector survives to support our nation's air transportation system needs and that the passengers and cargo carried by the private service providers are provided with safe, predictable, available, competitive, and reasonably comfortable transportation.

Because there is no rational pricing of the provision of air transportation services, today's system of regulation simply does not provide the feedback necessary for cogent investment by either the industry or government that will properly increase the system capacity and increase passengers' QOS. Record numbers of people are flying today, but major airlines are losing so much money that they are cutting back on trivial amenities such as peanuts and blankets to rescue themselves. This situation is unique to the United States because the nation's air system does not charge for air traffic services on any simple, rational basis, such as number of ATC interactions or congestion at airports. In any other industry, with more rational government regulations designed to both protect the public interest and provide for fair and equitable competition, this absurd economic situation would not exist.

One of the principal arguments for deregulation was to lower barriers to new entrants. However, as mentioned, the lack of the FAA's ability to modernize (or to step out of the way of modernization) or the courage to regulate airport operations to safe and predictable operational rates has allowed hub congestion and airline gate dominance to provide a significant barrier to new entrants and increasing consolidation of old legacy airlines.

The economic decline in airline profitability that first occurred in the early 1980s occurred again a decade later. And by the early 2000s, our current system began sending airlines into bankruptcy during a reoccurrence of an "over-capacity" cycle. [The so-called legacy airlines (those operating well before deregulation) were burdened with personnel costs and fleet mixes that were often noncompetitive under the new postderegulation situation. New entrants did not offer commensurate salaries for their employees, targeted equipment that was appropriate for the route structure they selected, but they offered lower fares that could not be matched profitably by the older airlines. Thus, bankruptcies and liquidations of these older airlines became common by the 1990s, with airline giants such as United remaining on the brink of extinction.] John Hansman of MIT first pointed out the growing amplitude of this feast-or-famine cycle and modeled it as an unstable control system cycling between airline bankruptcy and massive delays. The authors agree with his analysis and feel that this cycle must be stopped in the interest of the nation's economic welfare.

Table 4.1 contrasts the status of major U.S. airline carriers in 1975 (the 50th anniversary of commercial flight in the United States) with that of the major carriers in 2005, 30 years later. Notice that five of the top ten airlines in 1975 are no longer in existence. Eastern, Pan Am, and TWA were founders and world leaders in the industry in 1975. Also notice that five of the airlines listed in 2005 were either in bankruptcy or have just recently emerged from it, and some of them for more than one time.

Table 4.1 also introduces three important metrics used by the industry to measure aircraft system capacity (as distinct from airport system capacity, which is discussed in the next chapter). The first is airline revenue passenger miles (RPM), the number of fare-paying passengers times the distance flown by the flight. A second is the airline's available seat miles (ASM). These are the total number of seats available for the transportation of revenue passengers multiplied by the number of miles for which those seats are flown. The third is the airlines' previously discussed average LF. This represents the fraction of the seats on the aircraft

Table 4.1   Comparison of the Top 10 Airlines Between 1975 and 2005 (ATA one-year operating data)[a]

Rank	Airline	RPM	ASM	Avg LF
Airline service 1975				
1	United	26,226,950,000	45,923,198,000	0.57
2	Trans World	20,956,907,000	39,246,937,000	0.53
3	American	20,870,598,000	36,682,339,000	0.57
4	Eastern	18,169,434,000	32,323,538,000	0.56
5	Delta	16,460,463,000	29,480,849,000	0.56
6	Pan American	14,862,750,000	31,377,842,000	0.47
7	Northwest	9,471,280,000	20,910,963,000	0.45
8	Western	6,998,309,000	11,572,063,000	0.60
9	Continental	6,356,319,000	11,778,704,000	0.54
10	Braniff	6,290,420,000	12,761,331,000	0.49
Airline service 2005				
1	American	138,222,000,000	175,912,000,000	0.79
2	United	113,899,000,000	139,811,000,000	0.81
3	Delta	103,561,000,000	133,513,000,000	0.78
4	Northwest	75,802,000,000	91,754,000,000	0.83
5	Continental	68,249,000,000	85,507,000,000	0.80
6	US Airways	64,393,000,000	83,912,000,000	0.77
7	Southwest	60,223,000,000	85,189,000,000	0.71
8	JetBlue	20,187,000,000	23,814,000,000	0.85
9	Alaska	16,905,000,000	22,277,000,000	0.76
10	AirTran	11,286,000,000	15,373,000,000	0.73

[a]Source: Air Transport Association Data.

that are sold and utilized. (Flights also routinely set aside a few seats for "passengers" who do not have tickets, most notably TSA air marshals and airline crew who must shuttle to the destination airport to meet crew scheduling needs. However, the numbers are small, and the impact on LF has been negligible to date.) The average LF can be computed by simply dividing RPM by ASM over a comparable time period.

Understandably, the LF is an important indicator as to the profitability of the airline and the comfort of the passenger. Higher average LFs translate into greater profitability for those flights. (After deregulation, flights with LFs above 0.7 were thought to be making a profit.) (Recently, this rule of thumb has shown not to be the case. The impact of low-cost airlines has dramatically altered the economics of all airlines.) Lower LFs translate into the increased comfort of the passengers, especially in coach, where the majority of passengers sit. Looking at the table, one can pretty much conclude that of all of the advances in creature comforts the country has made in the last 30 years, a more comfortable airplane experience is just not one of them (especially if the passenger has long legs or a belly that tends to wedge against the tray table when folded down to eat peanuts).

In addition, Fig. 4.3 shows the growth in airline ASM, and Fig. 4.4 shows the growth in aircraft departures over the same time period. The number of available seats has grown by a factor of 10, whereas the number of departures has grown by a factor of three. Thus, the average aircraft size has increased over this time period. Unfortunately, the number of runways at our hub airports has increased at a much lower rate. As discussed in Chapter 3, this situation has led to the gross delay and cancellation problem facing the United States today.

By contrast, Fig. 4.5 shows a different way of looking at the ATA data. This metric is somewhat representative of the efficiency in transporting people per flight. Note that it peaked in the 1990s and has been falling since the widespread introduction of the regional jet (RJ) (which will typically seat 30 to 50 passengers) around 2000. The desire to find profitability in servicing the thin network of smaller cities that feed the hub airports near major population centers has created a decrease in network-wide efficiency in the pursuit of individual airline network profitability. The airlines went to these small RJs for good marketing reasons. Unfortunately, these aircraft also accelerated the time to which the airports ran out of capacity.

Finally, Fig. 4.6 shows the bottom line for both the airlines' profitability and the air traveling passengers' point of view. The average LF initially decreased with the introduction of larger jet aircraft in the early 1960s. Under the regulated flight schedule and airfare system

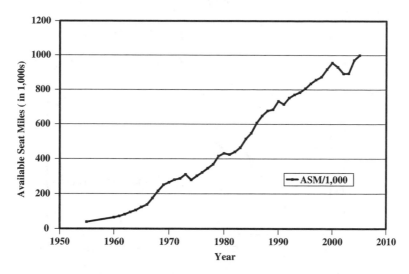

Fig. 4.3   Daily ASM scheduled for the U.S. airline industry, 1955 to 2005 (data taken from Air Transport Association Annual Reports 1960–2005).

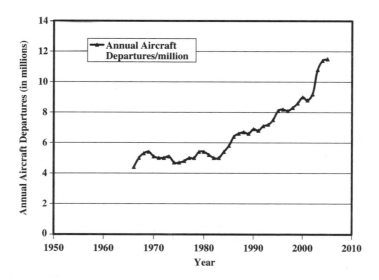

Fig. 4.4   Number of flight departures per year, showing more than twice the flight rate between 1975 and 2005 (data taken from Air Transport Association Annual Reports 1960–2005).

leading up to 1978, the airlines operated profitably with relatively low LFs. Passenger comfort and in-flight amenities (e.g., business-class and first-class passenger service) and frequent flyer programs acted as the factors for the airlines to compete with each other. This strategy

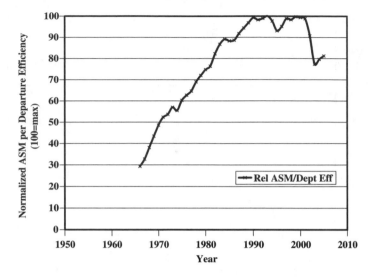

Fig. 4.5   Normalized metric that relates seats per departure over the period 1965 to 2005.

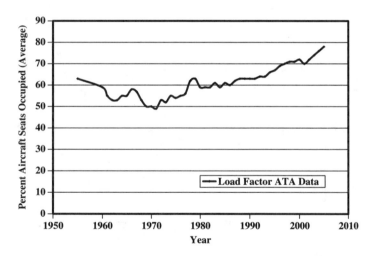

Fig. 4.6   Airline average annual load factor from 1955 to 2005 (ATA data taken from Annual Reports 1960–2005).

continued to work even after deregulation in 1978, but the LFs had to increase to make the flights profitable in an unregulated environment where the fares that the airlines could charge dropped on most routes and increased flight frequency was used to both attract more passengers as well as to provide added convenience to their preferred flyers.

The growth of the low-cost carrier (LCC) airlines (i.e., Southwest, AirTran, JetBlue, etc.) in the late 1990s and the increasing use of the Internet for ticketing (where fares were presented to the flyer ranked by price) changed the flying business model significantly (and perhaps permanently). Prior to these innovations, the airlines made most of their profits from business-class and first-class passengers. Economy-class passengers (many of whom were leisure travelers who were highly price sensitive) flew at or below the marginal cost of their transport. Increasingly, the upper-end business traveler (with a substantially lower sensitivity to price but a much higher sensitivity to travel predictability and comfort) began to eschew commercial aviation in favor of using private business aircraft. What was once viewed as a perk for only the company's top executives, the use of business jets by lesser mortals is now increasingly common. Thus, the airlines were forced to rely heavily on economy-class customers to make their flights profitable, which led to even higher LFs, yield management of their fares, and the use of small RJs on low-profitability markets to attract the leisure passengers. The systemically high LFs also led to an extremely fragile transportation system that has little resiliency or adaptability when confronted with either weather- or congestion-induced flight cancellations. (See Wang [2007] for a more detailed discussion of the effects of LF on a cancelled flight passenger's re-booking probability.) And, unfortunately, it will require more than a Passenger's Bill of Rights to fix this problem.

High flight frequency, which is important to business passengers, was never sacrificed in an attempt to compete for the remaining business traveler who could not afford to fly in a private business aircraft. Looking forward from today, we expect the advent of fractional aircraft ownership and a new breed of very light jets (VLJ) to further accelerate the deterioration of the old legacy airline business model.

U.S. Airports: Just How Long Can the Lines Get?

Within the next 10 years, many experts predict that there will be as many as **1.1 billion** air travelers per year in the United States (*FAA Aerospace Forecasts Fiscal Years 2006–2017*). However, the limited capacity of major airports within the United States is sure to constitute many heavy chokepoints, creating a major portion of the congestion in the system. Moreover, though the authors applaud (for several reasons) the numerous improvements planned for the airspace in the future, they will regrettably have minimal impact on the delays that plague the air system today. In short, "It's the airports, stupid!" (This was pointed out by former FAA Administrator David Hinson in 1996, but few listened or understood.)

A projection of the growth in the demand for air travel in the major metropolitan areas, coupled with FAA assessments of future airport capacities [FAA 2006; DOT 2004], reveals that 15 airports will need additional capacity by 2013, and eight more will face capacity limitations by 2020. Later in the book, the authors address the likelihood of achieving the needed capacity enhancements by these dates, but for those eager to know the answer now, the probability of meeting the projected demand is—drum roll, please—pretty small at best.

Table 4.2 shows the top 30 airports ranked by Airport Councils International (ACI) in 2000 and 2005. Notice that most of our major airports have reached operational levels exceeding those of 2000. As mentioned earlier, the delays in 2000 were characterized as the worst in the history of aviation. The 2005 delays and cancellations, however, were almost as bad. The shaded areas in the table indicate that either the number of aircraft movements is above where it was in 2000 or the number of enplaned passengers was above the level in 2000. In many cases, the number of passengers has risen faster than the number of flights (the result of the average LFs going from 72% in 2000 to over 80% today). This is a historic high for aircraft LFs and is a direct cause for the feeling that all of the flights are full with no extra seats (and no leg room!). But these average LFs understate the actual LFs that most frequent flyers experience when they fly. A fair number of flights are not even close to being half full (e.g., there are aircraft repositioning flights that would fly empty if no passengers could be found to populate the aircraft) and aircraft being flown primarily to protect market access [Le 2006].

Also note that several European airports are shown as high enplanement capacity airports. For future reference, the 2006 ATM arrival delay statistics [EC 2007] for these airports are as follows: Paris (CDG, 2.2 minutes), Frankfurt (FRA, 2.7 minutes), London (LHR, 3.0 minutes), and Amsterdam (AMS, 0.7 minutes). By contrast, note that New York/New Jersey Newark airport has a comparable number of operations **with 25% fewer passengers and over 10 times the average flight delay**.

Note also that some major airports are above the 2000 level of arriving flights (e.g., Atlanta, Chicago, Las Vegas, Houston Bush, Denver, and Philadelphia), whereas others (e.g., Phoenix and Detroit) have fewer flight movements but more passengers (i.e., higher LFs). And some U.S. airports have made this list for the first time in 2005. Airports such as Van Nuys and Long Beach, California, are in the same category as the Madrid, Spain; Toronto, Canada; and New York Kennedy airports.

So just what is going on here? Unless passengers fly in private planes (e.g., business jets) or Jet Blue (into Long Beach), they probably have not flown into Van Nuys or Long Beach airports. These are categorized as general-aviation airports. One might be surprised that a general-aviation airport is as busy as the data show, but these numbers stand as proof positive that the asserted growth in heretofore business airline passengers switching to noncommercial business aircraft is real. Moreover, it is increasingly obvious that a good cost-effectiveness argument can be made for this switch, making it ever more likely that this trend away from increasing unpleasant and unpredictable commercial airline travel is likely to continue for the elite.

As mentioned, many people feel that the performance of the U.S. air transportation system in 2000 (the year before the 9/11 terrorist attacks on the World Trade Center and the Pentagon) was the worst it has ever been. Several things were happening that year: 1) air transport movements were at an all-time high (over 5.5 million movements); 2) aircraft LFs were at an all-time high of 72%; and 3) New York LaGuardia Airport had its historic aircraft arrival slot controls relaxed by Congress (the 2001 congressional transportation authorization bill called AIR-21). This led to massive delays and flight cancellations at LaGuardia that affected the entire nation's air transportation network performance. (That's right, one airport's problems is reputed to have bogged down the country's entire air travel system! The authors doubt that LGA has this big of an effect on the entire system, but ATL and ORD certainly do.) By 2001, the economy had started into a recession, taking demand off the system, and Congress allowed the FAA to institute a slot lottery at LaGuardia to bring the delays and flight cancellations back to only ~10% above its historic average. These factors reduced the network's congestion. But then those infamous jetliners broke through the September morning skyline over New York, and the bottom fell out for all air travel for a while.

From the DOT/FAA standpoint, the impending congestion disaster foretold by the experiences of CY00 was averted, only to be replaced by airport security concerns. Much of the subsequent passenger angst about aircraft delays was diverted to the extra hour or two that most passengers are now spending at the airports, coupled with the irritating process of passing through the airport security process. The public was told at the initiation of these security measures that these were for our own protection. And most passengers, like the good sheep that they are, accepted this without serious challenge. However, a half a decade has now passed, and some things have changed, which suggests that

Table 4.2   ACI Data for the Top 30 Airports in the World (ranked by total aircraft movements)[a–c]

Airport	Total movements		Total passengers	
	2005	2000	2005	2000
Atlanta Hartsfield (ATL)	980,386	915,454	85,907,423	80,162,407
Chicago O'Hare (ORD)	972,248	908,989	76,510,003	72,144,244
Dallas–Ft. Worth (DFW)	711,878	837,779	59,176,265	60,687,122
Los Angeles (LAX)	650,629	783,433	61,489,398	66,424,767
Las Vegas (LAS)	605,046	521,300	43,989,982	36,865,866
Houston Bush (IAH)	562,966	483,570	39,684,640	35,251,372
Denver (DEN)	560,669	520,073	43,387,513	38,751,687
Phoenix (PHX)	555,256	637,779	41,213,754	36,040,469
Philadelphia (PHL)	535,666	484,308	31,495,385	
Minneapolis–St. Paul (MSP)	532,240	523,146	37,604,373	36,751,632
Paris (CDG)	522,619	517,657	53,798,308	48,246,137
Detroit (DTW)	521,899	555,375	36,389,294	35,535,080
Charlotte (CLT)	521,878	452,009		
Washington DC Dulles (IAD)	509,468	456,436		
Cincinnati (CVG)	496,364	477,842		
Frankfurt (FRA)	490,147	458,731	52,219,412	49,360,630
London (LHR)	477,884	466,815	67,915,403	64,606,826
Salt Lake City (SLC)	455,472			

Airport			
Newark (EWR)	437,402	33,999,990	34,188,468
Amsterdam (AMS)	420,736	44,163,098	39,606,925
Madrid (MAD)	415,677	41,940,059	32,893,190
Van Nuys (VNY)	411,317		
Toronto (YYZ)	409,401	29,914,750	28,930,036
Boston (BOS)	409,066		27,412,926
New York Laguardia (LGA)	404,853		
Munich (MUC)	398,838		
Memphis (MEM)	392,360		
Miami (MIA)	381,610	31,008,453	33,621,273
Phoenix (DVT)	378,225		
Long Beach (LGB)	353,011		
New York Kennedy (JFK)		41,885,104	32,856,220
San Fransico (SFO)	429,222	32,802,363	41,040,995
Beijing (PEK)		41,004,008	
Hong Kong (HKG)		40,269,847	32,752,359
Bangkok (BKK)		38,985,043	29,616,432
Singapore (SIN)		32,430,856	28,618,200
Tokyo (NRT)		31,451,274	
Seoul (SEL)			36,727,124

[a]Source: Airports Council International.
[b]Data from list of top 30 airports.
[c]Blank data fields indicate the airport was below the top 30 in that category.

perhaps it is time to challenge that assertion. For example, with the strengthening and locking of the pilot's cabin door, experts believe that the likelihood of a terrorist in the passenger's cabin being able to hijack the airplane is quite low. It was never obvious why certain personal items (e.g., finger nail clippers) were banned. And items such as pocket knives, understandably prohibited when the pilot's cabin was still unprotected, no longer pose a credible threat vis-à-vis hijacking the airplane. If these items were not banned prior to 9/11, why are they banned now?

Concerns about the current airport security implementation will not be repeated here. They are addressed elsewhere in this book. However, they include the resulting overall costs to the airlines and flying public, the additional hassle that U.S. passengers must endure (in contrast to other parts of the world), and ironically the added security concerns related to the generation of a large number of passengers congregated within the airport but outside of the security apparatus.

Some U.S. airports have been at their capacity maximums **for over 40 years**. In 1968, all three New York/New Jersey airports, Chicago O'Hare, and Washington National (Reagan) airports were so congested that Congress imposed slot controls on these airports. As mentioned earlier, these arrival time slot allocations have been referred to as the high-density rule in the United States. Unlike in the United States, however, the rest of the world's major airports (or at least most of them) are slot-controlled for safety, congestion, and environmental reasons.

Prior to 1985, New Jersey's Newark airport was taken out from under HDR (for reasons that are unclear) and is now one of the worst airports in the world for flight delays and cancellations. After deregulation in 1978, the airlines that were operating out of the slots at the HDR airports were granted defined operating rights of these slots by the DOT in 1985. Their use was predicated on an 80% "use-or-lose" rule, and a secondary trading market was established. In fact, because the secondary market was not public or blind (and politicians routinely hand out new "virtual" slots for free), there has been very little secondary trading of these slots outside of bankruptcy negotiations.

In addition, in the 2001 AIR-21 congressional authorization, the slots on Chicago, LaGuardia, and Kennedy were greatly relaxed and allocated to small aircraft at perceived underserved markets. This legislation has led to massive delays and flight cancellations at LaGuardia (2000 and 2001), Chicago O'Hare (2004), and JFK (by the summer of 2007). The FAA reduced the LGA flight schedule from 20% over maximum safe operating capacity to 10% over maximum safe operating capacity using a lottery to allocate the 10% new slots above the 1985 ownership level. The administrator of the FAA negotiated privately with the airlines to intimidate them into reducing their schedules in a return to the preregulation days without the benefit of the CAB economics analysis. But at least the FAA administrator only tried to control arrival and departure times and did not meddle with the airfares or profit margins. Still, the result negatively affected the business viability of some airlines, and the impact on passenger service continues to be felt throughout the entire airport network.

Finally, as a foil to the U.S. experience, note that the number of passengers traveling through the new Asian airports is much larger than many of the congested U.S. airports without the same number of delays. And many of these airports are no larger than Miami or Newark.

Case Study of New York LaGuardia Airport

Along with Washington, D.C.'s National Airport, New York's LaGuardia Airport (LGA) is one of the oldest and most used airports in the world. Although quite advanced in its day, LaGuardia has a simple layout that dates back to the 1930s. But today its geography seriously limits its expansion capacity. It is one of the highest-value airports in the United States but also one of the most congested. Figure 4.7 shows the basic design of LaGuardia. One runway (typically RW22) is used for arrivals, and the other (preferably RW13) is used for departures. Accordingly, this simple geometry is relatively easy to measure, analyze, and model.

LaGuardia Airport has a long history of severe congestion. As mentioned, in 1968 the FAA instituted the HDR to limit the number of takeoffs and landings during certain hours of the day. The landing slots were rapidly filled by the airlines already flying from LaGuardia. Over time, the airlines used these "slots" in bankruptcy proceedings as financial assets. Specific "grandfather" rights were given to the long-time users of LGA in 1985. Understandably, the airlines guarded their "perceived" slots jealously, partly to ensure that competitors did not have access to them and partly because many of the airlines had invested money into LaGuardia (for hangers, etc.) and wanted to make certain that these investments were not threatened.

In 2000, that HDR was amended by adding 300 additional landing slots (a 30% increase of airport daily operations) at LaGuardia. These additional slots were granted to nonincumbent airlines that fly aircraft

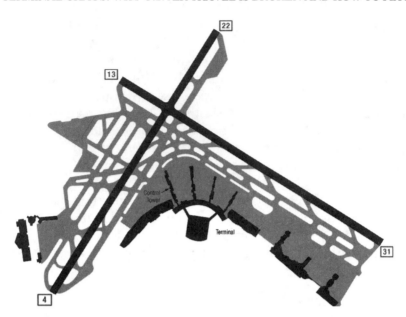

Fig. 4.7   New York LaGuardia Airport, showing the two major runways, taxi-ways, terminals, and ramps.

with 70 seats or fewer to provide better access to new entrant airlines and the medium-sized cities in the surrounding states. But the real result of this rule change was record delays at LaGuardia (see Fig. 4.8). Everyone (even some sheep) agreed that the situation was untenable and that the HDR had to be modified to restore order.

As an initial step, the number of slots was reduced, and a lottery was introduced to allocate the remaining *new congressional virtual* slots as a temporary congestion measure to help control the delays. The events of 9/11 in 2001 and the following economic slowdown in mid-2002 reduced demand and congestion and diverted attention from airport congestion to airport safety. Since then, the growth in air traffic has steadily grown, once again putting substantial pressure on the airport's infrastructure, not to mention the good spirits of the passengers. Average arrival delays per flight reached 28 minutes in July 2002 and 31 minutes in July 2005.

Unfortunately, LaGuardia has little room for expansion, as it is largely surrounded by water. And assuming a normal expansion of the population's interest in air travel (driven by demographics if nothing else), these delays are likely to continue to rise as the airlines using LaGuardia continue to try to expand their flights into the airport. This

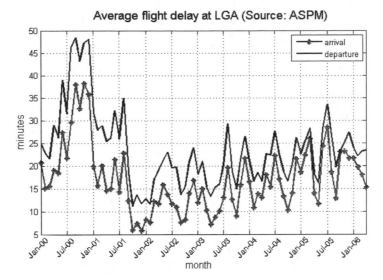

Fig. 4.8   Delays at LGA following the addition of slots to nonincumbent airlines [Le 2006].

might sound contradictory to some, assuming all of the slots are taken. But the reality is that more slots have been granted than the airport's listed operating capacity can accommodate. Some airlines are not using their slots efficiently. It costs the airline little to hold them, and it serves the purpose of restricting competition from new airlines at that airport.

The average aircraft size serving LaGuardia in recent years has decreased from 129 seats to 96 seats per plane (see Fig. 4.9). (See Robyn [2007] for a good discussion of this general trend.) On the other hand, while having no expansion possibility, LaGuardia has seen the number of operations constantly increasing from the peak year 2000 of air transportation.

Research done at GMU indicates that regulations which encourage up-gauging (i.e., using larger aircraft), coupled with market mechanisms, can greatly reduce these delays while still ensuring that the airline industry operates profitably. As discussed in Chapter 7 and Appendix E, the authors hypothesized that the current congestion situation is caused in large part by the existing rules. Specifically, they questioned whether the current grandfather rights with an 80% "use-or-lose" requirement, slot exemptions, and weight-based landing fees lead to inefficient use of airport capacity at slot-controlled airports. Such inefficiency affects both airlines and airports. Thus, as the U.S. system faces projected traffic

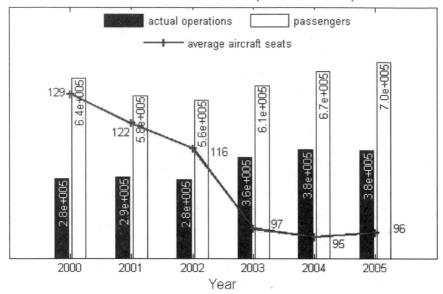

Fig. 4.9   Decreasing aircraft size at LGA and increasing operations despite no expansion possibility [Le 2006].

growth in the future, it is increasingly obvious that the current rules at slot-controlled airports require serious reexamination of market-based congestion control mechanisms.

U.S. Government: A History of Organization, Reorganization, and Inactivity

As early as 1919, the Europeans developed the first operational air/ground radiotelephone voice system for passenger air transport service between London and Paris. In the United States, Thorp Hiscock of Boeing Air Transport and John Summer Anderson [later to become president of Aeronautical Radio, Inc. (ARINC)] demonstrated voice weather communications to aircraft in 1928. In 1927, the Federal Radio Commission [later to become the Federal Communications Commission (FCC)] granted the first license and frequency allocations to aviation services. ARINC was incorporated in Delaware in December of 1929 to represent the airlines in providing a single corporate entity to develop and provide radio communications to commercial aircraft. The FCC transferred all frequency licenses to ARINC in the same year.

Then, to develop improved voice communications standards and equipment, the Radio Technical Commission for Aeronautics (RTCA) was established in 1935, and the Air Transportation Association (ATA) was established in 1936 to help the industry improve technical and safety standards. All of these organizations are still active today. Also in 1936, the federal government (via the CAA) first assumed responsibility for air traffic control, although the first government-operated ATC centers were not established until 1946.

In 1938, ARINC (in conjunction with Bell Labs) and TWA tested the first very high-frequency (VHF) voice services to aircraft. The military adopted the VHF amplitude-modulated (AM) radio system developed by ARINC and Bell Labs for use in World War II. After the war (1945), the International Civil Aviation Organization (ICAO) and the International Telecommunications Union (ITU) were organized to harmonize the growth in international air travel and tele-communications. It was at this time that the ATA and RTCA conducted a study under Special Committee 31 (headed by Del Rentzel of ARINC) that basically set out the technical roadmap and architecture of today's ATC system. Del Rentzel was appointed by President Truman to head the CAA, and later the CAB, and he ultimately became the undersecretary of commerce for Transportation. In 1958, President Eisenhower abolished the CAA and established the FAA. It is reputed that this action was predicated by the Grand Canyon midair collision that could have been prevented by the use of radar. Previously, the CAA had been unable to adopt this technology that was developed in World War II, almost 15 years earlier, and so the new FAA was instructed to do so.

ARINC turned over most of the aviation frequencies it had been using for almost 30 years to the new FAA at this time. The FAA adopted both the technology and the system architecture defined by ARINC and the RTCA. And since the mid-1950s, the system has been changed very little [CAA 1956].

Toward the end of World War II, the International Civil Aviation Organization was formed as part of the newly formed United Nations to regulate international civil aviation. Currently, there are approximately 180 member countries. Each member country must have a civil aviation authority to provide communications, navigation, surveillance and air traffic management (CNS/ATM) services at internationally accepted standards. For the United States, this agency is the FAA.

In addition to the provision of CNS/ATM services, each country must provide aircraft safety oversight for the certification of aircraft airworthiness and aircraft operation. Until recently, these two functions (CNS/ATM and safety oversight) have been supplied by the same government agencies.

Since 1990, there has been a trend among industrialized nations to privatize (through different means ranging from wholly owned government organizations to complete private ones) the provision of CNS/ ATM services and retain government safety oversight as an essential governmental service. (See Oster [2006], McDougall [2006], and Poole [2005; 2006] for a good discussion of this desirable trend.) In the United States today, the vast majority of the ATC system equipment is owned and operated by the federal government. Many of the industrialized nations are turning this function over to private or government-owned corporations so that the rapid changes in technology and productivity-enhancing procedures (and, subsequently, required increased access to investment capital) can be incorporated into the ever-changing ATC systems that will be required in the future. Federally operated systems are typically financed by a combination of user taxes and general tax fund contributions. The newly privatized system (e.g., in Canada) and quasi-privatized systems (e.g., in Germany, Australia, or New Zealand) are totally supported by user fees and have access to private financial capital for modernization investments. And this access to investment capital has turned out to be a key ingredient in modernizing an individual country's air traffic systems. In a sense, this is a return to the way in which air traffic management was initially conceptualized by the private sector and conducted at its inception. And contrary to popular belief, the provision of CNS/ATM services has never been an inherently governmental function.

The CNS/ATM function has evolved from the 1920s provision of primitive navigation and communications services to a highly computerized ATM systems with central flow control management (CFCM) or traffic flow management (TFM) using a combination of ground and space-based communications and navigation equipment (as shown in Fig. 4.10). With the advent of radar in World War II and the follow-on 1950s deployment of surveillance radars in various parts of the United States and Canada (for air defense against Soviet long-range bombers), the air space surveillance function was well-established when added to the FAA's provision of services in the early 1960s.

The physical limitations of radar at this time set the aircraft separation standards that are still in use today. These separation standards (in conjunction with the number of runways that are available) set

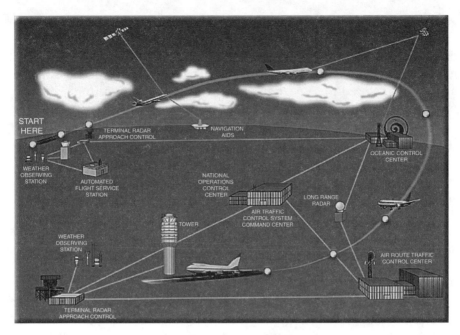

Fig. 4.10 Pictorial of the many components and subsystems that exist in the current U.S. National Airspace System (NAS), and that are typical of a modern air traffic management system. [Source: U.S. FAA NAS 4.0 (FAA 1998).]

the maximum operational capacity that the air transportation system can support, at a specified level of safety. These separation standards are typically five nautical miles (nine kilometers) in high altitude airspace (i.e., above 18,000 feet) and three nautical miles (six kilometers) in low-altitude airspace [typically within 60 nautical miles (110 kilometers) of an airport]. Airspace that does not have radar surveillance must maintain procedural separation using aircraft onboard navigation position fixes and ATC communications. These separation standards usually exceed 60 nautical miles (110 kilometers) and are used in oceanic airspace and undeveloped countries that lack radar services.

The basic radar physical properties that dictate these standards are beam width and sweep rate. In practice, the en-route aircraft are routinely maintained at 7 to 30 miles (13 to 56 kilometers) of separation as a result of ATC cognitive workload limitations. A typical controller can maintain situational awareness on four to seven aircraft at a time. When the workload of an airspace sector (a region of space in area and altitude that is allocated to one 25-kHz radio frequency) exceeds this amount, two (or sometimes three) controllers work as a team to maintain aircraft separation. In the United States, there are over 730 high-altitude sectors, and in Europe there are over 460 sectors. Adding in sectors at lower altitudes and those devoted to airport approach or departure corridors, there are in total over 2500 sectors in the United States.

The number of sectors that are available to high-density airspace in the United States and Europe is limited to the number of communication channels that are available to the FAA/CAA. The number of communications channels that are available is dictated by the technical efficiency in which the allocated radio spectrum is used. The radio spectrum is allocated and controlled by the ITU, also a United Nations charter organization. The current U.S. FAA radio spectrum is inefficiently used because of the obsolete VHF radio specifications. The FCC has repeatedly urged the FAA and DOT to upgrade their systems to allow their valuable spectrum to be used by an ever-expanding array of new applications. It has been suggested that the FAA could use the proceeds from a new spectrum auction to pay for the modernization of the current ATC communication system [Robyn 2007].

Unlike in the United States, where the FAA operates the entire airspace ATC (from airport tower to upper-altitude airspace), Europe has formed a central, trans-European organization called Eurocontrol to coordinate the national provision of ATC services and operates the Central Flow Management Unit (CFMU) and upper airspace over central and (increasingly) eastern Europe.

Both the United States and Europe have experienced considerable delays in introducing new technology over the last 25 years because of the difficulty of civil government agencies developing complex computer software that can demonstrate extreme levels of safety. The FAA's software is grossly outdated and in severe need of replacement. What is needed is new software to significantly increase the level of ATC automation and thereby reduce air traffic controller workload. A ubiquitous digital transfer of information from the air traffic service provider to the aircraft is an essential element required to make increased automation work. Accordingly, the European Commission is expected to mandate that all air navigation service providers have controller-pilot data-link communications (CPDLC) in place by 2010, with all aircraft equipped by 2014. About 350 European airliners are already using CPDLC in the Maastricht Upper Area Control Center airspace. Unfortunately, the FAA currently has no definitive plan for exploiting this technology for the foreseeable future.

The privatized ATS organizations have demonstrated [see McDougall 2006] much better capability to modernize their systems, and aircraft manufacturers have been much more successful in introducing computerized flight management systems (FMS) that reduce pilot workload and provide onboard aircraft collision-avoidance systems (ACAS). Thus, not surprisingly, much of the increase in air transportation safety over the last 40 years has been attributed to the introduction of these aircraft automation systems.

CHAPTER 5

Why Do the Airlines Not Just Fix This Problem?

Game theoreticians like to talk about the "prisoner's dilemma." There are several variants of the story, but the authors' favorite version involves three prisoners who have escaped from a prison on a remote island. To fully gain their freedom, however, they must pass over shark-infested waters to get to the mainland. Unfortunately, the boat they have acquired for their escape is designed to carry only two people. All can get off the island safely if two cross first, but one will have to return to get the remaining prisoner. So the question is, which one would be willing to volunteer to remain on the island and count on the honor and good nature of one of his fellow prisoners to come back for him? For many, the answer would be simple—none of them (after all, they did not get to be prisoners for nothing). So, the overwhelming temptation would be for all three to crowd into the boat and risk capsizing, drowning, and being eaten by sharks.

Economists tell a related story called "the tragedy of the commons." (It is about sheep, and so many readers should be able to identify.) As this story goes, there is a pasture (historically referred to as a "commons") that is free to all sheepherders for the grazing of their sheep. The grass is good and plentiful there, and inevitably more and more sheepherders bring their sheep to graze on the free grass. By contrast, the sheepherders must pay a fee to graze on the meadows surrounding the village. But the commons are free, so when the grass becomes overgrazed there, nobody wants to return to paying a fee on the meadows surrounding the village. Furthermore, removing one's sheep from the commons (and paying for the grazing elsewhere) would make it better for everyone else and would also make one less competitive on price

71

when it comes time to sell the sheep. The sheepherders could, of course, get together and change this situation by charging a usage fee to control overconsumption of the grass on the commons. But they simply cannot all agree to give up the free access. It is just too tempting. Thus, in the pursuit of higher profits from free grazing, they all lose a valuable pasture (and we gain some valuable insight into why the airlines are unable to fix the industry themselves).

Deregulation and the Pros and Cons of the Hub-and-Spoke System

Without a doubt, the U.S. airlines today find themselves both in a prisoner's dilemma and suffering the tragedy of the commons. They deal with their competitive problems in a largely deregulated market by making decisions that are least bad for their stockholders but also not very good for their passengers. From their standpoint, these are logical decisions. However, a recent Nobel Prize in economics was awarded for applying a combination of both game theory and economics. Referred to as a Nash Equilibrium, it was found that in a multisided competition (or "game"), the players might often opt for the least of all evils rather than compete for a maximum in which they might individually lose even more. Most enlightened governments today recognize that it is their responsibility to look out for both the welfare of their citizens and their vital national industries. But this is not really happening in the U.S. air transportation system today. In fact, in the case of the United States, the current Nash Equilibrium is a major part of the problem.

As discussed earlier, prior to airline deregulation, the airlines were making steady progress in both air service and profitability. Both the airline's ticket fares and service routes were controlled by the government's CAB. Alfred Kahn, one of President Carter's economic advisors, played a prominent role in airline deregulation, and he recently defended this act by noting that the airlines' freedom to enter/exit domestic markets and to set prices in a competitive market has generated enormous benefits for consumers (estimated to exceed $20 billion annually) [Kahn 2004].

He is right. And not surprisingly, the benefits of these lower prices and greater access to a wide set of cities were manifested in the extraordinary growth in airline travel, coupled with the commensurate economic growth in the cities served. But the whole system has also paid a price for this growth, as it has brought with it significant congestion to the hub airports. Moreover, the larger airlines that used the hubbing strategy quickly dominated these airports, resulting in one or two airlines at each of the hub airports imposing de facto barriers to new airline entrants by means of controlling most of the gates through long-term leases. One of the principal arguments for deregulation was to lower barriers to new entrants, but airline hubbing strategies inhibited this. And the lack of the FAA's ability to modernize (or to step out of the way of modernization) or to show enough courage to regulate airport operations to safe and predictable operational rates has allowed hub congestion and airline gate dominance to provide a significant barrier to new entrants.

As might be expected, not all airlines were able to adapt well to the new highly competitive situation that followed deregulation. In the late 1980s, there was a decline in airline profitability, sending some airlines into bankruptcy. The economic decline in airline profitability around 1990 and 2000 also sent more airlines into bankruptcy. Frequently, this was because the airlines tried to expand their fleets too rapidly (they incurred more debt than they could handle), or they simply owned planes with more seat capacity than the demand justified. Table 5.1 is a list of airline bankruptcies between 1982 and mid-2006.

As an industry, the airlines initially prospered under deregulation. The drop in ticket prices resulting from vigorous competition was more than balanced by the sharp growth in passengers who were eager to take advantage of the lower fares. But airlines have always suffered from economic cycles. Figure 5.1 shows the cumulative airline profits, as published by ATA, from 1960 to 2004. A large decrease in air travel experienced by the first Gulf War in 1990 led to a catastrophic loss in profits by the airlines that was not recovered until 1996. After that, large profits were accumulated until about 2000, when the worst delays and cancellations in history were reported and the economy started into a downturn. The events of 9/11 in 2001 only exacerbated this decline. And by 2005, the airlines had lost almost $14 billion **more** than they had ever earned in modern times. Many major legacy airlines have failed completely (e.g., PanAm, TWA, Eastern, Braniff), and several are continually in and out of bankruptcy court (e.g., United, Continental, US Airways, and Delta). And ultimately, the success of low-cost carriers (LCC), led by Southwest and now several others, has forever changed the fare structures that once allowed the legacy airlines to make a profit for many years.

And speaking of the LCCs, Fig. 5.2 illustrates that, dollar-wise, they are doing just fine. In fact, the LCC airlines have consistently made profits during these difficult times using a very different business model than the legacy network carriers. For one thing, the LCCs will only fly to metropolitan areas that promise a good return on investment.

Table 5.1   Airline Bankruptcy from 1982 through 2006

Company	Chapter 11	Out	Chapter 7
America West	6/27/1991	8/25/1994	——
Braniff (1)	5/13/1982	9/?/1983	——
Braniff (2)	9/28/1989	5/?/1992	——
Continental (1)	9/24/1983	6/30/1986	——
Continental (2)	12/3/1990	4/27/1993	——
Delta	9/14/2005	?	——
Eastern	3/9/1989	——	1/18/1991
Midway (1)	3/25/1991	——	11/27/1991
Midway (2)	8/14/2001	——	10/30/2003
Northeastern	1/8/1985	?	——
Northwest	9/14/2005	?	——
Pan Am (1)	1/8/1991	?	——
Pan Am (2)	2/26/1998	6/28/1998	——
TWA (1)	1/30/1992	11/3/1993	——
TWA (2)	6/30/1995	8/24/1995	——
TWA (3)	1/10/2001	4/9/2001	——
United	12/9/2002	2/1/2006	——
US Airways (1)	8/11/2002	3/31/2003	——
US Airways (2)	9/12/2004	9/27/2005	——
Independence	11/8/2005	——	1/6/2006
ATA	10/26/2004	?	——

For example, Topeka is the capital of Kansas, and according to the 2000 census, it is the 180th largest city in the United States (with a population of 122,000). Nonetheless, it lost all scheduled air service in 2004. In effect, the LCC airlines essentially have a cream-skimming business model, and because they have no network to service, they have no need to service what they consider to be unprofitable city pairs. This makes good business sense, although not necessarily a robust national transportation system.

This, of course, begs yet another question: "What if all airlines were to adopt the LCC model?" We can only speculate, but if the LCC includes only flying the cities that are profitable for the airline, it strongly implies that a fair number of middle-size cities in the United States would either lose their air service altogether or (more likely) have it severely reduced. We do not know the implications of this for the overall U.S. economy, but the protests and resulting political pressure on the airlines to restore such service would likely be severe.

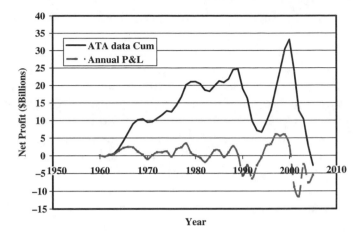

Fig. 5.1   Cumulative airline profits from 1960 through 2004. (Source: ATA Annual Reports 1960–2005.)

From a passenger standpoint, the good news is that the airline yields are at historic lows. In constant 2004 dollars, airline yield has decreased from over \$0.30 per RPM (preregulation) to less than \$0.10 per RPM today. Interestingly, **air travel is probably the least expensive mode of transportation in the United States**. And the LCCs have brought these yields down to a new level of expected performance that

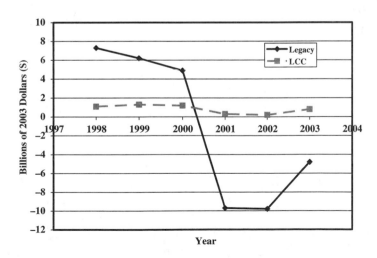

Fig. 5.2   Legacy airlines are the primary ones losing money [GAO 2004a].

might change the nature of mass commercial air transportation for the foreseeable future.

In addition, ever since deregulation in 1978, the federal government has had a little-known essential air services appropriation to provide economic subsidies to cities that could not attract air service based upon the inherent profitability of the service. This program has been growing in recent years with the growth of the LCC business model and the low fares that are a direct result of this competition. It is not clear, however, how air services will be provided to smaller communities in the future. Flying small aircraft into congested hub airports will probably not survive any market-based slot allocation system that will ultimately be adopted. Specialty small city hub airports with cross-links to the major hubs might emerge in the future. This is an important issue that requires future research.

As discussed, the widespread adoption of the hub-and-spoke system was certainly one of the important dynamics that occurred after the 1978 deregulation. The network is so large and complex, however, that it is difficult to understand its basic nature. The large numerical simulation models that have been constructed to represent this complex network (with over 65,000 flights per day included in the simulations) are now being used to map out the nonlinear, systems-wide network response functions. And recent work with a stochastic Monte Carlo simulation model and optimum airline scheduling models under development at GMU is showing that practices such as independent airline scheduling and airline network interactions have a much greater non-linear impact on delays than was previously believed. The simple analytic model described in Appendix D illustrates how improving schedule synchronization at major airports (by DOT-run arrival auctions at all of the major congested airports) will increase capacity and schedule predictability.

Many economists and operations research experts agree [e.g., Rassenti et al. 1982; Ball et al. 2005] that a well-designed public–private auction system needs to be developed to properly load-balance the system to achieve both maximum efficient use of existing infrastructure and to achieve maximum safety by not overscheduling airport runways (as seen at LaGuardia in October of 2000). If underutilized runway capacity is to be exploited—at cities such as Kansas City, Raleigh–Durham, and Denver—then new regulations will need to be developed to provide incentives for airlines to invest in hub airports that offer significantly less origin and destination (OD) traffic than 50%.

O&D passengers are those that tend to value the high flight frequency supplied by the hub for business travel and are willing to pay higher fares, schedule last-minute flights, and pay for first- or business-class fares. And under the old business models, these passengers generated a substantial amount of the profit margins for the legacy airlines. The economy-class seats could then be filled with leisure travelers paying lower fares that hopefully would cover at least their marginal costs. (When Donohue was at the FAA, the associate administrator for airports told him that a good rule of thumb used by airlines to open and maintain a hub airport was the expectation that the hub city would supply at least 50% of the O&D passenger traffic.)

The advent of LCCs, however, has changed this business model, and hub airport cities might no longer be required to generate a 50% O&D passenger base. Under these conditions, cities such as Kansas City and Raleigh–Durham, which have hub airport runway configurations, become attractive airports for airlines to expand national network capacity without increasing delays at cities such as Chicago.

Move over Big Boys: Emergence of Smaller Aircraft and Airports

Although surprising to many, the National Business Aircraft Association (NBAA) has been observing the rapid growth in business-class jet aircraft (GA) over the last 10 years, as shown in Fig. 5.3. In addition, the growth in regional-jet (RJ) usage has been nothing less than phenomenal over the same period.

This overall movement to smaller aircraft has been exasperating the nation's major airport congestion problems by enplaning fewer passengers

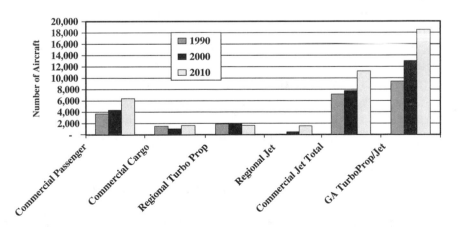

Fig. 5.3   Business jets outnumber commercial jets in the United States.

per aircraft over the last decade. The airline economic efficiency of using smaller aircraft at low operating costs, profitable load factors, and utilization rates has led to this trend. (Small RJs are inherently less efficient than larger jets but have had pilot salary scope clauses that made them look more cost effective. As fuel costs and RJ pilot salaries are increasing, however, this false economy is decreasing [Doganis 2002].) And as this trend continues, service to low-population-density regions will be serviced by an increasing number of small aircraft operating out of small and sometimes nontowered airports.

The United States does have a large number of airports that can be utilized by these aircraft. These airports are typically within a 30-minute drive from an urban population center, and they have paved runways greater than 3500 feet long. What the majority do not have, however, is an ATC tower, nor can they provide aircraft radar separation. Under IMC conditions, this lack of ATC infrastructure greatly reduces the value of these airports to provide reliable air transportation system capacity without a change in the ATC aircraft separation paradigm that relies on new technology and procedures.

Furthermore, some research suggests that flights to and from these small airports either originate or terminate in a high-density metropolitan community that already has saturated airports and airspace. Regional airports in these large metropolitan areas should absorb this increased traffic of smaller aircraft and not be allowed to congest the large major airports designed to handle large to very large aircraft with 1,000–10,000-acre facilities that are costly to procure, modernize, and maintain.

Thus, for small airports to be of significant help, regional metropolitan governments will need to provide adequate ground transportation modes to interconnect these disparate airports. We say more on this point in Chapter 7, where we discuss future policy options.

Overall, the systemic nature of the private-service air travel providers (i.e., the legacy airlines, the modern LCCs, and the growing number of business jet providers) in the United States is rapidly changing. Unless the rules are modified, these changes will certainly alter the way passengers are able to travel by air in many aspects.

And there are at least three assertions that the authors believe they can make with confidence. First, **the LCCs will continue to operate primarily on routes that are profitable**. They show no interest in expanding to cities where the passenger traffic is not likely to be profitable. So, to the extent these smaller cities can get air service at all, it will probably be associated with the legacy carriers.

Second, **legacy carriers are in serious trouble, and their future is uncertain**. In the past, these carriers made a major fraction of their profits by serving first-class and business travelers. The business-class passengers have become more price conscious (in part driven by government regulations prohibiting companies charging the government travel costs beyond the average air fare). And first-class passengers are increasingly choosing the option provided by the leasing of private business jets, avoiding not just the airlines, but (for the most part) the travails of passing through airports.

Third, **business jets are here to stay, and their numbers are growing rapidly**. As such, they pose a serious problem for the future of the aviation system. They carry far fewer passengers per plane (and thus are "inefficient" in their use of the airspace), where the number of "aircraft hulls" are the best measure of how crowded the airspace is. They also subtract from the legacy airlines passengers who are most needed to make the airlines profitable.

Finally, returning to the original question of the chapter, why do the airlines not just fix the problem? There seem to be two simple answers: 1) in some cases they cannot, and 2) in some cases they will not. For some airlines (especially the legacy carriers), a working business model seems unachievable, and their future (much like that of the three prisoners) seems pretty shaky. For others (such as the LCCs), the free green grass of the commons seems pretty tasty these day. But the ultimate question is, how long will it hold out? And what will the sheep do when there is nothing left to eat?

CHAPTER 6

Anatomy of Winners and Losers

In every system, there are winners and losers. The winners generally are those who are satisfied with the status quo, and the losers are the ones who want change. Identifying the winners and losers in the current U.S. air transportation system provides insight into why the current situation exists and why it might continue to worsen. However, it is worthwhile to remember that in today's rapidly changing economic and business environments today's winners are often tomorrow's losers and vice versa. In addition, if the system is allowed to continue along the path it is now traveling, the entire U.S. public will likely end up in the loser category.

Defenders of the Status Quo (aka the Winners)

It is clear that some agents or components of the air transportation system have little incentive to support major change. For them, potential solutions to the congestion problem will be costly, disruptive, or otherwise not preferable to the current situation. In November 2004, a "congestion game" was conducted at GMU to shed light on the creative tensions that exist between airlines (with different business models), airports, and federal government officials [Donohue et al. 2007; reprinted as Appendix E]. Several important observations were derived from that game. For example, the stakeholders that are currently unlikely to support change include the following:

- **Airlines** are complex organizations with very different business models. Airline executives have fiduciary obligations to their stockholders, not to their passengers or to the national air transportation system. Virtually every airline in operation today believes that restrictions on scheduling flights into the cities they serve would be bad for it (and some of the airlines are probably right). Thus, many think that political access is better for them than market-based solutions.

- **Airports**—In a sense, they win no matter what. They have the strongest political support for funding through the Airport Improvement Program (AIP) fund and deliver a monopolistic service to their local community. They operate shopping centers and parking lots that will be full even with extensive delays and flight cancellations. And much like the airlines, airports compete between cities for airline business. Thus, they tend to like solutions that give them an edge over their competition rather than network solutions that are good for the nation as a whole. Of course, some regional authorities that oversee the airports would probably disagree with this winner-like representation. Some recognize that, in the long run, failure to expand airport capabilities will hurt the economy of the region that the airport services by not providing the needed growing transportation capacity.

- **FAA Air Traffic Control Union (NATCA)**—NATCA is unique. It is a monopoly in that its membership contains almost every qualified FAA air traffic controller in the United States. [The previous union (PATCO) was not allowed to continue representing federal air traffic controllers after the 1981 controller strike. Over 10,000 controllers were fired, and a new union was established in 1987. If NATCA were to strike or (more likely) simply retire en masse (and the advanced age of a large fraction of the controllers and their attractive retirement benefits make the threat of retirement all too real), only a small number (and far too few to operate the existing ATM system) of military air traffic controllers would be available as replacements.] For a precedent, we would have to go back to the railroad unions of the 1940s and the Taft–Hartley Act, which was aimed at ensuring that a strike would not close down the U.S. economy by allowing the President to essentially hire the union members as government employees and forcing them to go back to work. However, in sharp contrast with the railroad workers union, NATCA members are already federal government employees who enjoy good pay, short working hours, excellent retirement benefits, excellent health benefits, and substantial paid leave. And the members protect all of this by routinely (and almost unbelievably) rejecting ATM modernization programs as "unproven" technological advances. (The authors agree that no system should be deployed into the system until it has been proven to be safe. But the real issue here is who gets to judge what is safe. Obviously, the controllers must play a prominent role because they are the ones who will be using the equipment. Safety always should be their first priority. But there also needs to be a third party involved who can independently judge whether the controller's assertions are valid. And it is highly notable that under the air traffic controllers' strong influence, the technology used to control U.S. air traffic today—namely, radars and AM radios—has not substantially changed since World War II.) (This is an issue discussed in more detail later in the chapter.)

- **Current manufacturers of FAA ATM equipment**—The current suppliers of FAA ATM equipment are dealing with a government staff that depends on its contractors for technical competency. These contractors therefore have a virtually guaranteed customer base with little to no competition.

- **Current manufacturers of general-aviation (GA) aircraft**—Today, GA (privately owned and operated) aircraft pay only a fraction of the ATM operating costs. Most government studies estimate that the economic cross-subsidies from the commercial air carrier airlines to the GA aircraft operator are in the billions of dollars annually. Not surprisingly, GA likes it that way. The congestion of the common carrier airlines is providing an expanding customer base for new business jets and the new VLJ air taxi market. GA manufacturers will thus oppose any change to the status quo until they become the scapegoat for congestion and major user fees are imposed on them. And if current trends continue, there will be more FAA ATM-controlled GA aircraft in the air than airline aircraft by the year 2010.

Agents of Change (aka the Losers)

In contrast to those who defend the status quo, several constituencies are—or should be—supportive of change to the management of the air transportation system.

- **U.S. travel and tourism industry**—Today the amusement parks, rental car companies, western ski resorts, beach communities, and other tourism industry components (e.g., hotels, rental cars, etc.), depend, in part, on low-cost air transportation to support their business models. The constraints on air transportation growth and increasing air fares are sure to cut out the leisure traveler first. Although this lobby has potential power to do something about this situation, it is highly fractionated and dispersed. Thus, it has not yet played a major role in the debate.

- **Leisure travelers**—These are the primary customers of the U.S. system. They are also the most sensitive to price and will be the first to abandon air travel as an option. Trips to visit distant family will be fewer. Population shifts will be affected. And because leisure travelers have no effective lobby in the government decision-making process, they are probably the biggest losers in today's system. [The president of the Air Travelers Association and the chairman of the Business Travel Coalition present themselves as representatives of the traveling public (see [Sharkey, 2007]). In the authors' opinion, however, they certainly do not represent any of our knowledgeable colleagues or the best interests of the traveling public in the current debate over congestion management.] The U.S. Congress is their best bet to solve the crisis in air transportation.
- **Business travelers**—Although less price-sensitive than the leisure travelers, even these travelers will be paying a higher price, not only in airfares but also in increased opportunity costs stemming from systematic delays and flight cancellations (which are sure to become worse than those of today). Executives will thus increasingly turn to private business jets to provide their flights. This will add further congestion pressure on both airports in high population centers and already congested airspace. The lower-level business traveler (aka the "road warrior") will likely continue to put up with increasing delays and cancellations, which will impose additional costs on business as a result of lost productivity.
- **FAA ATC infrastructure managers**—The FAA's income from the current tax structure is inadequate to support both high salaries of a low-productivity workforce and required modernization (see GAO [2005b] and Robyn [2007]). Any future air traffic service provider must be able to depend on an income stream linked to operational costs that will allow for the insertion of even existing digital telecommunications technology and provide technical/operational innovations to accommodate future demand. It is very important that the income be directly linked to the cost of providing a service so that the proper investment in innovative technology is identified.
- **U.S. manufacturers of large aircraft and their subcontractors**—The historically poor financial performance of today's U.S. airlines and the lack of growth potential in the U.S. system is significantly depressing the U.S. market for large commercial aircraft. The business aircraft market might remain strong, however, for the manufacture of high-end and VLJ aircraft. (See *Flying* magazine

articles on the Gulfstream G150 [April 2007] and the Cessna Mustang [May 2007] for good descriptions of two new aircraft in both categories.) Accordingly, Boeing Aircraft is looking more and more to overseas sales to support its manufacturing base. And it is only a matter of time until this industry contemplates a headquarters move offshore to be closer to its market and skilled employees with a lower-cost workforce. In fact, it has already moved a major portion of its manufacturing capacity.

There are, of course, others who could be added to the list of those who are or should be interested in changing the current air travel system. And they have rights too. Thus, there is increasing pressure to get Congress to pass the Passenger's Bill-of-Rights, similar to the one that exists in Europe. (Typically, these proposals call for the airlines to compensate passengers for delays or cancellation under some sort of sliding scale. They also include compensation for lost or delayed luggage. The thinking is that financial penalties will give the airlines an incentive to better performance. See Appendix F.) However, as mentioned earlier, this proposal was "gamed" several years ago at GMU and found to have little effect on the airline's behavior because it did not address the basic problem that exists in the U.S. set of airport access regulations (see [Donohue et al. 2007] in Appendix E). Thus, enacting a Bill of Rights without addressing the airlines' previously discussed prisoner's dilemma and fixing the airport overscheduling loophole in the 1978 deregulation act would seriously hurt airline profitability without addressing the delay and/or cancellation problem. When asked why the airlines overschedule the airport's infrastructure capacity and create terrible delays, some airline executives have responded that they are "simply playing by the rules." Moreover, they add, "If we do not like their behavior, we will have to change the rules." They are right.

Government "Solution": Faces of the FAA

So where is the federal government in all of this talk of winners and losers? To really understand why the government's main participant, the FAA, is satisfied with the status quo, one must first understand the reluctance of the FAA to modernize the ATC system and the already discussed aircraft separation and traffic flow controls that are in use today. Figure 6.1 shows the lack of ATC productivity increase from 1982 to 2006. As shown, an average controller handles about 2500 aircraft per year (a 44-week work year at 20 hours per week on station, which equates to about three aircraft per hour). Notice also that the cost per operation has increased from about $100 per operation to

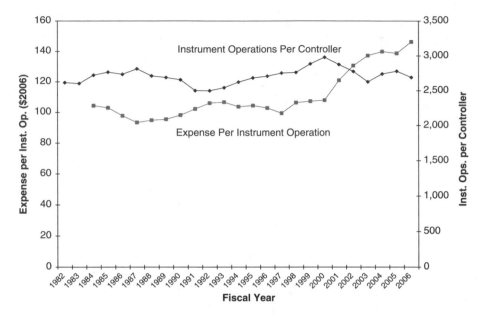

Fig. 6.1   History of FAA controller productivity [Robyn 2007].

about $150 per operation in inflation-adjusted dollars. This is amazing in light of the comparable increases in productivity in the rest of the world's economy (especially in telecommunications, perhaps the closest analog to ATC in the private sector). In reality, one could extend this trend back to 1960 with about the same result. To be frank, the FAA is a government monopoly with little or no incentive to innovate or invest in new technology and procedures that could increase productivity and ultimately air transportation capacity.

Many managers in the FAA Air Traffic Control Organization (ATO) have risen up through the ranks from being air traffic controllers. To become an air traffic controller, one must possess a minimum of a high-school education and one year of government-financed training. To really be successful, however, one also needs a relatively high IQ, good spatial perception, good spatial and temporal long-term memory, and the ability to deal with the potential stress of issuing verbal orders to keep at least two aircraft—each carrying hundreds of passengers at speeds of over 600 mph—from colliding into one another. A controller also needs to remain highly alert while sitting in front of a computer screen for up to two hours at a time, in many sectors and at some times of the day, with little aircraft activity.

So one logical question that might be asked is why do so many people line up to take the FAA exams to get these jobs? The answer is simple: high pay, good benefits, and low educational requirements. And how about this one? Why do many controllers make substantially more money than the FAA managers, senior executives, lawyers, and engineers while working a shorter work week? Again, a simple answer: they have a strong union with good political connections and no real incentive to reduce operation costs in a government-run monopoly. (Note that the authors are not negative on unions, per se. Unions serve a very important role in our society. NATCA is not a typical union, however. It represents members who are highly paid and protected by civil servants operating a monopoly with no market checks and balances to influence their bargaining demands.) Finally, how can the air traffic controllers' union get away with advertising that they operate the safest air traffic control system in the world when the United States is clearly behind Europe in safety metrics? (Europe had 0.32 hull losses per one million departures compared with North America's 0.49 [IATA 2007].) Perhaps this answer is the simplest yet: the American Public are sheep and allow them to do it.

Mind you, there are many good, hard-working people among the FAA and ATC ranks, and the authors have had the privilege of working with many of them. However (based on the authors' extensive experience in the field, personal observations, and ongoing communication with other industry professionals), both organizations have serious problems.

Interestingly, Robert Rose directed a five-year $2.8 million study about air traffic controllers in the early 1970s, and one of the most notable (and surprising to many) findings in the 750-page report was that the controller's job was not uniquely or debilitatingly stressful. He did, however, find that controllers suffered from high rates of drinking and depression. Many of these questions were studied again in the 1980s after the 1981 strike [Shostak and Skocik 1986]. Several quotes reported in Paul McElroy's book *TRACON* (2000) and taken from the congressional hearings after the strike offer some possible insights into the mind of a typical controller.

> ATCs are "... highly intelligent men who control their anxieties by meticulous compulsive behavior...[They] tend to be bold and dominant individuals by nature and have no great intrinsic respect either for authority or regulation..." [Congressional hearings 1983–84, p. 968.]

> I have been unable to find a job or position that offers the same excitement and personal satisfaction that controlling aircraft did. [Congressional hearings 1983–84, p. 1372; Shostak and Skocik 1986.]

> Some ATCs are "... like gods, like giants; like nobody else ... macho, crazy, eager, proud, dedicated" [Shostak and Skocik 1986].

In addition, in the aftermath of the strike many fired controllers stated that it was not about the money (they demanded an approximate 30% raise) but about the retirement benefits and control over their work environment. Wanting more *control* (of multiple things) was a recurrent theme in these interviews.

In addition, in the introduction to the book, *TRACON*, John Carr (a past president of NATCA) further describes the controller's typical personality as follows (Taken from the afterward of the book *TRACON*, written by Paul McElroy [2007], *TRACON* was a book paid for by the NATCA to advertise itself to the general public. John Carr, the president of NATCA at the time, wrote the introduction in August 2001.):

> Air traffic controllers are prone to living and dying at Mach 3 with their hair on fire. It's been said that controllers at busier facilities produce more adrenaline asleep than most people do in their waking hours. Controllers do everything hard, whether it's work or play. If they smoke, they smoke a lot and love it. If they're occasionally prone to a cocktail or two, why, they know how to socialize. If they cuss, no Navy sailor could have said it any better ... Controllers are fiercely independent, demanding people. Their job description requires perfection as the minimum acceptable level of competence, and they're notorious for expecting perfection from others. They are routinely disappointed in that regard. Divorce rates are high, and spouses and children of controllers can tell you a thing or two about being ordered around like an airplane. It should come as no surprise that some of us can only find true happiness with those who really understand us—other controllers.

It is also notable to look at how some former air traffic controllers manage as they get promoted into supervisory positions. Again, from *TRACON* [McElroy 2000],

> David Bowers [a former controller] found it ironic that the "paramilitary style that seemed to be prevalent in the FAA is not one that I have encountered with any frequency in the Navy nor in the work that I have done with the Army."

> [Controllers] are accustomed to vectoring aircraft ... [so then] they attempt to manage by vectoring people. But

people don't vector. Nevertheless, they have a management philosophy that emphasizes top-down direction, top-down control, autocratic behavior, and says that this is indeed what gets results—and an inefficient, top-heavy bureaucratic structure which inhibits communication.

Perhaps the most telling statement made in this regard was made to the authors personally. In mid-1996, Bill Jeffers and Donohue were walking back to the FAA building after a meeting with Mort Downey, then deputy secretary of Transportation under Secretary Pena. Jeffers was a former controller himself and the FAA director of Air Traffic Services. The topic being discussed during the walk was the FAA's progress on fixing the overbudget advanced automation system (which Donohue had been brought to the FAA to fix). The point was emphasized that good progress was being made on the computer display replacements in the en-route computer control centers. However, the new concept of "free flight" would require aircraft to have satellite-based precision navigation systems (GPS/WAAS) equipage and digital data links *with transfer of separation authority in high altitude and final approach airspace from the controllers to the pilots*. At hearing this, Jeffers was very quiet for a while and then noted that he doubted that "free flight" would ever work. The reason? He said that he had 15,000 air traffic controllers working for him who would *"never give up control of anything."*

Mini Case Studies on Modernization and the FAA's Response

To gain even more insight into the psyche of many of the autocrats and controllers at the FAA (especially concerning technological modernization of the system), it is useful to briefly consider five mini case studies. Except for the description of the development of collaborative decision making (CDM), these were personal experiences that Donohue encountered while he was in charge of modernization at the FAA. Thus, they are given in his own words and from his personal perspective. Others, no doubt, might remember the details somewhat differently. Note that the inclusion of individual names and organizations in some of the studies is not meant to cause embarrassment or offense, but is intended to provide specificity and support for the claims made herein.

Case 1: AMASS Runway Collision Warning System

In 1996, I was awakened one morning at about 1:00 a.m. to the sound of my STU III telephone ringing. This was a secure, encrypted line that the FAA Operations Center had put into my house, and it had never rung before (except for system checks). I answered the phone with great misgivings and was informed by the Operations Center that there had been a collision between two aircraft at St. Louis Airport involving a commercial passenger transport and a general-aviation business jet. There were fatalities, and the public affairs officer was coming on the line to brief me fully. She informed me that I needed to get my ASD-3 radar expert on the FAA jet first thing in the morning to meet the National Transportation Safety Board (NTSB) investigators at the accident site. [The ASD-3 radar is mounted on top of airport control towers and is a fast-scan (60 rpm), high-resolution, down-looking radar used for aircraft ground movement monitoring.] The collision was the result of simultaneous runway occupancy, and the ASD-3 radar was part of the surveillance system that was designed to alert controllers of such a possibility.

The NTSB investigation wanted to know why the airport movement area safety system (AMASS) system had not been deployed, as it had been in development for almost eight years and had passed its second key decision point milestone in April 1992. We had installed a working prototype at San Francisco Airport several years earlier, but no progress toward its third key decision point milestone, full-scale development, was being made. The system was developed by a small radar company (Norden) that had been purchased by what is now Northrop Grumman Systems and was in both financial and technical difficulty. The system was designed to take the high-resolution tower radar and use pattern recognition to warn controllers of situations that could lead to simultaneous runway occupancy and therefore potential aircraft collisions. A number of such accidents had occurred in the past, and the NTSB had been urging the FAA to develop and deploy such a system for years. (One of the most serious accidents in aviation history occurred when two fully fueled 747 aircraft collided on the runway, killing everyone onboard.) The system was projected to cost about $75 million for 40 deployed units at high-capacity airports. But over $25 million had been reprogrammed by the agency to cover cost growth on other systems prior to that year. Thus, it was obviously not a high-priority item for the ATC organization and the FAA's budgeters. Although I was watching the program and trying to help my integrated product team (IPT) work through the inevitable development problems, this accident suddenly brought the system to my full attention.

One of my best radar engineers, Rick Castaldo, was familiar with the system and was asked to testify as to the ability of the AMASS system to have prevented the St. Louis accident. Air traffic controllers had testified that the system did not work and would not have prevented the accident even if it had been deployed. Castaldo, however, testified that the radar tapes of the accident had been played through the prototype AMASS system, and it did indeed recognize the dangerous situation and would have properly sounded an alarm. Thus, had the AMASS system been deployed at St. Louis Airport, the collision might have been avoided.

After the testimony, the associate administrator for air traffic indicated to me that he was very upset that my engineers had testified against his controllers. I countered that I had been informed that my engineers had merely testified under oath and presented the facts as they were. Subsequently, I found out that the tower manager at San Francisco had instructed his controllers not to even look at the system. The display was placed in a back room so it could not be seen from the tower cab. The air traffic controllers' union position was that the system should not be deployed until we could certify that it would be perfect, have no false alarms, and prevent any situation from becoming a surface collision accident in the future.

Although we knew that the system would have prevented all of the previous runway collision situations, we did not know how to prove that every eventuality in the future would be prevented. The ASD-3 radar itself was so sensitive that it had frequent false targets, because of ground clutter and something called "target breakup" (as a result of its very high resolution). To some extent, AMASS software was designed also to help make up for some of the poor design specifications set by the air traffic control organization for the ASD-3. Thus, this was a classic case of "the best" being the enemy of "the good enough." But NATCA had found that the safety and perfection arguments were highly effective in slowing down the introduction of new technology. But what I did not know at the time was how often the tower controllers were cutting corners to "move traffic," and the AMASS system might well have detected and recorded these frequent rule-bending practices. And at the time of this writing, a decade later, the program is still not fully developed.

Case 2: Digital Data Links

It seems almost inconceivable that in today's world of the global Internet and the Blackberry®, commercial aircraft are not connected to the FAA and other aircraft by digital data links. One of the recurring contributing causes of fatal accidents is faulty communications [Nazeri 2007]. The increasing volume of international air operations is exacerbating this problem by requiring both controllers and pilots to communicate with each other in English, a language in which, often, neither is very proficient. The highly stylized communications lexicon and voice recognition/synthesis technology could do much to eliminate this growing international "Tower of Babel" problem by allowing the messages to be sent digitally and reconstructed in the language of the pilot or controller involved.

Unfortunately, almost all "official" information exchange between aircraft and the FAA is by voice-over-obsolete VHF, low-bandwidth, analog communications links. The error rate for such a communication system is about two percent (i.e., there's a 98% chance of getting an error-free message to or from the controller and the pilot). For almost 30 years, commercial aircraft have transferred messages between the aircraft and their air operations centers via an old digital system called ACARS. This system has been supplied by ARINC, Inc., working for the airlines and has now been upgraded to what is called Very High Frequency (VHF) Data Link Mode 2 (a Carrier Sense Multiple Access digital data link that is not very advanced by today's technological standards). The FAA has been planning to transition critical messages to digital data links for over 45 years but has been unable to do so for several reasons:

1) The air traffic controllers (as represented by NATCA) demand a system that is 99.999% accurate (vs what could be supplied off the shelf at 99.9% accuracy, **almost 20 times more accurate than their current 98% accurate voice communication system**).

2) The United States and Europe have been unable to agree on a common standard, and thus the FAA is unwilling to mandate aircraft equipage.

The FAA is notably incompetent in modern digital communications technology and has relied on MITRE to do its thinking for it. Unfortunately, in this case, MITRE proposed a technical solution (VDL-3) that was significantly inferior to the commercial state-of-the-art wireless systems that were being fielded at the time.

I remember a highly confrontational set of meetings between Larry Stotts [an expert in digital communications technology whom I had brought over from the Defense Advanced Research Projects Agency (DARPA)] and FAA/MITRE communications staff regarding the desirability of using commercial off-the-shelf (COTS) digital networking techniques (i.e., TCP/IPv6) and the new Code Division Multiple Access (CDMA) digital cell phone communications protocols as the best and fastest way to move the FAA into the 21st century. (DARPA is the top Department of Defense research and development organization. Stotts completed his Ph.D. under the founder of QUALCOM and the inventor of the Code Division Multiple Access digital communications system that is in wide use today.) MITRE/ CAASD representatives, the principal advisors to the older FAA communications engineers, insisted that their new proprietary Air Transportation Network networking system and Time Division Multiple Access (TDMA) message formatting were the only way to proceed (and they had convinced the technically unsophisticated airlines and FAA communications engineers). Moreover, they argued that the system Stotts was advocating would not even work. Now, with 10 years of hindsight, it is clear that Stotts was completely correct. And, not surprisingly, the FAA still does not have a working system.

This technology is a critical ingredient in almost all ATM automation systems under development, but the FAA has formally taken the introduction of data links off the table for at least 10 to 15 years. And Europe knows that it cannot wait that long. So, the FAA's untenable position has helped to undermine the European technical community's confidence in accepting any U.S.-proposed standard. Europe and Australia are proceeding with their own solutions to this problem, and the FAA and U.S. airlines will ultimately be forced to adopt whatever the European industry and Eurocontrol mandate. Right now that looks to be the European LINK 2000+, which will allow data exchange between ground computers and aircraft computers and will provide faster, more accurate, and more detailed four-dimensional trajectory contracts to be established for more efficient airspace and aircraft operations. Without a doubt, data-link technology will lead to a major change in the air traffic controller's job. Thus, the substantial resistance to adopting any new communications technology is not that surprising.

Case 3: STARS Terminal Radar Display System

A third example where I had a run-in with air traffic controllers involved the TRACON radar display replacement program called STARS (standard terminal automation replacement system). I had put David Ford, one of my best engineering program managers, in charge of this $1+ billion program. He headed an IPT made up of engineers, air traffic controllers, lawyers, and accountants. Linda Hall Daschle (at that time, deputy administrator of the FAA) had already determined before I arrived at the FAA that we could probably buy a TRACON radar computer display system as a commercial-off-the-shelf (COTS) system. The system that had been under development in the old Advanced Automation System program was frankly not worth salvaging. Ford's team did an extensive product survey (working with the ATC Requirements Division) and boiled down the selections to three possibilities.

First, there was a high-tech prototype system working at Edwards Air Force Base in California that had many good features, and Boeing had teamed to offer this as a fully developed product. Second, Lockheed Martin (which had been producing the existing system and was several years behind schedule in producing the "Common ARTS" interim upgrade system) had formed a new team under the leadership of Bob Stevens and Don Antonucci (who had come from the Loral/Lockheed Martin merger). Stevens and Antonucci were doing an outstanding job on fixing the en-route center display system replacement (DSR) system, and the common ARTS system was beginning to show signs of improvement under their management. They chose to propose a new system, however, using a team from several recently merged companies. Finally, Raytheon and Hughes teamed to offer a third option based upon two systems that they had been selling to European countries for several years.

Raytheon turned out to be a clear winner in the competition and was awarded a full-scale development and production contract in September 1996. Its product passed the most number of tests to which all of the systems were subjected, and the primary part of its system had been used to separate traffic at Frankfurt Airport in Germany, at that time the seventh busiest airport in the world. I personally interviewed the German engineers and controllers to discover how they liked the system. They said the system worked very well, and they were very pleased with the technical support they were getting from Raytheon.

However, within six months of contract award, senior NATCA union officials went to Congressman Frank Wolf, then chairman of the House Transportation Appropriations Subcommittee, and complained that we should have been buying the Common ARTS system from Lockheed Martin and that the Raytheon system was unsafe for use in the United States. I was called back from a meeting in New Delhi, India, to testify at Congressman Wolf's hearing.

At the hearing, I promised to test the system again with full union representation on the testing team to see the problems to which they were referring. In addition, I promised to fix anything found to be unsafe by an independent audit conducted by Maureen Pettitt, my chief scientist for human factors, and by the MITRE Corporation. I also pointed out that we could not just keep changing requirements, the way the FAA did on the Advanced Automation System. The lack of requirements stability was one of the major failures of that program. Congressman Wolf agreed that the union did not have carte blanche on changes and said that if I made sure that there was nothing unsafe, I should proceed.

And so we did. Pettitt brought in a team of human factors' specialists who were not involved in the system selection and ran extensive tests with union controllers. They identified 98 items that could have been better from a human factors' perspective. None of them concerned safety, however, and many were simply personal preference. (For example, the controllers preferred the old ABCDEF keyboard and a stationary trackball to a standard QWERTY keyboard and mouse, which were low-cost COTS items. The custom-engineered and custom-manufactured trackball and keyboard per unit cost was many thousands of dollars more than the standard items in the bid, which were known from the start to be in the proposal.) Raytheon informed me that seven software fixes would take care of all 98 items, and the job could be done in four to five months for less than $20 million.

I asked the union officials to formally agree to accept the system if these changes were made, knowing that the FAA could not afford to just continue chasing a changing requirement. But they refused to do so, telling me that they reserved the right to find other flaws in the system. The union went directly to FAA Administrator Jane Garvey, and she agreed to their demands. (The STARS program contract was for about $1 billion, which was mostly for installation of the slightly modified COTS system into 172 TRACON control sites.) That was the beginning of the end of development cost control for the STARS program.

Case 4: FAA–Airline Collaborative Decision Making

This historical perspective was provided by Mike Wambsganss, one of the founders and developers of the concept and operation from its inception. The year was 1991, three years before I arrived at the FAA. The FAA's Traffic Flow Management (TFM) organization, led by Central Flow Control [now known as the Air Traffic Control System Command Center (ATCSCC)], had only been operating for a few years.

TFM is the science of managing the relationship between the demand for a *National Airspace System* (NAS) resource and the capacity of that resource. Successful TFM occurs when the relationship is maintained without wasting capacity or incurring excessive operating costs (e.g., diversions that have very high cost). It also requires some semblance of market equity (or fairness), and above all, system safety must be maintained. TFM is a highly interdependent process where the users are the drivers of the demand side of the equation and the service provider is the keeper of the capacity side of the equation.

Created by the fires of deregulation, high fuel prices, and the controller's strike of the early 1980s, the mantra of this new organization was "no airborne holding." This was evidenced by the increasing use of Ground Delay Programs (GDPs) and other techniques that involved the predeparture delay of flights. As mentioned earlier, the intent of a GDP is to sequence flights into an airport at a reduced rate of flow (usually necessitated by some type of weather event or by airline over-scheduling of the airports actual runway arrival capacity) in a manner that substantially reduces or eliminates the need for airborne holding.

To the airlines, TFM was a new FAA initiative that was totally out of control. The only communication the airlines received from the FAA when a GDP was in effect was a teletype list of their control delay times—no rationale, no explanation, no insight into the "whys" of these rather significant delays. So negative were the airlines to this "new" FAA function that many were exerting significant influence on Capitol Hill to get Congress to "de-fund" it.

On the other hand, the FAA had become convinced that its wise, intelligent revolutionary means of managing capacity/demand imbalances was being undermined by airline cheating and gaming. If the airlines would stop breaking the rules and be more forthright about their true intentions and schedules, the FAA reasoned, the TFM system would improve, and everybody would stop complaining.

And such was the cloud that hung over the conference room at Air Transport Association headquarters in late 1992, when there was a meeting between airline representatives and FAA flow managers, a meeting that is widely viewed as the "kick-off" meeting for Collaborative Decision Making (CDM). Mike Wambsganss was the presenter/facilitator, under contract to the FAA, with marching orders to "get the airlines' data and get them to stop cheating."

After much give and take, the attendees finally agreed on a win-win strategy. The FAA would get dynamic schedule updates from the airlines so that it could make better, more informed decisions. It would also monitor for compliance with the rules through what Charles Hall (then Director of Central Flow Control) called "trust but verify." The airlines would also win: they would receive a new set of rules governing the allocation of scarce airport arrival resources, an increase in flexibility through new mechanisms that govern the use of those resources, and common situational awareness via access to the FAA's aggregate airport capacity/demand data and its congestion management tool, the flight schedule monitor (FSM).

In 1997, with the encouragement of MITRE/CAASD and the airlines, the Associate Administrator for Air Traffic and I recommended to Administrator David Hinson that the FAA provide TFM data to the airlines to formally begin what has come to be known as collaborative decision making (CDM). CDM is the collection of data, information, tools, rules, procedures, and policies that provide a daily "spot market" between the command-and-control systems of the ATM service provider (the FAA) and the command-and-control systems of the operators. Its general goals (which sometimes conflict) are to improve system predictability while enhancing the ability of the system (and the users) to adapt to changing conditions. Unfortunately, as I was later to discover, CDM would have the unforeseen consequence of the increase in the use of flight cancellations by the airlines, ultimately leading to deterioration in passenger QOS as the aircraft LFs increased.

The formal FAA deployment of CDM was in January 1998. The five airlines initially involved were all major airlines. Then the regional airlines and hundreds of general-aviation operators joined. It was the ideal blending of operations, researchers working with dispatchers, academia, industry, and FAA, all working together. What a beautiful sight. CDM was moving forward, and it appeared that the FAA had developed a successful model that could be applied to other programs.

The old TFM paradigm was completely hierarchical. The FAA would determine what new capabilities were needed in TFM, principally through the Office of Air Traffic Requirements, and the operators would get what they got. There was no common situational awareness. There was no insight into the airport demand/capacity profile that drives the need for traffic management initiatives (such as GDPs). (See Appendices C, D, and H for a better understanding of this issue.) And certainly there was no reporting on whether capacity was thoroughly used; how the delays were distributed; or, in general, whether the system was undercontrolled, overcontrolled, or appropriately controlled. Issues such as user flexibility, options, or incentives were not in the air traffic requirements' lexicon.

But CDM changed that paradigm. The operators were now seen as not just the source of the problem (i.e., too much demand) but a key player in the solution. Wambsganss's organization (METRON Aviation) and Mike Ball (from the University of Maryland) had shown—through simulations, analysis, and demonstrations over a period of years—that successful TFM truly requires a melding of the command-and-control functions of the FAA with the command-and-control systems of the airline operators. This melding is needed operationally and also in the evolution and development of their respective technologies. The group thought they had forever changed the problem space of TFM. It was no longer viewed as strictly an ATC problem but a problem possessing much broader and deeper complexities: stochastic elements, multiple criteria, operator networks that drive the need for options, the management of uncertainty, incentives for operator investment, nonlinear delay effects, performance measurement, equity, and feedback loops (as in adaptive control systems). Through the involvement of academia (e.g., Mike Ball), the technical community also became exposed to economic theory and began to understand that the fundamental challenge of TFM is properly stated as "the free market vying for scarce public resources." With so many failed FAA programs to compare with, they were certain that the FAA would follow its procollaboration rhetoric by actively supporting the "CDM process."

But around 2002, things started to change. New FAA leadership was appointed for the CDM body. Gone were the forward thinkers whose background was in research and development. CDM was now led by an air traffic controller. Gradually at first (and more rapidly later), the technical and research communities were squeezed out of the process, no longer showing presentations at CDM meetings or being called upon for new "innovative" ideas. A new customer (operator) forum, S2K, was established, and it included only "important" people. And there would be no direct link to CDM. The technical community was told they need not apply. And thus the path to bureaucracy had begun.

When Russell Chew was about to become the FAA chief operating officer (COO), many were encouraged. They thought that finally somebody senior in the FAA would understand the complexities of airline network operations and the value of CDM. However, their encouragement quickly gave way to disappointment. For years, CDM funding had been unstable and uncertain, evidence that it was not really embraced at the highest levels of the FAA. Although it was a very small program by most standards (never over $15 million or so in annual funding), it was routinely cut for one reason or another. Moreover, under Chew's leadership, CDM was to experience its largest cut ever, around 33%.

And then came the ATO's reorganization. This reorganization altered the checks-and-balances equation, where the acquisition side of the FAA, in control of program funds, provided somewhat of a counterweight to air traffic services. Now with the new "flattened" organization, air traffic had all the power, and CDM was to feel it directly. Research projects were stopped. Performance analysis, the glue that kept CDM moving forward for many years, was virtually eliminated. And everything became program schedule predictability. Essentially, the technical people (including forward-thinking contractors) were told, "Don't propose something new because there might be risk." The FAA, always a risk-*averse* organization by its nature, had become risk-*avoidant*.

At the main CDM meeting in January 2007, Wambsganss observed how the change was now complete. The paradigm had shifted back.

This was a two-day meeting with well over 200 attendees consisting of only FAA presentations. He was later to find out that Mike Gough, the director of system operations programs, had dictated that only FAA personnel could be presenters at the CDM main meeting. Wambsganss asked a few questions, but they were treated as annoyances. And finally he was given a polite "please shut up, we don't have time for discussion." Expressing his dismay at the lack of open discussion, he was informed that such discussion now takes place in the subgroup meetings. He thus figured he would go to the next ground delay program enhancements (GDPE) subgroup meeting. He had noted that an agenda item was "data quality," and as a provider of ASD services to hundreds of operators (who deal with poor data quality from FAA systems on a routine basis), this was a subject in which he wanted personally to engage. But that did not happen. The subgroups, he was later told, were by invitation only, and they did not want any "vendors."

CDM is no longer an open process. The technical and research communities have been shut out. For good reason, many of the airlines are derisively referring to CDM as "FDM," as in "FAA decision making." A return to hierarchical control is fairly definitive proof that the paradigm shift they had ushered in was only temporary.

In hindsight, there were many signs along the way that the conceptual aspects of CDM had never been embraced by FAA senior management. Collaboration simply became another buzz word used by the FAA to show that it was working with the airlines. But the actual technical, scientific, and operational work of the CDM group was never truly embraced. Perhaps we should have anticipated this. CDM ultimately presented a new operating paradigm, one that does not center on the air traffic controller. In fact, more and more participants began to question why the FAA staffs its TFM functions with air traffic controllers. A new college graduate with a background in statistics, probability, optimization, and economics would be far better equipped to handle the fundamental TFM challenge: "*balancing uncertain capacity and demand forecasts, between multiple players with multiple criteria.*" They should have understood that the controllers of the FAA would never accept this new paradigm because they really were not part of it.

Case 5: Automatic Dependent Surveillance-Broadcast (ADS-B) and the Alaska Capstone Operational Evaluation

Shortly before the 1996 Olympic Games in Atlanta, one of my most energetic and innovative engineers, Rick Weiss, proposed a bold idea. We had been discussing the major shift from radar separation of aircraft to the use of aircraft-based GPS position and state vector (i.e., aircraft velocity, acceleration, and destination intent) broadcast to all other aircraft as a major advancement in being able to reduce aircraft separation standards and to ultimately increase the en-route and terminal airspace capacity. We would use a small number of ADS-B/Data Link–equipped helicopters to demonstrate the new technology and call it Operation Heli-STAR. (These were not FAA-certified avionics and were early prototypes.) ADS-B is now stated to be the cornerstone of the new FAA NEXTGEN air traffic control system.

Because of White House security concerns, the Secret Service had decided that the FAA could not allow any aircraft in airspace above the Olympic venues that were not under positive control and surveillance. The Atlanta TRACON radar could not provide this surveillance because of low altitude, ground clutter, etc. Therefore, the international press would not be able to have any aerial photography of the games. Thus, we took a small demonstration of an inner-city helicopter transportation system with ADS-B-equipped helicopters, and we were able to quickly expand this capability to 100 aircraft and airships for the duration of the games. But even more important, this successful demonstration showed us what had to be done to ultimately achieve FAA certification of the aircraft-based avionics equipment and air traffic control procedures to achieve a paradigm shift in the air traffic control modernization.

In late 1996, Linda Hall Daschle, then the acting FAA administrator, set up a meeting with Vice President Al Gore to discuss the final report of his commission on the future of the U.S. air traffic control system. Vice President Gore was interested in having some bold new initiative to announce as part of his report due out in early 1997, and quite frankly nothing very spectacular was being proposed. I told him at this meeting that the technology that was needed to make a major change in the air traffic control paradigm was nothing more than his laptop computer combined with a small GPS receiver and the equivalent of a handheld digital wireless telephone installed in every aircraft in the world.

The major obstacle was a commitment by the federal government (i.e., the FAA) to certify the equipment and approve the new aircraft separation procedures. I suggested that the ideal location for a major operational evaluation (OPEVAL) would be Alaska and Hawaii. Theses locations had a number of aspects that made them operationally and technically desirable for an OPEVAL (e.g., the high fatality rate for private aircraft operating in western Alaska that was, for the most part, caused by Alaska's lack of an ATC system, which would help them avoid crashing into the terrain). (The annual number of aircraft fatalities in Alaska exceeded 500 at that time.) Senators Ted Stevens (R-Alaska) and Daniel Inoue (D-Hawaii) were the ranking members of the Senate Appropriations Committee and should be interested in supporting this plan.

Vice President Gore included this recommendation in his final report, much to the chagrin of most FAA executives and managers and the major airlines (who did not want to pay anything to equip their aircraft either then or anytime into the future). (In this sense, Al Gore can realistically be considered the "father" of the next-generation air traffic control system, which is based on the Alaska Capstone ATM paradigm.) However, the Alaska FAA regional flight standards organization and the air traffic controllers (at that time) were strongly supportive. So, with substantial help from David Tuttle, who worked for me at the FAA, and Paul Fiduccia, president of the Small Aircraft Manufacturers Association (SAMA), this OPEVAL has emerged as the Alaska Capstone Demonstration. Capstone began in 2000 and has expanded ever since, but against substantial and continual opposition from many elements of the FAA and the national air traffic controller's union.

Moreover, the resulting development of FAA-certified avionics, which the FAA purchased for the Capstone OPEVAL, has allowed the United Parcel Service (UPS) to begin equipping its cargo jets, which largely fly at night, with ADS-B equipment that provides UPS air operations substantial operational efficiency at its hub airports. With any luck, this universal equipage of the cargo jets (which could be completed as early as 2015) could be the beginning of the movement to a new paradigm in air traffic control in the United States.

NATCA's Power to Resist Change

So, why does NATCA continue to resist all of this change? Well, it cannot be low salaries or long hours, can it? Amazingly, at the time of this writing, NATCA was in the process of requesting a 5.6% raise and a shorter work week. According to a recent FAA audit of the New York TRACON [FAA 2005c], resulting from numerous complaints about unreported safety violations, the FAA states that 25% of the New York controllers are earning over **$200,000/year** and are working an effective average of **only 3 hours and 40 minutes per day** separating aircraft (the average salary was reported to be $160,000/year). This is compared to a more productive TRACON in Southern California, where the average salary is $155,000/year for an average of five hours per day. As civil servants, senior controllers also get over six weeks of paid leave per year.

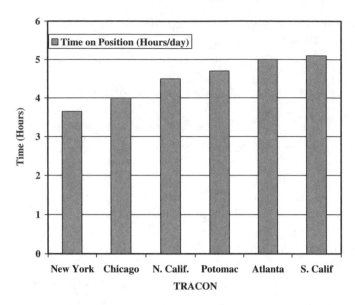

Fig. 6.2   Average air traffic controller time on station at selected high-capacity TRACONS [FAA 2005c].

Although the popular perception is that the workload of a typical air traffic controller is quite high and the working hours long, Fig. 6.2 shows FAA data on the average work day for several high-capacity TRACON control centers, where controller workloads are the highest in the system [FAA 2005c]. (As mentioned earlier, the average controller is on position about 800 hours per year and controls about 12 aircraft per hour. A typical aircraft residency time in a sector is about 15 minutes.) Note the standard work day consists of 40 to 60% "break time." Controllers state that this time is used in paperwork and training.

In addition, Fig. 6.3 (which was also computed from an FAA report) shows the number of aircraft that an average controller handles at any one time. This number is an average, and certain sectors in high-density airspace routinely handle more traffic. The national average of aircraft assigned to a controller when an operational error occurs is seven. (Note that an operational error is not necessarily dangerous. The system is designed to maintain safety buffers. An operational error is frequently the occurrence of a buffer separation being cut close and might not involve a hazardous encounter. See Nazeri [2007] for a discussion in the trends of controller operational errors.) However, high sector loads can go up to 15 to 30 aircraft in highly structured airspace, and in

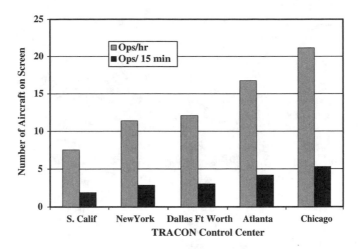

Fig. 6.3   Typical number of aircraft handled by a controller at any one time; 15 minutes is assumed as a typical aircraft sector residence time (authors' calculation from [FAA 2005] data).

these events these sectors will almost always be handled by a team of controllers.

But numbers alone are not adequate to describe the air traffic controllers' cognitive workload, and these factors have been studied extensively over the last 30 years. Highly sophisticated computer models of air traffic operations, including controller's decision-making functions, can control for these factors and produce much better sector designs, designs that take advantage of structured corridors of flight, that minimize the controllers' cognitive workload, and that allow computers to handle more of the routine functions.

MITRE-developed software called the User Request Evaluation Tool (URET) greatly assists the planning position to anticipate potential loss of separation as much as 20 minutes in advance and reposition aircraft trajectories before a separation violation potential exists. Not surprisingly, full use of this tool has been resisted by the controllers. One (quite remarkable) reason they have cited is that the tool reduces the radar controller's workload to the point of his losing situational awareness. NASA has also done extensive work over the last 20 years that has produced significant new paradigms for en-route and terminal separation that would make the ATC job easier and safer [Andrews et al. 2005]. NATCA has strongly resisted these technical upgrades as well.

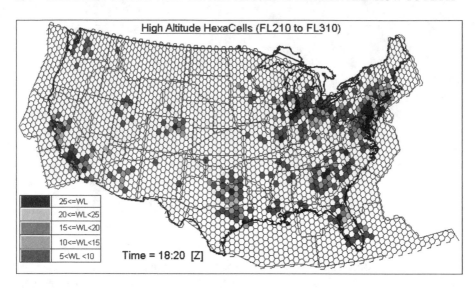

Fig. 6.4   Nationwide workload distribution from computer simulations at GMU [Yousefi 2005].

Figure 6.4 shows how the workload is distributed nationally at a "busy time of day" in the United States. This graph is the result of detailed computer simulations [Yousefi 2005; Yousefi and Donohue 2004] that take into account not only the number of aircraft but the complexity of the operations involved. Each hex cell represents 20 nautical miles on a side, and a typical irregular-shaped sector would contain three to five of these cells. The current ATC center and sector boundaries need a complete redefinition to increase average controller productivity and decrease the large operational costs of the FAA. Any private-sector service provider could reduce the number of centers by at least half to two-thirds within several years if the Congress would allow several competitively selected air traffic service providers to modernize the ATC system. This is discussed more in the next chapter.

Although it is illegal for any government employee to lobby for his or her agency's position, NATCA union officials are immune from this restriction and have been increasingly using their heavily funded political action committee (PAC) to influence both public and congressional perceptions of the necessity to remain government employees [vs having the ATC function performed by a private service provider (see Chapter 7)]. In fact, over \$2.5 million was contributed to political campaigns in 2003–2004 and almost \$3.3 million in 2005–2006 by the NATCA PAC. According to the Federal Election Commission records, NATCA was in the top 25 of all PACs for contributions in this period (above the American Postal Workers contributions). And this giving would have put them in with the top 20 corporate PACs contributing in 2006 (http://www.fec.gov/disclosure. html). Over half of the House of Representatives received some donations and almost 40% of the Senate, with both Democrats and Republicans receiving contributions. Considering the small size of the NATCA union, this is quite an impressive investment in political influence.

Now, the authors are not implying that these contributions are "buying" any votes. However, they most certainly ensure NATCA access to influential members. In addition, they can help the union present "facts" without much debate as to the veracity of those facts. Last year, there was strongly organized opposition within both the House and the Senate to the FAA outsourcing of the flight service stations and "Level One" tower functions to the private sector, even when objective analysis by the FAA management had repeatedly shown that the job could be done cheaper and just as safely by the private sector. Hmmm.

So why, one might ask, has FAA management historically put up with this behavior? (To her credit, Administrator Blakey has fought valiantly to resist further salary increases and has persevered in the face of considerable opposition to outsource both the flight service stations and the level one towers. The fight is not over, however.) Once again, it is pretty simple: because it is operating a government monopoly with a union workforce that has more political clout with its bankers (the Congress) than even it (the management) does. And it is without any real accountability! Shame on the FAA, and shame on the American public for allowing this to go on for as long as it has.

CHAPTER 7

Flight From Chaos: Expansion, Modernization, and the 30% Solution

So, where does the system go from here? Is American society willing to do something about the current state of affairs in the air travel system, or will it simply allow the chaos to continue and to truly become terminal? The Airports Council International's (ACI) Global Traffic Forecast 2006–2025 projects a doubling of current passengers within the next 20 years. Passenger demand volumes are predicted to grow by an average of 4% annually over this period, leading to passenger volumes of over 9 billion by 2025, up from 4.2 billion in 2005. How will the U.S. system accommodate this growth? Simply put, unless the basic rules governing the system are changed, it will not.

Figure 7.1 shows a projection of future passenger delay hours from both flight delays and flight cancellations [Wang 2007]. **The combined total is over 280,000,000 hours in 2010!** Unless the Congress takes some bold actions soon, this will be far worse than the delays experienced in 2000 or 2007. The passenger growth rate in North America (USA) is projected by the ACI to be flat at 3%, significantly below the Asia Pacific, European, and world growth rates. It is also below the projected growth rate in the U.S. economy and the U.S. population. If this comes to pass, it will adversely affect our national economic growth and will be caused by a massive failure in U.S. government policy. It also leads one to ask the question: If Halliburton can move its headquarters to Dubai to be closer to the Middle East oil fields, would Boeing likewise consider moving its Commercial Airlines

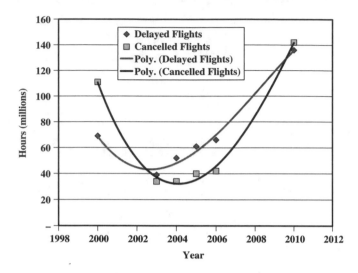

Fig. 7.1   Projection to 2010 of passenger lost productivity from both flight delay and flight cancellations [Wang 2007].

Division headquarters to Beijing at some point to be closer to its major customer base [*Wall Street Journal* 2007]?

As discussed, a modern airport designed to accommodate hub operations requires thousands of acres of land near a large metropolitan city complex. This land is becoming very expensive and very hard to acquire. The last major new airports constructed in the United States were Kansas City; Houston; Dallas–Forth Worth; Washington, D.C.; Denver; and now Las Vegas. Note that most of these airports are in the western United States (where land is still relatively plentiful and cheap). [Note that Washington's Dulles Airport was built before Washington, D.C. became a major population center and was paid for by the federal government. Recent history on building new airports shows a timeline from start of planning to completion to be about 20 years. To the authors' knowledge, there are not any major airports in consideration at this time (except Las Vegas), suggesting that a new major airport would not be available until after 2025, far beyond any help with the problems of today.]

By now, it should be obvious that the numerous problems described throughout this book cannot be solved without the efforts of many individuals and organizations, including the full engagement of the federal government. Significantly, these problems are highly interconnected; thus, no single policy initiative is sufficient in itself to provide meaningful long-term remedies. **And one important fact stands out: none of the** major players—not the airlines, the airports, the FAA, the DOT, the White House Office of Management and Budget, or the Congress— seem to believe it has the responsibility for fixing the problem. Each seems to be waiting for somebody, anybody, to take charge. To make progress, this needs to change. And it probably will take a few sheep to stand up and say, "I'm mad as hell and I won't take it anymore."

First Things First: Holding Responsible Those Most Responsible

At present, no federal agency or individual within a federal agency feels it has the authority to alleviate congestion. The simple fix to this dilemma is to unambiguously designate the DOT as the agency responsible for fixing the overscheduling problems at the top 10 to 15 congested airports and have the FAA oversee and publish monthly a passenger's QOS metric, as shown in Appendix G, Fig. G.5 (see http://www.greenflights.info). And Congress needs to give the DOT secretary unambiguous legal authority to use market-based congestion management techniques at critical air transportation network nodes (i.e., currently overscheduled airports).

Furthermore, prior literature has identified three general strategies for fixing the congestion problems: 1) expanding the physical capacity of congested airports, if and when it is feasible; 2) improving the throughput of the system, which would involve new technology, aircraft separation procedures, and multiple actors; and 3) increasing airport infrastructure utilization to improve efficiency at the congested airports, and to the overall ATM system to a lesser degree. Obviously, each of the three strategies has costs and benefits. Also, some elements can be implemented relatively quickly, whereas others will take significantly longer to be put into place. But, whatever the case, they need to be put into place, and soon.

Expanding the Physical Capacity of Airports

Expanding the physical capacity of the airports is perhaps the most difficult to carry out. For one thing, it requires heavy capital investment. In addition, airports might lack the capability of expanding the size of their physical plant (i.e., there simply might be no more land available to accommodate new facilities). Physical expansion also raises complicated issues of local land-use politics. Residents surrounding an airport will raise strong protests against any plan to expand the airport's footprint, especially if it brings runways closer to their neighborhoods or increases the number of flights at the airport. Still, in a select number of cases, it might be possible to build our way out of some congestion problems. Consider, for example, the new airport planned outside of Las Vegas. The new Denver airport is also a good example of a large airport that can take more operations than currently scheduled. The acquisition of Stewart International Airport by the Port Authority of New York/New Jersey should be applauded, although to help reduce congestion at the New York airports, better access to Manhattan needs to be developed.

It is less clear where additional airport building opportunities exist east of the Mississippi River. A recent study by Butler and Poole (2008) illustrates how the new technology could be used to add some capacity to land-constrained airports like JFK and SFO. Some airports, such as in Kansas City and St. Louis, have large infrastructure investments that are currently being underutilized for both east–west and north–south hub operations. Raleigh–Durham Airport had been used by American Airlines in the past for East Coast hubbing operations and could be used again to take some of the load off of Atlanta–Hartsfield Airport. The authors see limited potential for much capacity increase from this option, however. **To significantly increase the air transportation capacity, the airlines must begin to schedule larger aircraft on the high-density market routes.**

Modernizing the Air Traffic Control System

This strategy involves policymakers and planners finding (or, in most cases, just using) new technology, better air traffic management procedures, better airspace design, synchronized scheduling, and other mechanisms to increase throughput at the airports, thereby increasing capacity and reducing congestion. The options here range from use of new, larger, more fuel-efficient planes (with corresponding reductions in the number of daily round trips between city pairs) to implementation of various emerging technologies (e.g., the already described avionics and data links as well as aircraft separation technologies to locate, track, and inform) that enable aircraft to land in closer proximity to one another. In general, the FAA-planned NEXTGEN satellite-based air traffic management system will add little capacity to the system. (Weather is widely thought by the public to be a serious congestion factor in the en route airspace. It is not. Almost all weather lies below the normal flying altitudes of commercial jet aircraft. The exception, thunderheads, are sufficiently dispersed that they cause only modest revectoring of the traffic flow. Weather is often a convenient excuse used by the FAA or by the airlines for delays and cancellations.) Most of its benefit will be to reduce airline fuel consumption and thus lower airline operating costs. If the NEXTGEN system relies less on en-route radars, it will lower the

FAA cost to replace the current worn-out radars with expensive (both to buy and to maintain) new long-range radars. (However, as pointed out repeatedly by former FAA Administrator Langhorne Bond, the lack of a land-based e-LORAN backup area navigation system to the satellite-based GPS navigation system will expose the NEXTGEN system to serious single-mode failure vulnerabilities. Thus, e-LORAN should be added to the architecture to complement commercial aircraft inertial navigation systems not shared by all aircraft.)

Of course, failure to make meaningful progress on modernizing the ATC system has been widely discussed in numerous reports from within the federal government, presidential and congressional Blue Ribbon commissions, the airlines, and from private organizations. Substantial government funding for modernization has been provided in the past, with little to show for it. And the past decade has seen a plethora of management changes to solve this problem, but without notable success. Still, examples of successful ATC modernization certainly exist elsewhere (e.g., in Europe, Canada, and Australia), proving that technology per se is not the barrier [McDougall 2006; Oster 2006; Poole 2007; Robyn 2007]. So, what is the problem?

Without rehashing the many modernization issues already discussed in detail throughout this book, the following list reiterates some of the major problems already identified:

- There is a lack of senior people within the FAA who have the required background and technical knowledge to manage the large, complicated programs that makes up most of the ATC modernization.
- Persistent funding problems within the FAA cause program turbulence and uncertainty. [The FAA's funding problems are not entirely from internal problems. Congress often alters the FAA budget requests by inserting politically motivated actions related to ATC system (e.g., denying the FAA's request for phasing out older expensive-to-maintain equipment, for reasons related to political favors to its constituencies)].
- The controller union (NATCA) resists endorsing new systems, ostensibly because they might be unsafe (or at least have not been shown to be safe in a realistic environment), or increase productivity thereby decreasing the FAA's reliance on a highly paid, craft-skilled workforce.
- The airlines and private aviation resist agreeing on outfitting their airplanes with the airborne equipment needed to make the modernization successful. To some extent, this is based upon a demonstrated failure of the FAA to deliver on the promised benefits of modernization.

Without a doubt, however, continued failure to modernize the ATC system could have substantial negative impacts on the United States. Some elements of the modernization would help the overall system capacity by decreasing the required aircraft separation minimums, lessening delays and making the airline operations more efficient. Others directly support an increase in safety of flight. Still others could lower the overall costs of the system, which could produce savings that could be better used to bolster the economy or serve some other needy purpose. America's failure to modernize its system has opened opportunities for foreign industries to gain a substantial competitive advantage over U.S. companies that are in the business of providing aviation-related equipment to U.S. carriers and/or the FAA.

For solutions, the authors simply encourage following the precedents of the other industrial countries and either corporatize the Air Traffic Management Services' function of the FAA or (failing that) seriously consider outsourcing major elements of the ATC system and its modernization. Without exception, these privatized ATM service provider organizations are providing better service (however it is measured) at a lower price and without any indication of reductions in safety or overall system capacity.

Failing complete corporatization (i.e., the Canadian model), outsourcing at least some (or some more) of the system might be the only way 1) to attract sufficient numbers of capable technical managers to a new air traffic services organization in order to meet the coupled goals of increasing system safety and capacity and 2) to have the capital resources necessary for modernization. This could be done in an incremental fashion by building on those cases where air traffic services have already been transferred successfully and safely to the private sector. And this incremental approach would allow the American traveling public to adjust to an understanding that the safety oversight function and the day-to-day operation and maintenance can be done better by splitting those functions between the public and the private sectors, allowing both sectors to do what each does best.

And no matter what option Congress selects, the safety regulation and enforcement responsibility would continue to be provided by the FAA because virtually everyone agrees those are essential governmental functions. But the day-to-day operation and maintenance, as well as the upgrade and expansion of the air traffic services (ATS) system to meet growing demands, should be put at "arm-length" from the FAA and made self supporting as many countries have already done [McDougall 2006]. A more corporate governance system can upgrade and operate an ATS system more efficiently and at lower cost to the users of the system and at considerable savings to the U.S. taxpayers than can a government bureaucracy. One of the advantages of outsourcing the ATS functions is that these services could be outsourced to several contractors, thus maintaining competition. We recognize that complete ATC privatization to one organization, considering the large size of the U.S. system, risks establishing a nongovernment monopoly that could ultimately become as bad as the current FAA system. (Consider the old AT&T model of the U.S. telecommunications monopoly vs the innovative, competitive system we have today.)

There are several good examples of where this has already been accomplished successfully. The first is the case of the least busy ATC towers with relatively little traffic. These towers, called "level-one" towers in FAA parlance, have been privately and safely operated, under FAA oversight, and with cost savings to the American public for many years. In addition, the FAA recently outsourced the flight service station function, used primarily by general aviation, to a private service provider. In like manner, the FAA could and should begin turning over to the commercial sector the operation and maintenance of air traffic services for digital communications (as the FAA recently did with the new ADS-B contract), management, and control of traffic over the ocean and for high-altitude air traffic operations in domestic airspace.

Another important function that needs to be outsourced is the FAA central flow control function that currently operates in Herndon, Virginia. The complexity of managing a virtual stock-market-like slot exchange "spot market" with over 20 major airlines is beyond the expertise of the FAA and air traffic controllers. As discussed, the major factor that triggers today's GDP slot barter is weather and congestion caused by airline overscheduling. Weather, and thus near-term airport availability, is inherently unpredictable over the two- to six-hour planning cycles that are required for U.S. air traffic flow management. The FAA simply does not have the technical expertise to operate this market exchange, which requires decision support system tools for making decisions under various levels of uncertainty.

The private sector would provide the investment capital and compete for this rapidly growing service business. In turn, they would charge airlines directly for the services they provide them. This simple step is possible almost immediately for oceanic airspace, because the communications services used over the oceans have traditionally been outsourced to commercial-service providers anyway and Congress has ratified charging for these services on a cost-reimbursable basis in the past. In addition, most of the nations that control airspace adjacent to U.S. oceanic airspace already have corporatized ATC operations. One of the major advantages to this approach is that these other nations are quickly and safely taking advantage of new technologies and operational procedures that directly result in efficiency and cost benefits to the airlines and other operators who make use of their services.

If Congress does not want to follow the example of the rest of the industrialized world, then the FAA could retain responsibility for ATC sevices in low-density terminal and low-density, low-altitude airspace, where a complex mix of military, private, and commercial operators place moderate demands on the system. At the same time, the commercial-sector ATC services entity could provide Congress and the taxpayers with commercial productivity metrics and accounting practices that could be used to evaluate the FAA's performance. This model is similar to what has happened successfully in the U.S. Postal Service vis à vis Federal Express and UPS. And it is based on the time-honored principle that what the government cannot or will not provide, the commercial sector will.

Unfortunately, the rapidly changing pace of technology exacerbates the failures in today's air traffic management system. Managers, air traffic controllers, and engineers in the air transportation control system require a whole range of new technical skills and talent that the federal government is finding extremely difficult to attract, as a number of recent surveys have shown. In addition, the federal government's planning, programming, and budgeting processes are far too archaic and glacially slow to accommodate the rate of change in digital communications and computer technologies. This results in a virtual paralysis of the FAA's new systems' development and acquisition process.

As mentioned earlier, the cargo airlines might be the key to modernizing the U.S. system. They primarily operate at night, can afford to equip their aircraft with the required avionics, and can train their pilots to the new procedures. UPS and FedEX virtually operate their own airports from 11:00 p.m. until 5:00 a.m. anyway, and they could equip their own TRACON/towers with the new technology to increase efficiency and safety at high operational tempos. All that the FAA would have to do is give them permission to operate their own systems to prove they are safe and to fine tune the new procedures that have already gone through detailed safety analysis and initial operational testing. This can be done under the FAA's austere budget situation and can show the degree of increased productivity that will be obtained with the new ATC paradigm.

But, all of this will be for naught if the combined resistance of NATCA, the heavily subsidized general-aviation community [led by the Aircraft Owners and Pilots Association (AOPA), the General Aviation Manufacturers Association (GAMA), and the National

Business Aircraft Association (NBA)] and the legacy airlines cannot be overcome. The good news is that experience with commercialization in other countries suggests that the sometimes unjustified concerns of the union can be overturned. And the reluctance of the airlines to equip would probably vanish if they felt that the promised ATC improvements were going to be accomplished as promised.

Using a 30% Solution to Reduce Congestion

Yet another (and highly promising) strategy to reduce congestion is to treat the physical plant of the congested airports (and really the U.S. air transportation system as a whole) as a limited and valuable asset that needs market forces to obtain needed efficiency in utilization. As already discussed in earlier chapters, the delays that plague airline operations today are primarily the result of the overscheduling practices of the major airlines at a limited number of the major airports in the United States. Every airport has a capacity limit, and today these airports are facing airline schedules that approach and exceed that limit. FAA Administrator David Hinson tried to explain this to Congress in the mid-1990s but was unsuccessful. Congress has got to understand that aircraft schedules must be governed by safety and schedule predictability standards and are not political commodities to be parsed out at will. The authors have explained why the airlines, acting in their understandable self-interest, are engaged in this practice. And so long as the incentives for airline behavior remain as they are, this problem will not be solved.

Before deregulation, airlines petitioned the FAA for and (sometimes) received landing slots at the HDR airports. The FAA made certain that the airports were capable of handling the traffic that the CAB approved. After deregulation, the CAB was abandoned, and it has been "advertise any schedule, feasible or not" ever since. Le [2006] provides a detailed explanation of what an optimum fleet schedule would look like for a highly congested airport such as New York LaGuardia. Research at GMU has found that a consistent upgaging (i.e., the use of larger, more fuel-efficient aircraft) with a 20% decrease in the number of flights using modern aircraft will substantially decrease congestion delays as well as noise and fuel emissions around airports. Figure 7.2 illustrates what an optimum upgaging at LGA would look like compared to today's aircraft size distribution. This distribution is estimated to preserve both airline profits and airport passenger throughput.

It is now recognized that, at the congested airports, a hands-off policy is no longer in the best interest of the passengers or the airlines. The

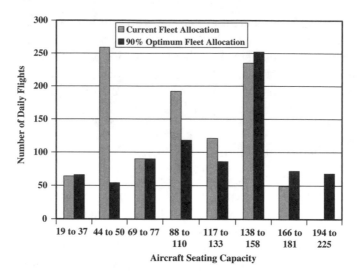

Fig. 7.2   Optimum aircraft size compared to 2005 fleet mix at LGA (see Appendix E for discussion).

proposals aimed at addressing airport congestion generally fall into two distinct categories: 1) reimpose government regulation on whoever is (and is not) authorized to land at the airport during a specific time of day or 2) introduce market mechanisms that will provide strong incentives for the airlines to alter their behavior. Not surprisingly, each of these proposals has its supporters within and outside the government.

The authors also recommend setting the landing slot allocation fraction at the most congested airports to 80–90% of their maximum technical safe capacity (see Appendices D and H and Jeddi et al. [2006]). Based on this analysis, a **30% reduction in scheduled flight frequency (combined with a commensurate 30% increase in average aircraft size) would appear to account for anticipated passenger demand and be realistic and feasible.** Even at these lower numbers, the overall loss of enplanements in the system would be modest. Using congestion pricing techniques, however, it would also give the airlines an incentive to increase the number of seats on some of their flights going into those airports, ameliorating the potential loss in available seat at those airports (see Appendix E).

Establishing arrival time slot controls is the key to achieving this recommendation. Matching airline schedules to arrival time slots can be achieved in three ways:

1) Reconstitute the CAB to award these valuable slots to airlines based upon public petition and economic review. Both aircraft

size and total national transportation efficiency would have to be taken into account with these decisions, as they likely will be difficult to make and defend. Note that the current use of FAA or DOT administrative mandates to reduce the schedule at Chicago O'Hare, New York LaGuardia, John F. Kennedy, and Newark Liberty is considered a poor form of this option and is not recommended.

2a) Institute a new DOT or regional airport authority Congestion Pricing Board(s) with the power to set "congestion prices" at various times of day to encourage the airlines to modify their schedules by raising the landing fees at congested times of the day to higher and higher prices. Currently, these fees are set by a complex weight-based formula that is airport dependent and time-of-day independent. This procedure leads to perverse incentives, favoring small, inefficient aircraft that are overscheduled. This landing-fee technique is woefully out of date.

These prices would probably have to be set based upon proposed schedules (perhaps including aircraft size) submitted by the airlines in advance and the resulting delays estimated by computer program predictions. An acceptable delay time would have to be established by the DOT. In this construct, the government would set the landing (or departing) ATC clearance prices, with the airlines choosing to keep or relinquish their existing schedule times and/or seek to add flights at a cheaper time of day. This board would have to review the schedules and congestion data several times each year (especially the summer months) to adjust the prices as congestion begins to rise again. (This procedure is effectively a short-term auction strategy. See Poole and Dachis [2007] for an excellent discussion of this option.) The airlines do not face long-term financial obligations under this option but also do not get any long-term predictability in airport access costs or property rights useful for long range strategic planning. These fees would not represent a "new tax," as the opponents of this proposal state, for these fees would be designed to replace existing landing fees and passenger facility charge "taxes" that are not reflective of runway scarcity.

2b) Award arrival (or departure) operating certificates that are good for a specific period of time (e.g., five years) and that allow the airlines to schedule a fixed number of operations within 15-minute time slots. Airlines would be required to win the bid for these operating certificates at a public auction. [Combinatorial auctions are becoming commonplace (see Ball et al. [2005]). However, they have never been used for this purpose, and there is clearly some reluctance on the part of those in the aviation world with whom the authors have suggested this approach. Nonetheless, both congestion pricing and slot auctions are estimated to generate revenues in excess of airport operations and capital investment requirements. Of course, the issue of who should get the money is a major political issue that would have to be resolved (see Plavin and Poole [2007] at http://www.reason.org.).] These auctions would award operation licenses within specified time slots (e.g., 15-minute intervals) to the airline that is willing to pay the highest price. Economic theory would predict that the airlines would, therefore, have incentives to make the best use of these scarce public assets with the best markets and optimal aircraft size. This policy is transparent and provides equal access to both the incumbents and new entrants as well as promotes both efficiency and competition. The downside is that this puts the legacy airlines in jeopardy of losing their historical access to these critical airports. In theory, similar schedules should result from the congestion pricing option or the slot-auction option. The slot auction would provide the airlines specific property rights that would have value in secondary markets and longer-term predictability of airport access costs. And airlines would need to demonstrate at the beginning of the auction that they had sufficient financial resources to pay the auction price, but that price could be paid out over the term of the operating licenses to alleviate cash-flow concerns.

The authors highly favor these combinatorial auctions to give the airlines some stability in a highly volatile industry. As analysts, the authors believe that either market mechanism would be likely to yield results that are better for the long-term health of the nation than many of the other mechanisms that might be used. The biggest hindrance to acceptance of this method is predicting with high certainty how economic incentives would work, given the complicated nature of airline scheduling. The full merits and demerits of this approach are probably not knowable until some real auctions occur. (The FCC discovered only after the first spectrum auction how smart auctioneers could "game" the system to their advantage and to the disadvantage of the nation's interests.)

Some Final Thoughts on Some Related Questions

At the conclusion, the following paragraphs provide some final thoughts on some relevant issues. Obviously, there are many more specific subjects that could be addressed here (e.g., issues regarding baggage, ticketing, 9/11 policies, in-flight procedures and amenities, etc.), but they will be for another day or another book.

How Should the FAA be Financed, and What Portion of That Financing Should Be Placed on the Airline Passengers?

Although this issue might appear to be straightforward, it really is not. Nonetheless, one simple answer is that those who gain the benefits of air transportation should also pay in proportion to those benefits. But who are those people? Obviously, it is not just the passengers, nor is it those working within the aviation sector of the economy. Aviation is part of the nation's overall transportation system, and this system provides goods and services that underlie the overall economy. Without air transportation, "just-in-time" delivery of parts and goods would be significantly impacted, increasing the general cost of goods to everyone and lowering the U.S. ability to compete with international competitors. In short, the transportation system is a vital part of the nation's economic well-being, and aviation is an increasingly essential element. So, who benefits? Everyone does.

Of course, some benefit more than others, and those people who travel (and ship cargo) on aircraft are unquestionably obtaining more benefits than those who do not. So, it is reasonable to assign some of the costs of the ATC system to the airline passengers. But what is that percentage? A reasonable answer to this question can be obtained analytically. [The reorganization of the FAA financial budgeting system, as proposed by FAA Administrator Blakey, is an important step in the right direction.]

Should the Government Undertake the Initiative to Significantly Modernize the Current Airport Baggage and Passenger Security System, and Who Should Pay the Costs of That Modernization?

To answer these questions, the following observations are offered:

- The current equipment is slow and not very good. Newer equipment exists and is already in use in Europe and elsewhere.
- The cost of maintaining and operating this equipment is substantial and growing.
- The passengers/airlines are paying most of these costs. (They are added to the price of the ticket.)
- Past work on optimizing the amount of equipment that should be fielded at airports indicates that the current deployments are

significantly less than this optimum [Shaver 2004b; Ervin 2006; Poole 2006; Jackson et al. 2007]. The lack of optimized employment does not need a fancy analysis; most trained observers can see this by casual inspection. If the optimization criterion were to maximize the deterrent of a terrorist attack on a national symbol at minimum overall cost to the nation [and it took into account the lost time of the passengers (the previously discussed government estimates of $30 per hour)], optimum equipment deployments would have generated average passenger delay times not greater than about three minutes (not to mention the attractive soft targets that long delay lines create simultaneously at major airports).

These observations suggest that our policies toward enforcing a high degree of (largely symbolic) security checks and our policies on how such security should be funded both need to be thoroughly and dispassionately reconsidered. Retaining expensive-to-maintain, improperly deployed, outmoded equipment and then penalizing the flying public by forcing them to wait in long lines are not good for the health of the nation. These financial penalties also put our privately operated airlines under additional financial pressure, at a time when we really need them to survive.

But the preceding observations do not address the degree of security that is needed. Honest, intelligent people can differ widely on this matter. One argument can be made that terrorist attacks against aircraft and airports have been occurring for decades (mostly in foreign lands), and the nation could have survived without a heavy emphasis on airport security measures. Others can argue that things have changed, and such attacks on passengers would have significantly increased had we not fielded our current equipment. However, if you believe the latter, then the consequences of the often-extensive queues that exist outside the security area make attacks against airports even more attractive than before. These queues often have 100 or more passengers waiting in a relatively small area, an area that is not secure against a bomber who simply wheels in a large bomb inside his carry-on luggage.

The implication of the last sentence is a serious effort to shorten the lines. This can be done by exploiting the new equipment (such as millimeter-wave backscatter fast imaging and multiphenomenology carry-on baggage screening equipment now available), coupled with a multilayered screening system designed to keep the lines relatively short during even the busiest hours at the airport [Castaneda et al. 2007].

But the question of who should pay is complicated. As was true in assessing that only a portion of the ATC operating and modernization costs should be placed on the backs of the airline traveler, here too there is an argument for some (if not most) of the costs to be borne by the nation as a whole (through income taxes). However, a serious economic study of this is warranted before any decision is made. That study could also include the work needed to actually identify the optimum amount and deployment of equipment needed. The past work on this matter suggests that the design of the current security deployments incurred unnecessary annual costs to the nation's economy measured in many billions of dollars per year [Shaver et al. 2004b].

Should the Congress Pass a Passenger's Bill of Rights, and if so, What Should Be in It and When Should It Become Law?

The answer to the first part of this question is "yes." The public deserves protection from some of the more outrageous actions that airlines have inflicted on it. In partial defense of the airlines, however, their actions are consistent with their struggles to stay out of bankruptcy, a struggle that many are failing regardless of how they treat their passengers. Hopefully, fixes to the system will minimize the need to maltreat the passengers, but abuses will still remain because of the economic incentives every airline has in filling its seats at a price that is competitive with its rivals.

The authors are inclined to recommend that Congress pass a Passenger's Bill of Rights that matches in almost all aspects the one passed in Europe, although they know of no analysis that suggests that Europe's Passenger's Bill of Rights is optimum in any way. But in all known accounts it is clearly working in the passengers' interests.

That said, the prominent downside of a prompt passage of a Passenger's Bill of Rights for U.S. air carriers is twofold. First, the European airlines operate out of slot-controlled airports where the prisoner's dilemma and the tragedy of the commons are not a serious problem. The bad scheduling actions of other airlines do not strongly affect the QOS to their passengers. This is not the case in the United States. Individual airline PBRs are worthless (because they can always argue that someone else caused the poor QOS), and a national law would be unfair without slot controls in place to regulate the predictability of airport service for all airlines. Secondly, the additional economic burden that would ensue from a real PBR might push some airlines with poor QOS over the financial brink. As mentioned, most of the larger airlines are near bankruptcy, and this bill might push them over the edge. Although the authors have studied these issues for many years, they simply do not know the consequences of the resulting bankruptcy actions and the long-term harm that might ensue for the country. Nor do they know how to weigh these concerns with their commensurate concerns about the passengers and their right to be treated better.

What Can and Should Be Done in Order to Accommodate the Anticipated Future Growth in Airline Transportation?

Up until now, we have been addressing the current problems related to the air transportation system and its users. These are problems that confront the flying public today, problems that merit serious attention by the various government organizations that oversee transportation needs and shortfalls. Our primary purpose has been to educate the flying public and those in government who set the transportation policy about the character of these problems and to inform them about options that might best address them. If this book has done that, then we have succeeded in our primary goal.

However, it would be a mistake on everyone's parts if they did not also look beyond the current problems. In a nutshell, even assuming that the myriad of vexing problems covered in this book were successfully addressed, the future of the commercial aviation system would still look bleak. We have provided the evidence for why this is true (i.e., the overall system is constrained by the capacity of the airports), and why capacity is essentially fixed at or near its current capability (see Appendices C and D). And it will soon be true that adding more flights into the largest airports simply will not be possible.

So, why should anyone care? In one sense, it is not so bad that adding more flights would not be possible, if for no other reason than the delays and cancellations that the system is now experiencing are not likely to become substantially worse. One plausible vision of the future is maintenance of the status quo at the already highly congested airports, accompanied by growing congestion at other currently not-so-congested airports as overall traffic volumes increase. Within a reasonable time, U.S. air travel should reach the relatively steady-state solution where the system is always congested, with substantial delays and predictable cancellations the norm, but with passenger discomfort not much worse than experienced at the busiest airports today. In other words, aircraft LFs cannot exceed 100%! Even if they get close, flying will be irritating for almost everyone, but will still be tolerable for many passengers.

Although this might be arguably acceptable from the narrow view of the passengers and the airlines, it is not a future that everyone should be willing to tolerate. It is time for the flying public to quit being sheep. The prime argument for this relates to the overall economic well-being of the United States. Not doing something about the limited capacity of major airports dooms the United States to a finite ceiling on commerce associated with air travel. One obvious sector of our economy that would be seriously impacted is the tourism and travel industry. Another, less obvious (but of equal or greater importance) sector is the business traveler (and the commerce that is enabled by his/her trips).

We have attempted to capture the impact of constraints on flying by estimating the number of "foregone passenger trips," using U.S. transportation data on forecasts of the future demand for air travel at the major U.S. airports, and then calculating the cost to the nation that they imply (see Appendix H for a description of the economic approach employed to obtain these numbers). Figure 7.3 shows the results, where the dollar amounts shown represent the reduction in the nation's GDP per year that can be attributed to restraining air travel plus the cost of passengers' lost time caused by flight delays and cancellations.

These numbers are in billions lost annually, assuming projected 2008 passenger enplanements and various levels of slot reductions to lower congestion (in constant 2006 dollars). As can be seen, the numbers are troublingly large. The use of new technology, as envisioned by the

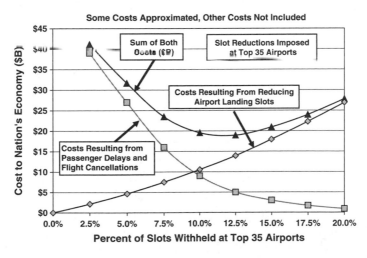

Fig. 7.3   Lost economic welfare from failing to address the problem.

Europeans (and to some extent by the FAA NEXTGEN program), could lead to higher airport capacity utilization (e.g., from today's average of about 80% to a future approaching 90 to 95%, because of reduced aircraft spacing capability). Better schedule synchronization and hub airport capacity limits using larger aircraft would also decrease the amount of delay and cancellations experienced.

Can the Government and the Public Ignore the Other Modes of Transportation and Still Provide the Robust Air Transportation System That This Country Needs and Deserves?

This question has not been addressed in this book or by the government for several decades. But the answer is probably "no." Addressing the capacity limitations of the entire aviation system also requires a long-term view of how the overall transportation needs of the country are to be addressed. It is hardly news that the nation's ground transportation infrastructure is also in disrepair, forecasting either large government spending to keep the highway system operational or a reduction in that system's throughput capacity. Moreover, our major highways are already heavily used, and in many major metropolitan areas suffering from almost overwhelming congestion. Political debates about who will cut taxes the most will not help this problem and will kill the goose that has laid the golden-economic-growth-through-transportation egg.

One measure of the status of a national transportation system is the cost and ease in going from one location to another. A major component of that "ease" is the traveler's average "block time." Block times between adjacent metropolitan areas have been growing, and many transportation experts are predicting additional congestion and delays in the future.

In choosing the mode of transportation, most travelers take into consideration the total transportation time between the place of origin and the destination. Air travel has historically "won" this competition where the cities were 200 or more miles apart. However, experience suggests that this is no longer the case; people are selecting automobiles over airplanes in increasing numbers for trips up to 500 miles, reflecting the overall problems in the air transportation system. This puts greater pressure on the interstate highway systems. If train service were a serious option (i.e., a service similar to what is available in Europe or Japan), it would likely win on block time contest for 100- to 300-mile trips, assuming that it did not stop at every midsized city en route.

These somewhat random comments are included solely for the purpose of getting the reader to recognize that transportation issues are not easily bundled separately into air traffic, interstate highways, or trains. They are all elements of our nation's overall transportation capabilities, and investments in them should recognize their relative strengths and weaknesses.

But whichever mode of intercity transportation one selects, one fact seems clear. Given the amount of investment capital needed to address this problem, only the government can afford it. In fact, this truth, coupled with his foresight on the nation's need for high-speed transportation between our major cities, led former President Dwight Eisenhower to establish our interstate highway system in the first place. This vital system was built primarily in the 1950s and 1960s. We are now at a state in our multimodal national transportation system to rethink whether a new (and similarly bold) set of transportation initiatives needs to be undertaken. This can only be done by the federal government (although financial or other support from state and local governments would no doubt play a major role). To the authors, it is obvious that the government needs a serious, well-researched set of plans and policies that cover all transportation modes. And these plans and policies need to be backed by significant financial resources. And, perhaps the hardest to obtain, they need a government commitment to make the needed investments, recognizing that the benefit of these investments might only bear fruit a decade or two later.

Bibliography

Andrews, John W., and John Robinson (2001), "Radar-Based Analysis of the Efficiency of Runway Use," AIAA Paper-2001–4359, AIAA Guidance, Navigation and Control Conference, Montreal, August 6–9.

Andrews, John W., J. D. Welch, and H. Erzerberger (2005), "Safety Analysis for Advanced Separation Concepts," 6th USA/Europe Air Traffic Management R&D Seminar, Baltimore, MD, June 27–30.

ARINC (1987), *The ARINC Story.* The ARINC Companies, Annapolis, MD.

ATA (1960–2005), Air Transport Assoc. Annual Reports 1960 through 2005.

Aviation Industry and Its Workforce Blue Ribbon Panel (1993), National Academy of Sciences, Washington, D.C.

Aviation Week and Space Technology (2004), Multiple articles on congestion, capacity, and delay, November 15.

Aviation Week and Space Technology (2005), "Formation Flight: US, European Efforts Are Setting the Pace for Global Air Traffic Modernization," March 14.

Aviation Week and Space Technology (2005), "Top Performing Airline Rankings," June 6, pp. 56–58.

Aviation Week and Space Technology (2006) "RISK REDUCTION: NTSB Seeks Multi-Layered Defense Against Runway Incursions," November 20.

Ball, M., Ausubel, L., Berardino, F., Crampton, P., Donohue, G., Hansen, M., and K. Hoffman (2007), "Market-Based Alternatives for Managing Congestion at New York's LaGuardia Airport," Air Netherlands Conference Paper, April.

Ball, Mike, G. L. Donohue, and K. Hoffman (2005), "Auctions for the Safe, Efficient and Equitable Allocation of Airspace System Resources," *Combinatorial Auctions*, edited by Crampton, Shoham, and Steinberrg, Massachusetts Inst. of Technology, Cambridge, MA, Chap. 20.

Blakey, Marion C. (2007), "Statement Before Senate Committee on Finance," July 12, 2007, accessed September 17, 2007. www.faa.gov/new/testimony/new-story.cfm.

Bowen, B., and D. Headley (2001), "The National Airline Quality Rating: Results 2001," Paper, Aviation Management Education and Research Conference, Montreal, July 16–17.

Bratu, Stephane, and C. Barnhar (2005), "An Analysis of Passenger Delays Using Flight Operations and Passenger Booking Data," *Air Traffic Control Quarterly*, Vol. 13, No. 1.

Bureau of Transportation Statistics (2007), "Air Travel Consumer Report," *Office of Aviation Enforcement and Proceedings*, Aviation Consumer Protection Division, U.S. Dept. of Transportation, August 2007 data reported October 2007. http://airconsumer.ost.dot.gov/.

Butler, Viggo with P. W. Poole, Jr. (2008), "Increasing Airport Capacity without Increasing Airport Size" Reason Foundation, Policy Study No. 368, March 2008.

CAA (1956), "A Development Plan for an Improved Air Traffic Control System," U.S. Dept. of Commerce, Technical Report 300, Washington, D.C., May.

Carnegie Mellon University (2006), "Rethinking Aviation Security," H. John Heinz III School of Public Policy and Management, Systems Synthesis Project, Carnegie Mellon University, Pittsburgh, PA.

Casaux, Francis (ed.) (2005), "Special Issue on Airborne Separation Assistance System," *Air Traffic Control Quarterly*, Vol. 13, No. 2.

Castaneda, E., J. Gonzalez, S. Harris, and J. Kim (2007), "Optimized Airport Security Infrastructure System (OASIS)," Proceedings of the IEEE Systems Engineering Conference, University of Virginia, Charlottesville, VA, April.

Center for Air Transportation Systems Research (2007), "Passenger Trip Delay Index (PTDI)," CATSR George Mason University, Fairtax, VA. http://www.greenflights.info.

Cobb, Roger, W., and D. M. Primo (2003), "The Plane Truth: Airline Crashes, the Media, and Transport Policy," Brookings Inst. Press, Washington, D.C.

Daniel, J. (1992), "Peak-Load-Congestion Pricing and Optimal Capacity of Large Hub Airports: With Application to the Minneapolis–St. Paul Airport," Ph.D. Dissertation, University of Minnesota, Minneapolis, MN.

Department of Justice (2005), "Congestion and Delayed Reduction at Chicago O'Hare International Airport," Federal Aviation Administration, FAA-2005-20704-13, Washington, D.C., March 21.

Doble, N., M. Brennan, N. Arora, C. Ermatinger, and S. Clover (2006), "Simulation and Operational Analysis of Airspace Flow Programs for Traffic Flow Management," 6th AIAA Aviation Technology, Integration and Operations Conference, September, Wichita, KS.

Doganis, R. (2002), *Flying Off Course*, 3rd ed., Routledge Press, New York.

Donohue, G. L. (1995a), "Testimony Before the House Committee on Transportation and Infrastructure, Subcommittee on Aviation, Concerning the Wide Area Augmentation System for the Global Positioning System," Washington, D.C., November 30.

Donohue, G. L. (1995b), "Testimony Before the House Committee on Science, Subcommittee on Technology Concerning the FAA's Research and Acquisition Budget," Washington, D.C., May 16.

Donohue, G. L. (1996), "Statement Before the White House Commission on Aviation Safety and Security Concerning ATC Modernization and the National Airspace Plan," Washington, D.C., December 5.

Donohue, G. L. (1997), "Testimony Before the U.S. House of Representatives Committee on Science, Subcommittee on Technology Concerning the Fiscal Year 1998 Research, Engineering and Development Authorization," Washington, D.C., March 13.

Donohue, G. L. (1999a), "A Simplified Air Transportation System Capacity Model," *Journal of Air Traffic Control*, April–June, pp. 8–15.

Donohue, G. L. (1999b), "Air Traffic Service Privatization: Will the USA Join Other Developed Nations?," *Journal of Air Transport Management*, Vol. 5, pp. 61–62.

Donohue, G. L. (2000), "Testimony before the U.S. House of Representatives Committee on Science, Subcommittee on Space and Aeronautics," Hearing on 2001 NASA Budget, *Congressional Record*, Washington, D.C., April 11.

Donohue, G. L., and A. Zellweger (eds.) (2001a), *Air Transportation System Engineering*, Progress in Aeronautics and Astronautics, AIAA, Reston, VA.

Donohue, G. L (2001b), "A Macroscopic Air Transportation Capacity Model: Metrics and Delay Correlation," *New Concepts and Methods in Air Traffic Management*, edited by L. Bianco, P. Dell'Olmo, and A. Odoni, Springer-Verlag, New York, pp. 45–62.

Donohue, G. L. (2001c) "Air Traffic Control Systems," *Handbook of Transport Systems and Traffic Control*, edited by, K. Button and D. Hensher, Elsevier Science, Amsterdam.

Donohue, G. L. (2002), "Proposed Architecture for a Future High-Density Air Transportation System," *Proceedings of the ATM and CNS Architecture IEEE Workshop*, Capri, Italy, September 22.

Donohue, G. L. (2003), "Air Transportation is a Complex Adaptive System: Not an Aircraft Design," AIAA Paper 2003–2668, AIAA/ICAS International Air and Space Symposium and Exposition: The Next 100 Years, Dayton, Ohio, July 14–17.

Donohue, G. L. (2007/2006), "An Approaching Perfect Storm," *Aerospace America*, August 2006; reprinted in *Managing the Skies*, January/February 2007. http.//www.faama.org.

Donohue, G. L., K. Hoffman, and B. Poole (2007), "Evidence That Airport Pricing Works," Reason Foundation Policy Brief No. 67, Los Angeles. http://www.reason.org.

DOT (1996), "DoT 1996 Appropriations Act," Dept. of Transportation, Washington D.C., November 15.

DOT (2004), "Airport Capacity Benchmark Report 2004," Dept. of Transportation, Federal Aviation Administration, MITRE/CAASD, Washington, D.C., September. www.faa.gov/events/benchmarks.

DOT (2005), "Comments of the United States Department of Justice on Congestion and Delay Reduction at Chicago O'Hare International Airport," Dept. of Transportation, Washington, D.C., May 24.

DotEcon, Ltd. (2001), "Auctioning Airport Slots: A Report for HM treasury and the Dept. of the Environment, Transport and the Regions," Technical Report, London, January.

EC (2003), "A Comparison of Performance in Selected U.S. and European En-Route Centres," Eurocontrol Performance Review Commission, May.

EC (2004a), "An Assessment of Air Traffic Management in Europe During the Calendar Year 2003," Eurocontrol Performance Review Commission, April.

EC (2004b), "ATM Cost-Effectiveness (ACE) 2002 Benchmarking Report," Eurocontrol Performance Review Commission, May.

EC (2005a), "ATM Cost-Effectiveness (ACE) 2003 Benchmarking Report," ACE2003 Final Report, Eurocontrol Performance Review Commission, April.

EC (2005b), "Performance Review Commission Eighth Performance Review Report for CY 2004," Final Draft, Eurocontrol Performance Review Commission, February.

EC (2005c), "Report on Punctuality Drivers at Major European Airports," Eurocontrol Performance Review Commission, May.

EC (2007), "ACI-NA, EC Performance Review 2006," May.

EC (2007), "Performance Review Report 2006: An Assessment of Air Traffic Management in Europe During the Calendar Year 2006," Eurocontrol Performance Review Commission, May. http://www.eurocontrol.int/prc.

Ervin, C. K. (2006), *Open Target: Where America is Vulnerable to Attack*, Palgrave Macmillan, St. Martin's Press, New York.

FAA (1996), "Report of the Blue Ribbon Panel on FAA Acquisition Reform," Federal Aviation Administration, Washington, D.C., March. http://fast.faa.gov/ams/reform/bluerib.htm.

FAA (1998), NAS 4.0 System Architecture, Federal Aviation Administration, Washington, D.C.

FAA (1999), "Administrators Fact Book," Federal Aviation Administration, Washington, D.C., December. http://www.ama500.jccbi.gov.

FAA (2004b), "A Plan for the Future: The Federal Aviation Administration's 10-Year Strategy for the Air Traffic Control Workforce: 2005–2014," Federal Aviation Administration, Washington, D.C., December.

FAA (2004c), "Economic Information for Investment Analysis," Federal Aviation Administration, ASD-400, Washington, D.C., March.

FAA (2005), FAA Aerospace Forecast Fiscal Years 2006–2017, Federal Aviation Administration, Washington, D.C.

FAA (2005a), "Administrators Fact Book," Federal Aviation Administration, Washington, D.C., August. www.atctraining.faa.gov/factbook.

FAA (2005b), "Notice of Proposed Rules, Congestion and Delay Reduction at Chicago O'Hare International Airport," 70 Federal Register 15520 Federal Aviation Administration, Washington, D.C., March 25.

FAA (2005c), "New York Terminal Radar Approach Control (TRACON) Operational Assessment (March 2–May 6, 2005)," Federal Aviation Administration, Washington, D.C., June 2. www.faa.gov.

FAA (2006), Aviation System Performance Metrics (ASPM), Federal Aviation Administration, Washington, D.C.

FAA (2006), "Terminal Area Forecast," Federal Aviation Administration, Washington, D.C.

FAA (2007), "FY 2005 Cost Allocation Report," Federal Aviation Administration, Washington, D.C., January 31.

FAA Aerospace Forecasts Fiscal Years 2006–2007, Federal Aviation Administration, Washington, D.C.

FAA/DOT (2004a), "Next Generation Air Transportation System Integrated Plan," Joint Planning and Development Office, Washington, D.C., December 12.

Fan, T. P., and A. R. Odoni (2001), "The Potential of Demand Management as a Short-Term Means of Relieving Airport Congestion," *Proceedings of EUROCONTROL-FAA Air Traffic Management R&D Review Seminar,* Santa Fe, NM.

Flying (2007), "Gulfstream G150 Defeats Mother Nature on Nonstop Coast-to-Coast Flight," Vol. 134, No. 4, April.

Flying (2007), "Mustang at Work: We Fly Cessna's New Light Jet on a Bunch of Real Trips," Vol. 134, No. 5, May.

Freiberg, K., and J. Freiberg (2001), *NUTS! Southwest Airlines Crazy Recipe for Business and Personal Success,* TEXERE Publishing, New York.

GAO (1996), "Aviation Acquisition: A Comprehensive Strategy Is Needed for Cultural Change at the FAA," U.S. Government Accountability Office, GAO/RCED-96-159, Washington, D.C., August.

GAO (2002), "Air Traffic Control: FAA Needs to Better Prepare for Impending Wave of Controller Attrition," U.S. Government Accountability Office, GAO-02-591, Washington, D.C., June 14.

GAO (2003a), "Human Capital Management: FAA's Reform Effort Requires a More Strategic Approach," U.S. Government Accountability Office, GAO-03-156, Washington, D.C., February 3.

GAO (2003b), "Air Traffic Control: FAA's Modernization Efforts—Past, Present and Future," U.S. Government Accountability Office, GAO-04-227T, Washington, D.C., October 30.

GAO (2004a), "Commercial Aviation: Legacy Airlines Must Further Reduce Costs to Restore Profitability," U.S. Government Accountability Office, Report to Congressional Committees, GAO-04-836, Washington, D.C., August.

GAO (2004b), "Information Technology: FAA Has Many Investment Management Capabilities in Place, But More Oversight of Operational Systems Is Needed," U.S. Government Accountability Office, GAO-04-822, Washington, D.C., August 20.

GAO (2004c), "Federal Aviation Administration: Plan Still Needed to Meet Challenges to Effectively Managing Air Traffic Controller Workforce," U.S. Government Accountability Office, GAO-04-887T, Washington, D.C., June 15.

GAO (2004d), "Federal Aviation Administration: Challenges for Transforming into a High-Performance Organization," U.S. Government Accountability Office, GAO-04-770T, Washington, D.C., May 18.

GAO (2005a), "Air Traffic Control: Characteristics and Performance of Selected International Air Navigation Service Providers and Lessons Learned from their Commercialization," U.S. Government Accountability Office, GAO-05-769, Washington, D.C., July.

GAO (2005b), "Air Traffic Operations; The Federal Aviation Administration Needs to Address Major Air Traffic Operating Cost Control Challenges," U.S. Government Accountability Office, GAO-05-724, Washington, D.C., June.

GAO (2005c), "National Airspace System: Expert Views on Improving the U.S. Air Traffic Control Modernization Program," U.S. Government Accountability Office, GAO-05-333SP, Washington, D.C., April.

Gundmundson, S.V. (1998), "New-Entrant Airlines' Life Cycle Analysis: Growth, Decline and Collapse," *Journal of Air Transport Management*, Vol. 4, pp. 217–228.

Hare, R. D. (1999) *Without Conscience: The Disturbing World of the Psychopaths Among Us*, Guilford Press, New York.

Haynie, R. (2002), "An Investigation of Capacity and Safety in Near-Terminal Airspace for Guiding Information Technology Adaptation," Ph.D. Dissertation, George Mason University, Fairfax, VA.

IATA (2007), "IATA 2006 Safety Report," *Aviation Week and Space Technology*, April 30, 2007.

Jackson, B. A., P. Chalk, R. K. Cragin, B. Newsome, J. V. Parachini, W. Rosenau, E. M. Simpson, M. Sisson, and D. Temple (2007), "Breaching the Fortress Wall: Understanding Terrorist Efforts to Overcome Defensive Technologies," RAND Corporation.

Jeddi, B., J. F. Shortle, and L. Sherry (2006), "Statistical Separation Standards for the Aircraft-Approach Process," *Proceedings of the IEEE/AIAA 25th Digital Avionics Systems Conference*, Portland, OR, October.

Jiang, Helen Hong, and J. Hansman (2004), "An Analysis of Profit Cycles in the Airline Industry," International Center for Air Transportation, Report ICAT-2004-7, Massachusetts Institute of Technology, Cambridge, MA, December.

Kahn, Alfred (2004), *Lessons from Deregulation: Telecommunications and Airlines after the Crunch*, AEI–Brookings Joint Center for Regulatory Studies, Washington, D.C.

Kaplan, D. P. (2007), "Toward Rational Pricing of the U.S. Airport and Airways System," *Advances in Airline Economics*, edited by Dan Lee, Vol. 2 (to be published).

Laskey, K., N. Xu and C. H. Chen (2006), "Propagation of Delays in the National Airspace System," *Proceedings of the 22nd Conference on Uncertainty in Artificial Intelligence*, Massachusetts Inst. of Technology, Cambridge, MA.

Le, Loan (2006), "Demand Management at Congested Airports: How Far Are We from Utopia?," Ph.D. Dissertation, George Mason University, Fairfax, VA, August. http://catsr.ite.gmu.edu/.

Le, Loan, G. L. Donohue and C. H. Chen (2004), "Auction-Based Slot Allocation for Traffic Demand Management at Hartsfield Atlanta

International Airport: A Case Study,"Transportation Research Record No. 1888 Safety, Economy, and Efficiency in Airport and Airspace Management Operations, Transportation Research Board of the National Academies, Washington, D.C.

Le, Loan, G. L. Donohue, K. Hoffman, and C. H. Chen (2008), "Optimum Airport Capacity Utilization Under Congestion Management: A Case Study of New York LaGuardia Airport," *Transportation Planning and Technology – Special Edition: Approaches for Developing the Airports of the Future* (to be published); draft of paper at http://catsr.ite.gmu.edu/.

Lohr, G. W., R. M. Osequera-Lohr, T. S. Abbott, W. R. Capron, and C. T. Howell, (2005), "Flight Evaluation and Demonstration of a Time-Based Airborne Inter-Arrival Spacing Tool," NASA TM-2005-213772, NASA Langley Research Center, Hampton, VA.

McCarteny, Scott (2005), "FAA Steps up Oversight of Air-Traffic Controllers," *Wall Street Journal*, August 2.

McDougall, Glen (2006), "Air Traffic Control Commercialization Policy: Has It Been Effective?," MBS Ottawa Rept., in cooperation with George Mason University, Syracuse University, and McGill University, Inc. January.

McElroy, Paul (2000), *TRACON*, Japphire. http://www.paulmcelroy.com.

Morrison, Steven A., and C. Winston (1995), *The Evolution of the Airline Industry*, Brookings Instit. Press, Washington, D.C.

Nazeri, Zohreh (2007), "Cross-Database Analysis to Identify Relationships Between Aircraft Accidents and Incidents," Ph.D. Dissertation, George Mason University, Fairfax, VA, November. http://catsr.ite.gmu.edu/pubs. html.

Osequera-Lohr, R. M., G. W. Lohr, T. S. Abbott, and T.M. Eischeid (2002), "Evaluation of Operational Procedures for Using a Time-Based Airborne Inter-arrival Spacing Tool," AIAA Paper 2002-5824.

Oster, C. V. (2006), "Reforming the Federal Aviation Asdministration: Lessons from Canada and the United Kingdom," IBM Center for the Business of Government, School of Public and Environmental Affairs, Indiana University, Bloomington, IN.

Pels, E. and E. Verhoef (2003), "The Economics of Airport Congestion Pricing," Tinbergen Inst., Discussion Paper No. 03-083/3, Amsterdam, October 10.

Plavin, David Z. with R. Poole, Jr. (2007), "Using Revenues from Airport Pricing," Reason Foundation Policy Brief No. 68. http://reason.org/ pb68_airportpricing.pdf.

Poole, Robert W., Jr. (2005), "Air Traffic Debate About Safety and Efficiency," Reason Foundation, Los Angeles. http://www.rppi.org/airtrafficdebate.shtml.

Poole, Robert W., Jr. (2006), "Airport Security: Time for a New Model," Reason Foundation, Los Angeles.

Poole, Robert W., Jr. (2007), "The Urgent Need to Reform the FAA's Air Traffic Control System," Reason Foundation, Policy Study No. 358, Los Angeles, March.

Poole, Robert W., Jr., and Benjamin Dachis (2007), "Congestion Pricing for the New York Airports: Reducing Delays while Promoting Growth and Competition," Reason Foundation, Policy Study No. 366, Los Angeles, December.

Poole, Robert, W., Jr., and V. Cordle (2005), "Resolving the Crisis in Air Traffic Control Funding," Reason Foundation, Policy Study 332, Los Angeles, May.

Rassenti, S., V. Smith, and R. Bulfin (1982) "A Combinatorial Auction Mechanism for Airport Time Slot Allocation," *Bell Journal of Economics*, Vol. 12, No. 2, 1982, pp. 402–417.

Robyn, Dorothy (2001), "Congress Plan to Reduce Flight Delays is not Airworthy" AEI–Brookings Joint Center Policy Matters 01-15, May 2001. http://www.aei-brookings.org/policy.

Robyn, Dorothy (2007), "Reforming the Air Traffic Control System to Promote Efficiency and Reduce Delays," The Brattle Group, Inc., October. http://www.brattle.com/Publications/ReportsPresentations.asp.

Rutishauser, David, G. L. Donohue, and Haynie (2003), "Measurements of Aircraft Wake Vortex Seperation at High Arrival Rates and a Proposed New Wake Vortex Seperation Philosophy," Fifth FAA/Eurocontrol ATM R&D Conference, Budapest, Hungary, June 23–27.

Schank, J. (2005), "Solving Airside Airport Congestion: Why Peak Runway Pricing Is Not Working," *Journal of Air Transport Management*, Vol. 11, pp. 417–425.

Scovel, C. L. (2007), "FAA's FY 2008 Budget Request: Key Issues Facing the Agency," Statement of the U.S. Dept. of Transportation Inspector General Before the Transportation and Infrastructure Committee, Subcommittee on Aviation, U.S. House of Representatives, Washington, D.C., February 14.

Sharkey, Joe (2007), "Memo Pad," *New York Times*, December 11.

Shaver, R., and M. Kennedy (2004a), "The Benefits of Positive Passenger Profiling on Baggage Screening Requirements," RAND Corporation, DB-411-RC, September.

Shaver, R., M. Kennedy, C. Shirley and P. Dreyer (2004b), "How Much is Enough? Sizing the Deployment of Baggage Screening Equipment by Considering the Economic Cost of Passenger Delays," RAND Corporation, DB-410-RC, September.

Sherry, L., D. Wang and G. Donohue (2007), "Air Travel Consumer Protection: A Metric for Passenger On-Time Performance," *Transportation Research Board Review* (to be published).

Shostak, Arthur and D. Skocik (1986), *The Air Controllers' Controversy: Lessons from the PATCO Strike*, Human Sciences Press, New York.

Stout, Martha, (2005), *The Sociopath Next Door*, Broadway Books, New York.

Tretvik, T. (2003), *Acceptability of Transport Pricing Strategies*, Pergamon, New York.

Wall Street Journal, "China's Auction Dreams Beginning to Take Flight," March 20.

Wall Street Journal (2007), "China's Aviation Dreams Beginning to Take Flight," March 20.

Wang, D., L. Sherry and G. L. Donohue (2006), "Passenger Trip Time Metric for Air Transportation," Second International Conference on Research in Air Transportation, June.

Wang, Danyi (2007), "Methods for Analysis of Passenger Trip Performance in a Complex Networked Transportation System," Ph.D. Dissertation, George Mason University, Fairfax, VA, July. http://catsr.ite.gmu.edu/pubs.html.

Washington Examiner (2007), February 5.

Washington Post (2007), "Top 20 Corporate PACs in 2006," March 20.

White House (1997a), "White House Commission on Aviation Safety and Security, Final Report to President Clinton—Vice President Al Gore, Chairman," Washington, D.C., February 12.

White House (1997b), "National Civil Aviation Review Commission: Avoiding Aviation Gridlock and Reducing the Accident Rate—Norman Mineta Chairman," Washington, D.C., December.

Xie, Y., J. Shortle, and G. L. Donohue (2003), "Runway Landing Safety Analysis: A Case Study of Atlanta Hartsfield Airport," IEEE/AIAA, Paper 0-7803-7844-X/03, 22nd Digital Avionics Systems Conference, Indianapolis, IN, October 13–16.

Xie, Y., J. Shortle and P. Choroba (2005), "Quantitative Estimation of Wake Vortex Safety Using the P2P Model," *Proceedings of the 6th USA/Eurocontrol Air Traffic Management Research Seminar*, Baltimore, MD, June.

Xie, Yue (2005), "Quantitave Analysis of Airport Arrival Capacity and Arrival Safety Using Stochastic Methods," Ph. D. Dissertation, George Mason University, Fairfax, VA, August.

Xu, N. (2007), "Method for Deriving Multi-Factor Models for Predicting Airport Delays," Ph.D. Dissertation, George Mason University, Fairfax, VA, November. http://catsr.ite.gmu.edu/pubs.html.

Xu, N., G. L. Donohue, K. Laskey, and C. H. Chen (2005), "Estimation of Delay Propagation in the NAS Using Bayesian Networks," *Proceedings of the Sixth USA/Eurocontrol Air Traffic Management Research Seminar*, Baltimore, MD, June.

Xu, N., K. Laskey, C. H. Chung, S. C. Williams, and L. Sherry, (2007), "Bayesian Network Analysis of Flight Delays," *Proceedings of the 86th Annual Transportation Research Board Meeting*, January 21–25.

Yousefi, Arash and G. L. Donohue (2004), "Temporal and Spatial Distribution of Airspace Complexity for Air Traffic Controller Workload-Based Sectorization," *Proceedings of the AIAA Conference*, AIAA, Reston, VA, September 16.

Yousefi, Arash (2005), Ph.D. Dissertation, George Mason University, Fairfax, VA.

APPENDIX A

Acronyms and Abbreviations

AAR	actual arrival rate
ACAS	aircraft collision-avoidance system
ACI	Airport Council International
ADS-B	Automatic Dependent Surveillance-Broadcast
AIP	Air Improvement Program
AM	amplitude modulated
AMASS	airport movement area safety system
AOC	air operations center
AOPA	Aircraft Owners and Pilots Association
ARINC	Aeronautical Radio, Inc.
ASM	available seat miles
ATA	Air Transportation Association
ATC	air traffic control
ATCSSCC	Air Traffic Control System Command Center
ATO	Air Traffic Control Organization
ATS	air traffic services
BTS	Bureau of Transportation Statistics
CAA	Civil Aeronautics Administration
CAA	civil aviation authority
CAB	Civil Aeronautics Board
CAS	complex adaptive system
CATSR	George Mason University's Center for Air Transportation Systems Research
CDM	collaborative decision making
CFCM	central flow control management
CFMU	Central Flow Management Unit

CNS/ATM	communications, navigation, and surveillance and air traffic management
COO	chief operating officer
COTS	commercial off-the-shelf
CPDCC	controller-pilot data-link communication
DARPA	Defense Advanced Research Projects Agency
DOT	U.S. Department of Transportation
DSR	display system replacement
EV-PTD	Expected Value-Passenger Trip Delay
FAA	Federal Aviation Administration
FCC	Federal Communications Commission
FMS	flight management system
FOM	figures of merit
FSM	flight schedule monitor
GA	general aviation
GAMA	General Aviation Manufacturers Association
GDP	ground delay program
GDPE	ground delay program enhancements
GMU	George Mason University
GPS	global positioning system
HDR	high-density rule
ICAO	International Civil Aviation Organization
IMC	instrument meteorological conditions
IPT	integrated product team
ITU	International Telecommunications Union
LCC	low-cost carrier
LF	load factor
MIT	Massachusetts Institute of Technology
NAS	National Airspace System
NATCA	FAA Air Traffic Control Union
NBAA	National Business Aircraft Association
NEXTOR	FAA National Center of Excellence in Operations Research

NGATS	Next-Generation Air Traffic Control System
NTSB	National Transportation Safety Board
OD	origin and destination
OEP	Operational Evolution Partnership
OPEVAL	operational evaluation
OT & E	operational test and evaluation
OTP	on-time performance
PAC	political action committee
QOS	quality of service
R & D	research and development
RJ	regional jet
RPM	revenue passenger miles
RTCA	Radio Technical Commission for Aeronautics
SAMA	Small Aircraft Manufacturers Association
STARS	standard terminal automation replacement system
TFM	traffic flow management
TLS	target level of safety
TSA	Transportation Safety Administration
UPS	United Parcel Service
URET	user request evaluation tool
VHF	very high frequency
VLJ	very light jet
WAAS	wide-area augmentation system
WV	wake vortex

APPENDIX B

Airline and Airport Designation Codes

Airline[a]	Code
AirTran Airways	FL
Alaska Airlines	AS
American Airlines	AA
American Eagle Airlines	MQ
ATA Airlines	TZ
Atlantic Southeast Airlines	EV
Comair	OH
Continental Airlines	CO
Delta Air Lines	DL
ExpressJet Airlines	XE
Frontier Airlines	F9
Hawaiian Airlines	HA
JetBlue Airways	B6
Mesa Airlines	YV
Northwest Airlines	NW
SkyWest Airlines	OO
Southwest Airlines	WN
United Airlines	UA
US Airways	US

[a]Air carriers required to report data to DOT.

Airport name[a]	Code
Atlanta: Hartsfield–Jackson	ATL
Balt/Wash: Int'l Thurgood Marshall	BWI
Boston: Logan International	BOS
Charlotte: Douglas	CLT
Chicago: Midway	MDW
Chicago: O'Hare	ORD
Cincinnati: Greater Cincinnati	CVG
Dallas–Fort Worth: International	DFW
Denver: International	DEN
Detroit: Metro Wayne County	DTW
Ft. Lauderdale: International	FLL
Houston: George Bush	IAH
Las Vegas: McCarran International	LAS
Los Angeles: International	LAX
Miami: International	MIA
Minneapolis–St. Paul: International	MSP
Newark: Liberty International	EWR
New York: JFK International	JFK
New York: LaGuardia	LGA
Oakland: International	OAK
Orlando: International	MCO
Philadelphia: International	PHL
Phoenix: Sky Harbor International	PHX
Pittsburgh: Greater International	PIT
Salt Lake City: International	SLC
San Diego: Lindbergh Field	SAN
San Francisco: International	SFO
Seattle–Tacoma: International	SEA
Tampa: Tampa International	TPA
Washington: Reagan National	DCA
Washington: Dulles	IAD

[a]Airports covered by Rule 14CFR Part 234.

APPENDIX C

Selected Airport Statistics

[Data sources: GMU analysis of BTS data and the DOT 2004 Airport Capacity Benchmark Report.

Hourly traffic data were obtained from the FAA ASPM database for January 2000 to July 2002 (excluding September 11–14, 2001), 7:00 a.m. to 10:00 p.m. local time.]

Table C.1 Probability of a Passenger Experiencing Greater than 45 Minutes' Delay for All Airlines Ranked by Airport Performance from 2000 to 2006 [Wang, 2007]

Year	2004		2005		2006		Average of 2004 to 2006	
Rank	Airports	Prob. of Passenger Delay >45 min%	Airports	Prob. of Passenger Delay >45 min%	Airports	Prob. of Passenger Delay >45 min%	Airports	Prob. of Passenger Delay >45 min%
1	ORD	14	EWR	18	ORD	17	EWR	16
2	EWR	14	LGA	17	EWR	16	LGA	15
3	LGA	13	ATL	14	LGA	15	ORD	15
4	PHL	12	PHL	13	PHL	15	PHL	13
5	ATL	11	BOS	13	JFK	14	ATL	12
6	MIA	9	ORD	12	IAD	12	JFK	11
7	FLL	9	FLL	12	MIA	12	BOS	11
8	MCO	9	JFK	12	ATL	12	MIA	11
9	DFW	9	MIA	11	MDW	12	FLL	10
10	LAS	9	SFO	11	DTW	12	IAD	10
11	BOS	9	SEA	10	DFW	12	DFW	10
12	SFO	9	IAD	10	BOS	11	SFO	10
13	IAD	9	TPA	10	DEN	11	DTW	9
14	JFK	9	MCO	10	CLT	10	MCO	9
15	CLE	9	BWI	9	IAH	10	LAS	9
16	SEA	8	PIT	9	CLE	10	CLE	9
17	TPA	8	PDX	9	PIT	10	PIT	9
18	STL	8	DTW	9	DCA	10	SEA	9
19	PDX	8	LAS	9	MEM	10	MDW	9
20	BWI	8	DCA	9	SFO	10	DCA	9

Atlanta Hartsfield International Airport

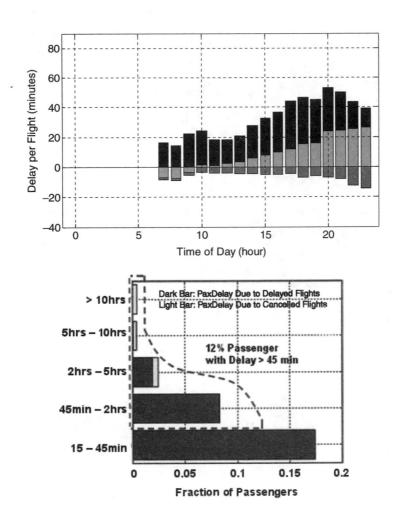

Calculated Capacity (Today) and Actual Throughput

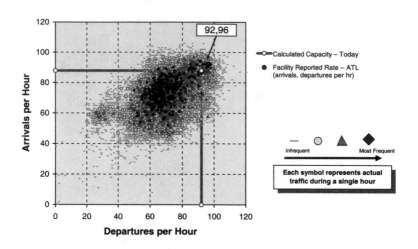

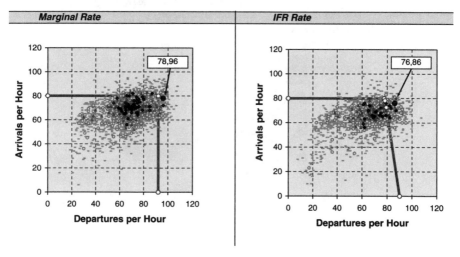

Boston Logan International

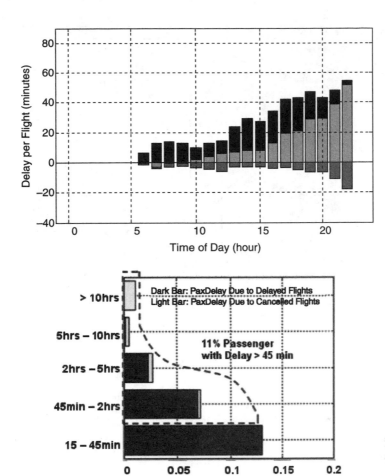

Calculated Capacity (Today) and Actual Throughput

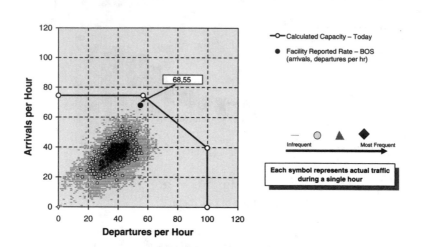

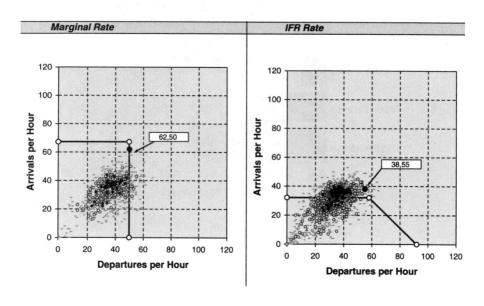

New Jersey Newark International Airport

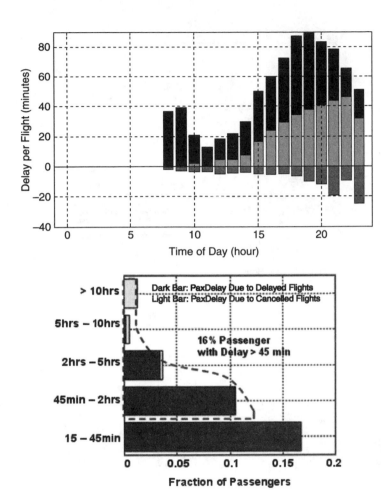

Calculated Capacity (Today) and Actual Throughput

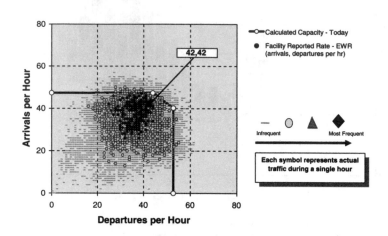

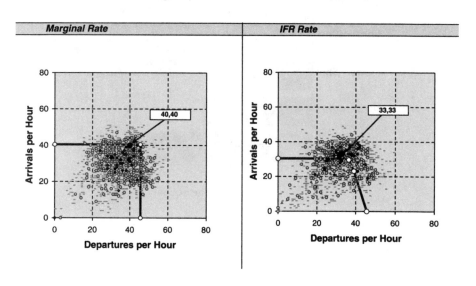

New York LaGuardia Airport

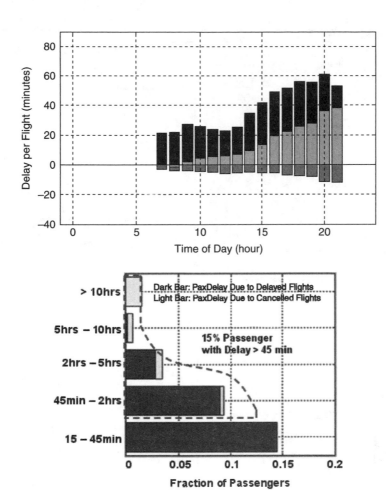

Calculated Capacity (Today) and Actual Throughput

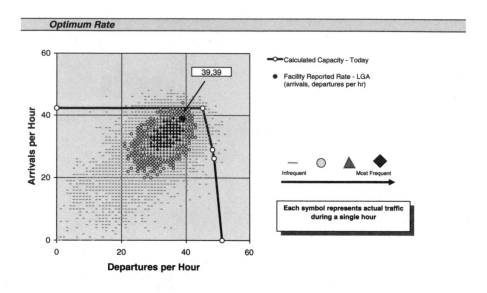

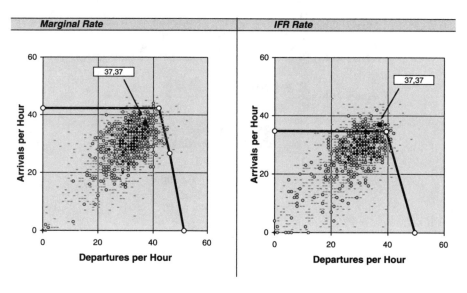

New York John F. Kennedy International Airport

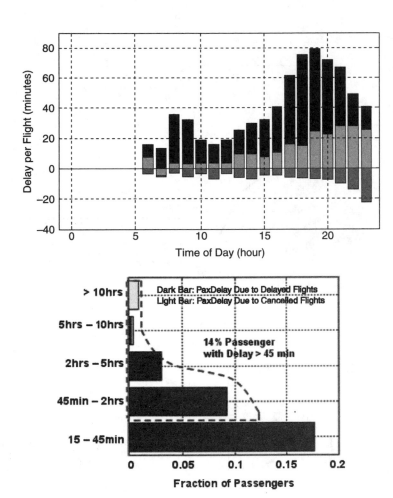

Calculated Capacity (Today) and Actual Throughput

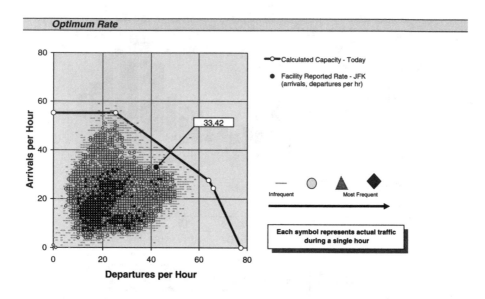

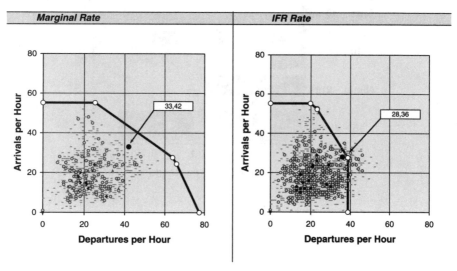

Chicago O'Hare International Airport

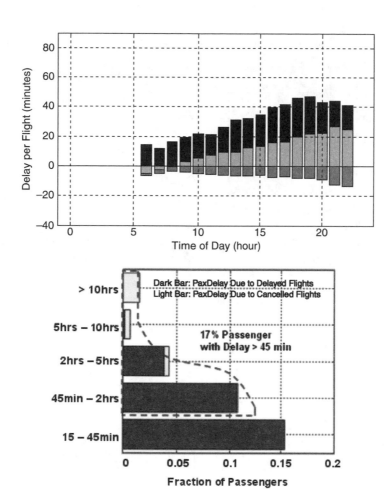

Calculated Capacity (Today) and Actual Throughput

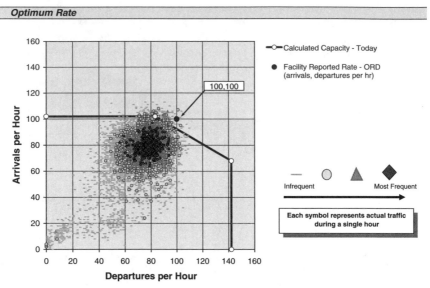

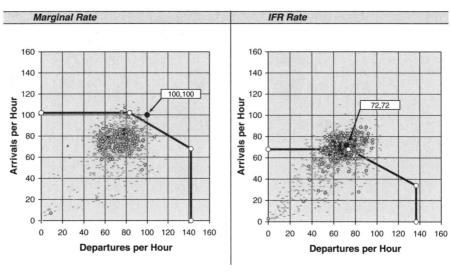

Chicago Midway Airport

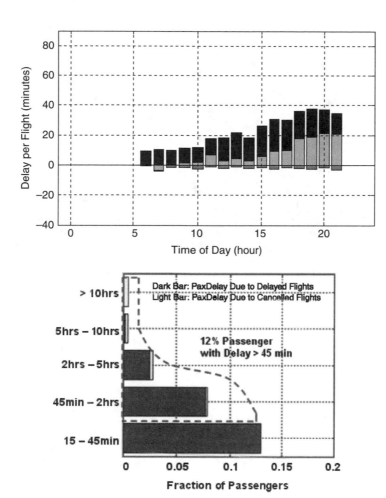

Calculated Capacity (Today) and Actual Throughput

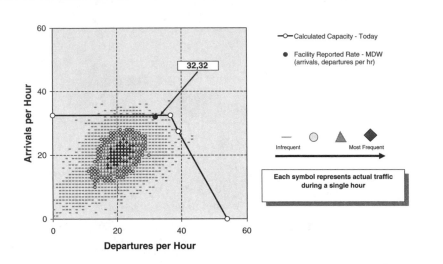

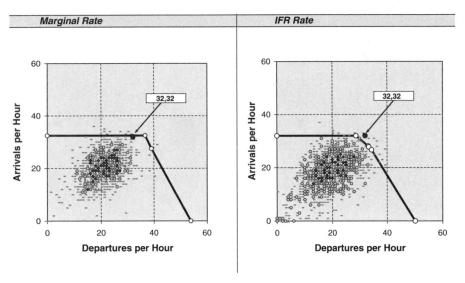

Detroit Metro Wayne County Airport

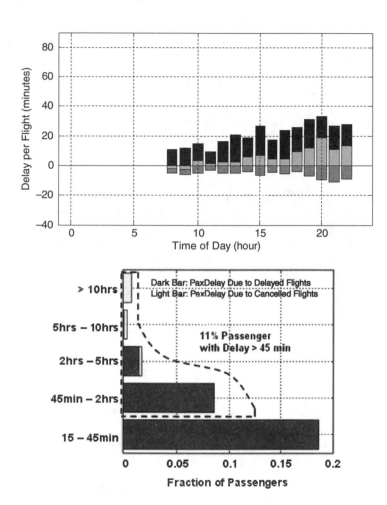

Calculated Capacity (Today) and Actual Throughput

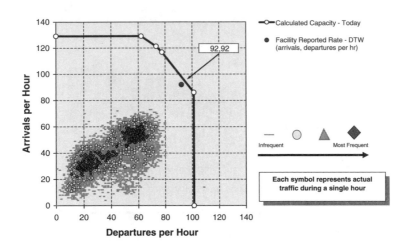

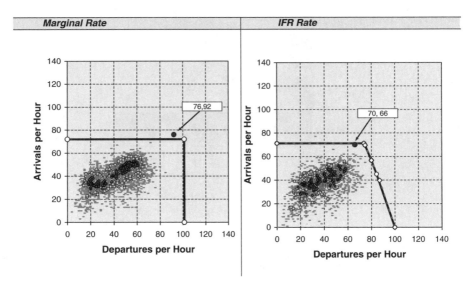

Fort Lauderdale International Airport

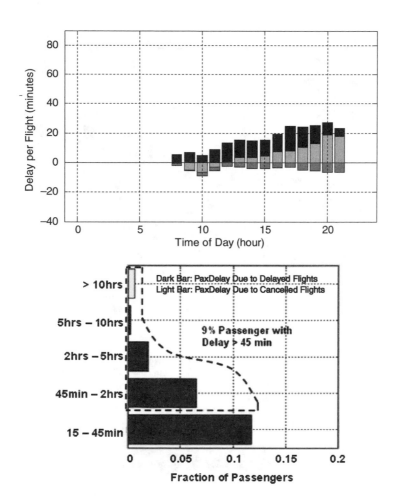

2004 Capacity Benchmark Data for FLL Not Available

Miami International Airport

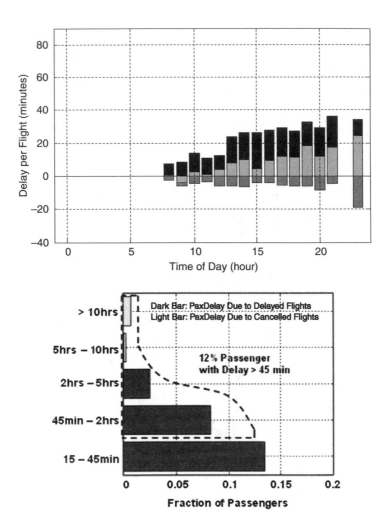

Calculated Capacity (Today) and Actual Throughput

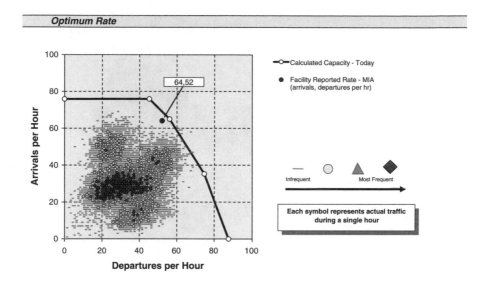

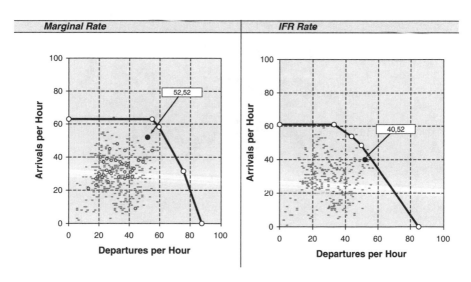

Philadelphia International Airport

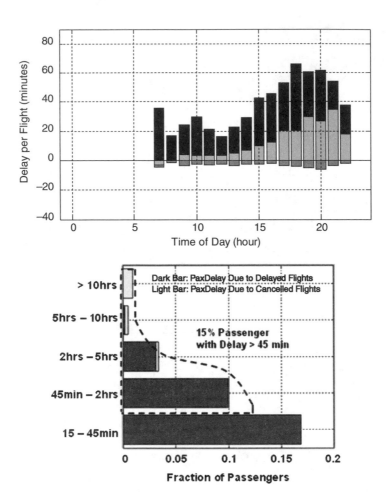

Calculated Capacity (Today) and Actual Throughput

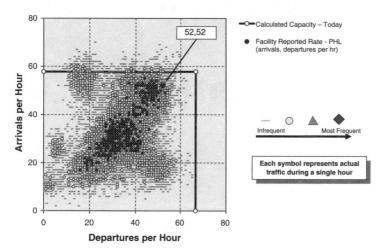

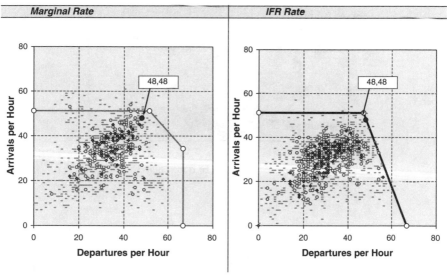

Denver International Airport

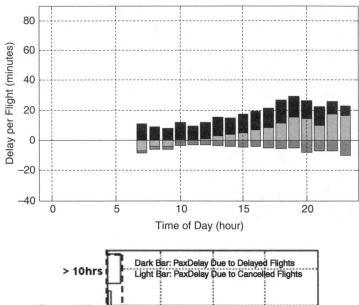

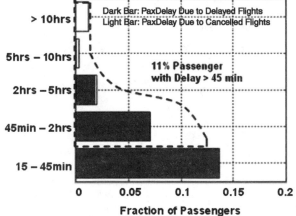

Calculated Capacity (Today) and Actual Throughput

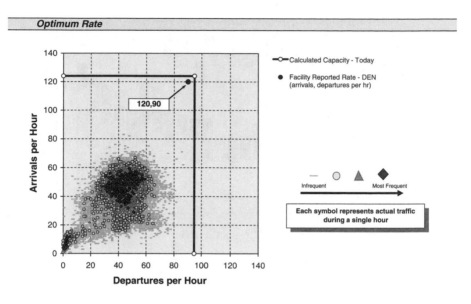

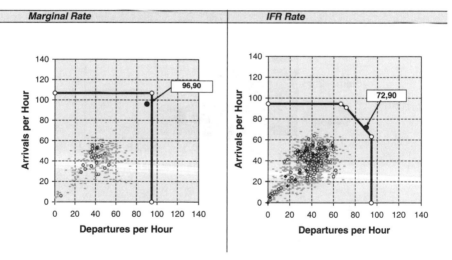

Washington Dulles International Airport

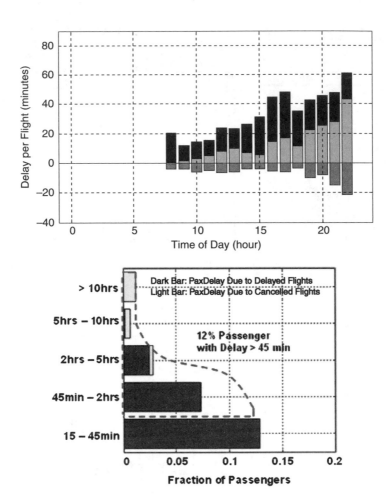

Calculated Capacity (Today) and Actual Throughput

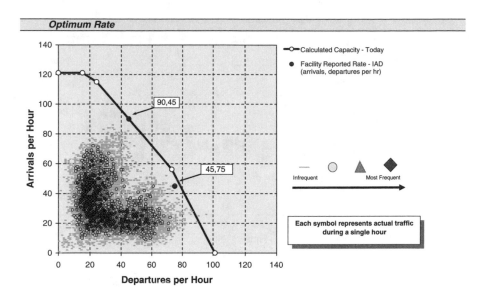

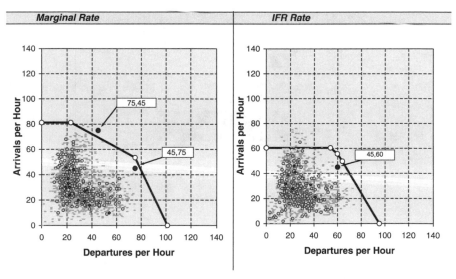

Washington Reagan National Airport

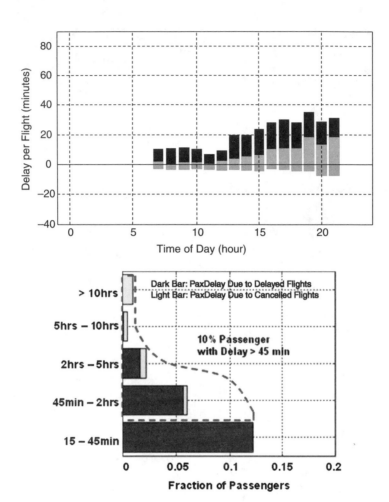

Calculated Capacity (Today) and Actual Throughput

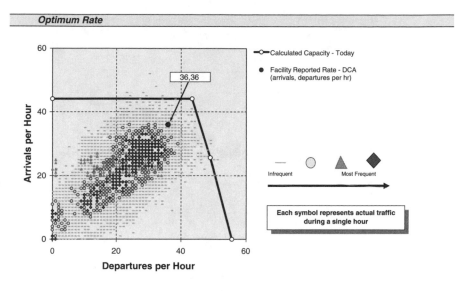

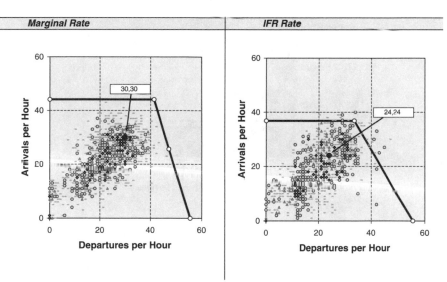

Baltimore Washington Thurgood Marshall International Airport

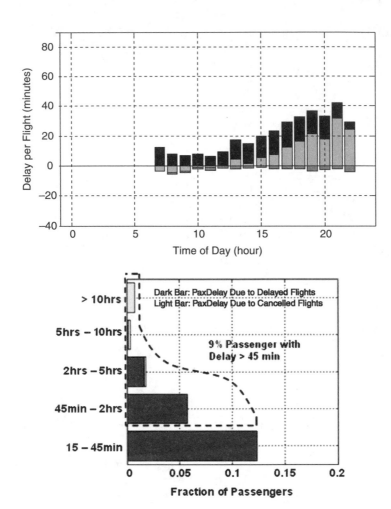

Calculated Capacity (Today) and Actual Throughput

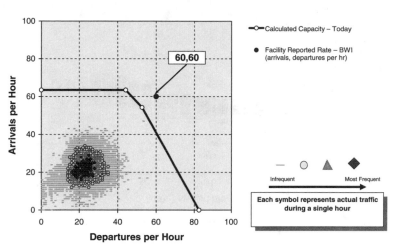

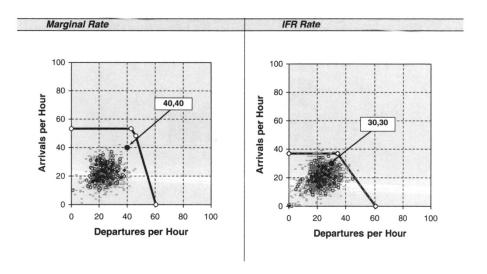

Dallas-Fort Worth Airport

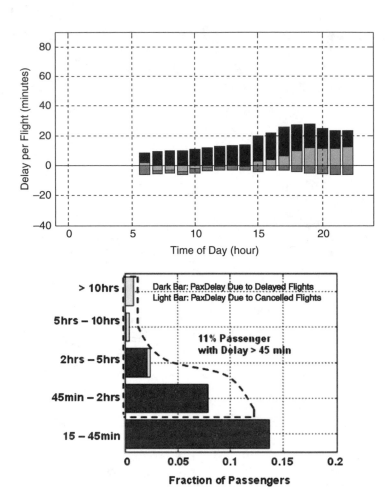

Calculated Capacity (Today) and Actual Throughput

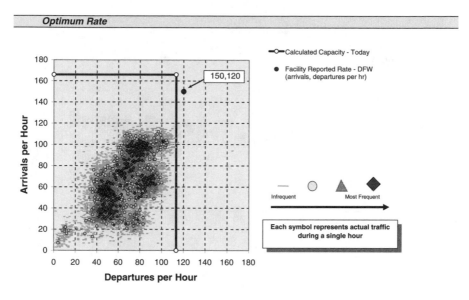

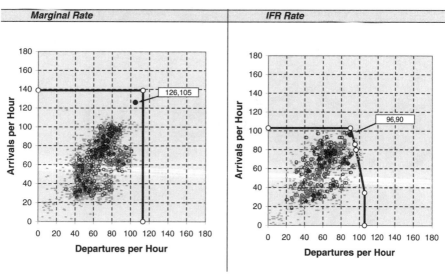

San Francisco International Airport

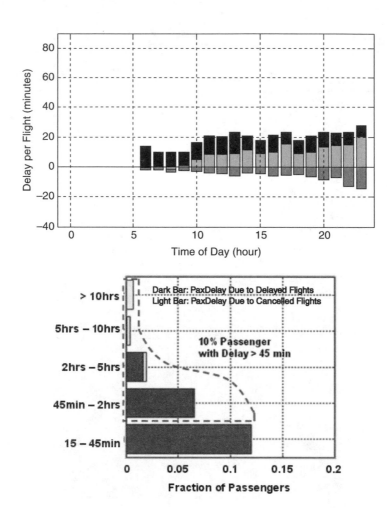

Calculated Capacity (Today) and Actual Throughput

Hourly traffic data were obtained from the FAA ASPM database for January 2000 to July 2002 (excluding September 11–14, 2001), 7:00 a.m. to 10:00 p.m. local time. Facility reported rates were reviewed by ATC personnel.

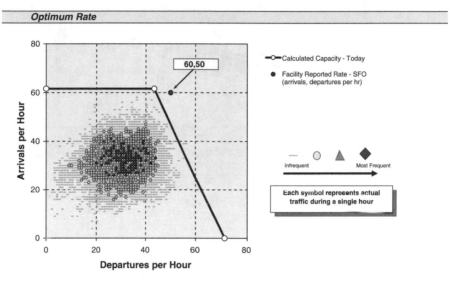

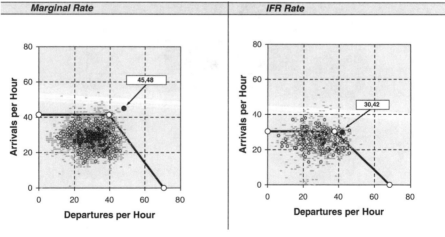

Los Angeles International Airport

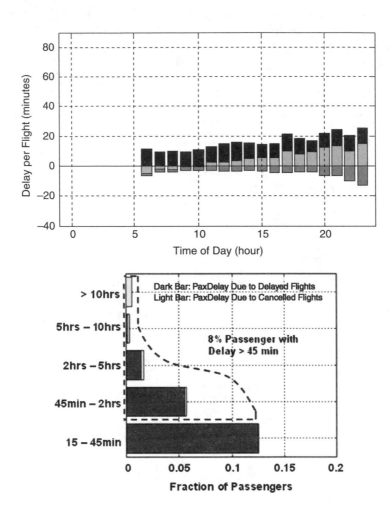

Calculated Capacity (Today) and Actual Throughput

Hourly traffic data were obtained from the FAA ASPM database for January 2000 to July 2002 (excluding September 11–14, 2001), 7:00 a.m. to 10.00 p.m. local time. Facility reported rates were reviewed by ATC personnel at LAX.

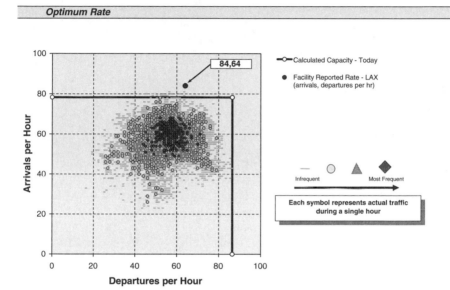

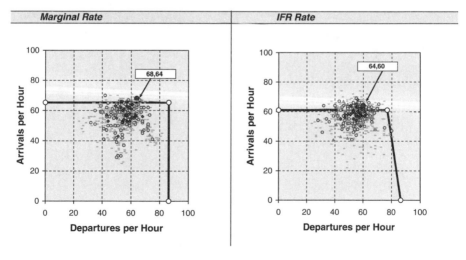

APPENDIX D

Airport Demand–Capacity Ratios and Their Importance: Mathematics of Estimating Aircraft Arrival Delays for Random and Structured Arrival Sequences

Arrival delays at airports will grow when demand for airline operations at a given airport approaches the airport's throughput capacity. Large simulation models do a reasonable job of taking into account the many factors leading to delays. Especially important are the dynamic effects associated with the cascading of delays from one region of the country to another, leading to arrival demands that are seriously skewed from the planned and scheduled sequences. This skewing leads to demand–capacity imbalances that cannot be mitigated, producing delays that cannot be predicted from ordinary static analysis. However, large simulation models reflect such behavior nicely. Alas, such models are not always available to the analyst. And even when they are, it has proven difficult to generalize from results that appear to be idiosyncratic to individual airports and overall airline scheduling structure.

Despite their shortcomings, simple algebraic expressions that compare average hourly demand (in units of operations or landings) against an airport's hourly capacity (in the same units) offer insights into an airport's ability to accommodate growth in demand. The demand–capacity ratio (D/C) provides a crude but instructive measure of airport performance. By definition, if demand exceeds capacity at some point in time, some planes would not be able to land. Even when demand does not exceed capacity, there is some probability that an arriving aircraft will find one or more aircraft waiting in an arrival queue to land. The probability that such a queue exists and what its length is can be calculated, using standard queuing techniques. The focus of this appendix is on estimating those queues.

This appendix starts by assuming an arrival structure for all scheduled aircraft and then calculates the expected delay that an unscheduled arrival would experience if it arrived at a random time. The scheduled arrival sequence can consist of totally randomly assignments to available landing "slots," or scheduled assignments that include aircraft landing in a contiguous cluster, called an arrival "bank." Airlines often schedule arrivals in banks, so that a full complement of connecting flights will be available for the arriving passengers. It has often been suggested that airline banks are a strong contributor to arrival (and departure) delays. Among the issues that this appendix addresses is the impact of arrival banks on delays.

Equations for Arrivals Whose Schedules Are Randomly Scattered Across All Slots

Assume initially that all scheduled arrivals have times that are randomly scattered over the day. For convenience, we assume that only one aircraft lands at a time. Each landing aircraft occupies a slot. The number of available slots at the airport is defined by the airport's capacity. If the airport can accommodate 60 landings an hour, then there are 60 available landing slots, each occupying (in sequence) one minute. If an aircraft arrives at a time when the slot at that time is already filled, it must wait until the next slot. If the next one is also occupied, then it must wait until the next, and so on, until an empty slot is encountered. Again for convenience, we assume that all scheduled arrivals have assigned slots and these slots are always considered occupied. (This assumption might seem contrary to our experience and certainly contrary to the common ATC practice of "first come, first served." But it is not. The "scheduled" assumption was for convenience, so that we could assume a static demand. All that matters for our calculation is that some aircraft arrived at the appointed slot time. As to the "first come, first served," if we had assigned one of the occupied slots to the unscheduled arrival, we would have had to "delay" the scheduled arrival by an amount equal to the unscheduled arrival.) Given the random assignment assumption, the probability p that any slot is occupied by a scheduled arrival is just the ratio of the demand to the capacity, D/C. Given p, we can easily write out the probability that there is no delay, that the delay is for one slot, for two, or more.

The probability that a randomly arriving nonscheduled aircraft is delayed for exactly n slots is $p^n(1 - p)$, where p^n is the probability that the first n slots are occupied and $(1 - p)$ is the probability that the $n + 1$st slot is not. The expected delay that an unscheduled aircraft would encounter is simply the series. (For simplicity we assume the series to be infinite.)

$$ExpDelay_{random} = \sum[p(1-p)+2p^2(1-p)+3p^3(1-p)+4p^4(1-p)+\cdots]$$

which simplifies to

$$= (1-p)\cdot p\cdot \sum\left\{1+2p+3p^2+4p^3+5p^4+\cdots\right\} = \frac{(1-p)\cdot p}{(1-p)^2} = \frac{p}{(1-p)}$$

Substituting D/C for p, we get

$$ExpDelay_{random} = \frac{p}{1-p} = \frac{(D/C)}{1-(D/C)} = \frac{D}{C-D}$$

Using the preceding formula, if D/C = 0.5, the average delay for an unscheduled arriving aircraft would be 1 slot. If D/C = 0.9, this delay would increase to 9 slots. If D/C = 0.95, the average delay would increase further to 19 slots.

If we were to assume that there were two unscheduled randomly scattered arrivals per hour, then the delay for the second arrival would be simply

$$ExpDelay = \frac{D+1}{C-D-1}$$

If $D = 90$ and $C = 100$, the first arrival would have had an average wait of 9 slots. The second aircraft would have had an average delay of 10.1 slots.

Additional unscheduled (and randomly scattered) arrivals would increase the demand in a similar way, until such time that the new demand equaled the capacity.

Example: To turn the preceding equations into something that feels realistic, assume that the capacity at the airport is 30 arrivals per hour (the equivalent of one arrival every two minutes). Thus, a delay equal to

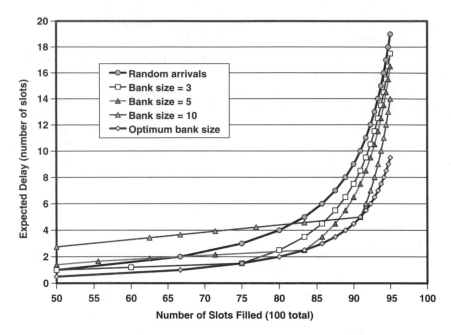

Fig. D.1   Expected value of delay for both random and structured arrival banks.

one slot is equivalent to a delay of two minutes. Figure D.1 shows the expected delay for a unscheduled aircraft as a function of the total number of randomly scheduled arriving aircraft. The equivalent of a 15-minute delay would occur in these circumstances if $D/C = 0.88$.

Suppose, in contrast, that none of the arriving aircraft were "scheduled." Then, $D = 0$, and the first aircraft would experience no delay. The second arriving aircraft would expect a small delay of $1/(30-1)$ slots, or 0.069 minutes. The third arriving aircraft would expect a delay of 2/28 slots, or 0.143 minutes. Figure D.2 shows the *average* delay suffered by all arrivals as a function of the total number of randomly arriving (unscheduled) aircraft. The delay for the nth arriving aircraft is the same as just shown, where the prior $(n - 1)$ aircraft are assumed randomly scheduled.

Equations That Include Clustered Arrival Airline Banks

With the assumption of clustered arrivals, we will also assume that the clusters are organized in sequences of consecutive slots occupied by the bank, followed (or preceded) by a set of "nonbank" slots. These nonbank slots can be occupied by other scheduled arrivals, but if they are, the nonbank scheduled arrivals are assumed to be randomly

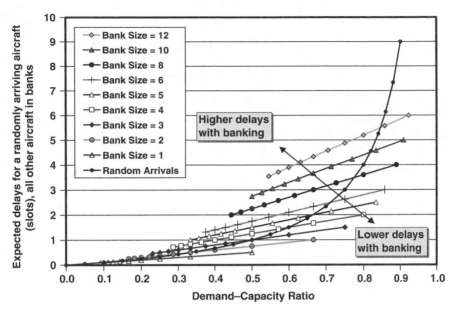

Fig. D.2   Expected value of delay for structured banks of different sizes. Structured banks (i.e., equally spaced landings in 15-minute time slots) provide reduced delays at high demand rates.

scattered over the ensemble of nonbank slots. This sequence of bank and then nonbank slots is assumed to be repeated throughout the day. (Actually, we assume that the sequence is infinitely long, in order to avoid debates over just how long the day is, whether the random unscheduled arrivals occur early or late in the day, etc.)

Let B be the number of slots that constitute the bank. By assumption, all of these slots are occupied. Let S be the number of nonbank slots. If all S slots are unoccupied, then

$$\frac{D}{C} = \frac{B}{(B+S)}$$

If, on the other hand, Q of these nonbank slots are filled with randomly scheduled arrivals, then

$$\frac{D}{C} = \frac{(B+Q)}{(B+S)}$$

We define the probability that any nonbank slot is occupied as equal to Q/S. We further define the variable q to be that probability, i.e.,

$$q = \frac{Q}{S}$$

Sequences with Banks Separated by Only One Nonbank Slot

Consider the following repetitive sequence of bank and nonbank slots:

$$\{s,b,b,b,b,s,b,b,b,s,b,b,b,b,\ldots\}$$

This repetitive part of the sequence includes one slot that is not part of the bank, followed by four slots that are. It is then repeated ad infinitum. (We will generalize this shortly to any number of B and S slots.) (Mathematically, it is not hard to select a finite length for the sequence. For example, the infinite series

$$\left\{1+p+p^2+\right\}p^3+p^4+\cdots=\frac{1}{(1-p)}$$

If we truncated that series after n steps, the equation would be

$$\frac{1}{(1-p)}-\frac{p^{N+1}}{(1-p)}$$

The second term is just the sequence starting at the term p^{N+1}.

Assuming that the unscheduled aircraft arrives at the first slot in the sequence, it will not be able to land with probability q. Furthermore, it will not just be delayed for that slot, but will also have to wait until the entire length of the bank has also landed. The total delay at this point would be $(1 + B)$, or five slots, and the probability of experiencing that delay is q.

The sequence repeats itself at this point. The probability that the unscheduled aircraft will find the sixth slot also occupied is q. If it is occupied, the plane will have to wait another $(1 + B)$ slots, for a total of 10. The probability of getting as far as the eleventh slot is q^2 (the probability of reaching the sixth slot, times the probability of finding the sixth slot occupied), and so forth. Writing out these various probabilities and their associated delays, we obtain the following expression for the expected delay for a randomly arriving unscheduled aircraft:

$$ED = ExpDelay_{\text{Banks}} = \sum_{i=0}^{\infty}\left\{q(1+B)+q^2(1+B)+q^3(1+B)+\cdots\right\}$$

$$= q(1+B)\sum\left\{1+q+q^2+\cdots\right\}=\frac{q(1+B)}{(1-q)}=\frac{q}{(1-q)}+\frac{qB}{(1-q)}$$

This equation only applies to the series $\{s,b,b,b,b\}$, where the nonbank slot appears first. If the unscheduled aircraft had arrived at the second slot, we would have obtained a different equation. There are a total of five possible unique sequences for the preceding series. The repetitive part of the sequences would be $\{s,b,b,b,b\}$, $\{b,s,b,b,b\}$, $\{b,b,s,b,b\}$, $\{b,b,b,s,b\}$, $\{b,b,b,b,s\}$.

Rather than develop an additional summation for each series, we have adopted a different approach. Preserving the sequence with a nonbank slot first and its expected value, we simply add some additional slots to the front of the sequence. The following sequences consist of the add-on slots plus the original repetitive sequence. Note that we start the new sequence by adding terms from the back of the repetitive sequence, with the initial sequence simply pushed back by the number of bank slots that precedes the nonbank slot.

The bracketed sequence inside the following sequences is just the original sequence, which we assume is repeated for the remainder of the infinite series. The slots that precede the internal brackets are not repeated.

$$\{s,b,b,b,b\},\ (b,\{s,b,b,b,b\}),\ (b,b,\{s,b,b,b,b\}),\ (b,b,b,\{s,b,b,b,b\}),\ (b,b,b,b\ \{s,b,b,b,b\})$$

To better understand what was done, consider the second sequence $(b,\{s,b,b,b,b\})$. The expected delay associated with this sequence is simply

$$\text{Expected delay for sequence } (b,\{s,b,b,b,b\}) = 1 + \text{ED}$$

The "1" stems from the observation that it is certain that the first slot encountered is occupied and the unscheduled aircraft will experience a delay of one slot, plus whatever delay it suffers from the subsequent infinite series. *ED* is actually multiplied by the probability that the plane could not land at the first slot. In this case, that probability is one. Using this logic for the remaining three unique sequences, and noting that each sequence is equally likely, the total expected delay is

$$ExpDelay_{\text{Total}} = \frac{1}{5}\big[ED + (1+ED) + (2+ED) + (3+ED) + (4+ED)\big]$$

$$= \frac{10 + 5ED}{5} = 2 + \frac{5q}{(1-q)}$$

This expression can be generalized for any size of the bank, i.e.,

$$ExpDelay_{\text{Total}} = \frac{1}{(B+1)}\left[\frac{B\cdot(B+1)}{2} + \frac{q(1+B)^2}{(1-q)}\right] = \left[\frac{q}{(1-q)} + \frac{B(1+q)}{2(1-q)}\right]$$

The first term reflects the delays associated with the slots that are not part of the bank and exactly equals the random delay formula. The second term represents the delays associated with the bank slot size. If $q = 0$ (i.e., all of the scheduled arriving aircraft are clustered in banks of size B), then $ExpDelay_{Total} = B/2$.

Including More Than One Nonbank Slot in the Repeatable Series

Consider the following sequence:

$$\{s,s,s,b,b,b,b,s,s,s,b,b,b,b,s,s,s,b,b,b,b,\ldots\}$$

where two additional nonbank slots have been added to the front of the repetitive part of the sequence. Furthermore, we assume for convenience (we will change this later) that all of the nonbank slots in the repetitive part of the sequence are contiguous. Thus we have a repeatable series that starts with three nonbank slots and finishes with four bank slots. For this particular sequence, the expected delay now looks like the following:

$$ExpDelay_{banks} = \sum_{i=0}^{\infty} q + q^2 + q^3 + q^3B + q^3\left(q + q^2 + q^3 + q^3B\right) + q^6\left(q + q^2 + q^3 + q^3B\right) + \cdots$$

$$= \sum_{i=0}^{\infty}\left(q + q^2 + q^3 + q^3B\right)\left(1 + q^3 + q^6 + \cdots\right)$$

$$= \left[\frac{q}{1-q} + \frac{q^3B}{(1-q^3)}\right] = \Omega_1(q, B, S = 3)$$

where we introduce the function Ω_a to aid in our exposition. $\Omega_1(q,B,S)$ is the expected delay for the specific sequence where all of the nonbank slots appear first in the sequence. Note that this equation is the same as the one where $S = 1$. [It is not an accident that $\Omega_1(q,B,S = 1)$ gives the earlier equation for the sequence where the number of nonbank slots was equal to one. The generalization of this function for arbitrary S is obvious.]

Given the preceding, there are a total of $B + S$ (in this case seven) independent sequences. To calculate the remaining six, it is useful to introduce an additional variable.

Let z_i = probability that ith slot is occupied. Obviously z_i is equal to one if the slot is part of the bank and q if it is not. As before, we retain the sequence where all of the nonbank slots appear first, and then add in front of that sequence individual slots consistent with the sequence. As an example, the second sequence would be

$$\{b; (s,s,s,b,b,b,b), (s,s,s,b,b,b,b), (s,s,s,b,b,b,b),\ldots\}$$

where the repetitive part of the sequence is shown in the interior brackets. The following relationships immediately follow:

$$\Omega_2(q,B,S) = z_2 \cdot [1 + \Omega_1 \ (q,B,S)] = 1 + \Omega_1 \ (q,B,S) \qquad \text{as} \quad z_1 = 1$$
$$\Omega_3(q,B,S) = z_3 \cdot [1 + \Omega_2 \ (q,B,S)] = 1 + \Omega_2 \ (q,B,S) \qquad \text{as} \quad z_2 = 1$$
$$\Omega_4(q,B,S) = z_4 \cdot [1 + \Omega_3 \ (q,B,S)] = 1 + \Omega_3 \ (q,B,S) \qquad \text{as} \quad z_3 = 1$$
$$\Omega_5(q,B,S) = z_5 \cdot [1 + \Omega_4 \ (q,B,S)] = 1 + \Omega_4 \ (q,B,S) \qquad \text{as} \quad z_4 = 1$$
$$\Omega_6(q,B,S) = z_6 \cdot [1 + \Omega_5 \ (q,B,S)] = q \cdot [1 + \Omega_5 \ (q,B,S)] \qquad \text{as} \quad z_5 = q$$
$$\Omega_7(q,B,S) = z_7 \cdot [1 + \Omega_6 \ (q,B,S)] = q \cdot [1 + \Omega_6 \ (q,B,S)] \qquad \text{as} \quad z_6 = q$$

Summing these with the original equation and dividing by $(B + S)$ yields the desired equation for the expected number of slots that a randomly arriving nonscheduled aircraft would experience. Generalizing this procedure for arbitrary B and S yields the following set of equations:

$$ExpValue_{\text{Total}} = \frac{1}{B+S} \cdot \sum_{i=1}^{B+S} \Omega_i(q,B,S)$$

where

$$\Omega_i(q,B,S) = \frac{q}{(1-q)} + \frac{Bq^S}{(1-q^S)} \qquad \text{for} \quad i = 1$$
$$\Omega_i(q,B,S) = 1 + \Omega_{i-1}(q,B,S) \qquad \text{for} \quad 1 < i \le B+1$$
$$\Omega_i(q,B,S) = q \cdot 1 + \Omega_{i-1}(q,B,S) \qquad \text{for} \quad B+1 < i \le B+S$$

Using the preceding equations, we get the following general equations:

$$\Omega_i = i - 1 + \frac{q}{1-q} + \frac{Bq^S}{1-q^S} \qquad 1 < i \le B+1$$

$$\Omega_i = \frac{q}{1-q} + \frac{Bq^{i-B-1}}{1-q^S} \qquad B+1 < i \le B+S-1$$

Summing like terms, and after some algebra, we obtain the following result:

$$ExpValue_{\text{Total}} = \frac{q}{1-q} + \frac{B}{B+S} \cdot \left\{ \frac{B+1}{2} + \frac{Bq^S}{1-q^S} + \frac{q}{1-q} \right\}$$

For this particular sequence, if $q = 0$,

$$ExpValue_{\text{Total}} = \frac{1}{B+S} \cdot \frac{B(B+1)}{2} = \frac{B}{2} \left[\frac{B+1}{B+S} \right]$$

In cases where the nonbank and bank slots are more randomly scattered, the summations are not easily simplified. These repetitive expressions, however, are very convenient for computer algorithms and are readily calculated numerically.

Comparing Delays from Banks Against Delays in the Totally Random Arrival Situation

It has often been suggested that the airline strategy of having aircraft arrive in banks (for purposes of hubbing) contributes negatively to delays at the airport. Sitting on the tarmac waiting for other 10:00 a.m. scheduled departure aircraft to depart is a well-shared experience that most travelers do not want to repeat. The preceding formulas give us the opportunity to identify the conditions where banking adds to delays and where it does just the opposite.

Case 1: Random vs Repetitive Series with $S = 1$ and $q = 0$

In this case, $p = B/(B + 1)$. Substitute p into the equation for random scheduled arrivals:

$$\text{Delays (random scheduled arrivals)} = \frac{p}{(1-p)} = \frac{B/(B+1)}{1-B/(B+1)} = B$$

Earlier we showed that the same sequence with $q = 0$ yielded the following expectation:

$$ExpDelay_{\text{Total}} = \frac{B}{2}$$

Surprisingly, for the conditions where the banks are separated by a single slot, banking reduces the expected delays by a factor of two, assuming equal D/C ratios.

Case 2: Random vs Repetitive Series with $S = 1$ and $q > 0$

Assuming that the probability that the next slot is filled is not zero, p becomes $p = B + q/B + 1$, and the random sequence expected delay is

$$ExpValue_{\text{Random}} = \frac{p}{1-p} = \frac{(B+q/B+1)}{1-(B+q/B+1)} = \frac{B+q}{(1-q)} = \left\{ \frac{B}{(1-q)} + \frac{q}{(1-q)} \right\}$$

From our earlier equations, the delay associated with banking where $S = 1$ is

$$ExpDelay_{\text{Total}} = \left\{ \frac{B}{2} + \frac{q(1+B)}{(1-q)} \right\}$$

Multiplying both formulas by $(1 - q)$, we have the following inequality:

$$\frac{B}{2}(1-q) + q + qB = \frac{B}{2}(1+q) + q < B + q \qquad \text{or} \qquad \frac{B}{2} < B$$

This shows that expected delays for sequences where $S = 1$ and B is arbitrary are always one-half that of delays associated with random scattering of scheduled arrivals. Of course, this only applies for this particular set of sequences.

Case 3: Multiple Contiguous Nonbank Spacings in Sequence, $q = 0$

The situation becomes somewhat more complicated when banks have multiple nonbank spacings in the repetitive sequence. For totally random scheduled arrivals and $q = 0$, the expected delay (in slots) is simply

$$\frac{p}{(1-p)} = \frac{B/(B+S)}{1-B/(B+S)} = \frac{B}{S}$$

From the preceding (with $q = 0$), the expected delays associated with sequences that include contiguous banking and nonbanking slots are

$$ExpValue_{\text{Total}} = \frac{1}{B+S} \cdot \frac{B(B+1)}{2}$$

Comparing these two, we can ask under what demand–capacity ratio would banking yield lower delays than those associated with totally random assignments. That is, assume

$$\frac{1}{B+S} \cdot \frac{B(B+1)}{2} \leq \frac{B}{S}$$

Cross-multiplying and simplifying terms, we obtain the following inequality:

$$S \leq \frac{2B}{B-1}$$

Satisfying this inequality says that sequences with banks generate lower delays than those that do not have banks. This roughly translates into a requirement that, if $q = 0$, the nonbank spacing needs to be at least twice the size of the bank in order for random arrivals to have lower delays than arrivals associated with banking sequences.

Extending the Results to Include Sequences That Are Not Uniformly Ordered in Contiguous Banks or Nonbank Spaces

The preceding equations are easily extended to include repeatable sequences that are not uniformly ordered into one bank of size B and a contiguous set of slots that might or might not be occupied of size S. Consider for example the following sequence of eight slots:

$$\{s,s,b,b,b,s,s,b\} = \Psi$$

The probability that a randomly arriving nonscheduled aircraft will go through the entire sequence without finding an open slot is simply q^4 (the probability of not finding an open slot among the four available, and the expected delay encountered is the following sum

$$q+q^2+3q^2+q^3+q^4+q^4 = \frac{q(1-q^4)}{(1-q)}+3q^2+q^4 = \Phi$$

where the third and sixth terms in the sum represent delays caused by the assumed banking slot. The overall expected value sequence is as before:

$$ExpValue = \sum\{\Phi+q^4\Phi+q^8\Phi+q^{12}\Phi+\cdots\} = \frac{\Phi}{1-q^4} = \Omega_1$$

This is just one of the eight terms in the overall expected value. The other seven can be generated by the same repetitive calculation introduced earlier. Recalling that the multiplier z is the probability that the slot is full and thus z 5 $\{1,q,q,1,1,1,q\}$, then for the expanded sequence we have the following:

$$\{b;\Psi\} \quad \Omega_2 = 1\cdot(1+\Omega_1)$$
$$\{s,b;\Psi\} \quad \Omega_3 = q\cdot(1+\Omega_2)$$
$$\{s,s,b;\Psi\} \quad \Omega_4 = q\cdot(1+\Omega_3)$$
$$\{b,s,s,b;\Psi\} \quad \Omega_5 = 1\cdot(1+\Omega_4)$$
$$\{b,b,s,s,b;\Psi\} \quad \Omega_6 = 1\cdot(1+\Omega_5)$$
$$\{b,b,b,s,s,b;\Psi\} \quad \Omega_7 = 1\cdot(1+\Omega_6)$$
$$\{s,b,b,b,s,s,b;\Psi\} \quad \Omega_8 = q\cdot(1+\Omega_7)$$

The expected delay for the entire sequence is as before the sum over the $B + S$ equally like sequences,

$$ExpValue_{Total} = \frac{1}{B+S}\cdot\sum_{i=1}^{B+S}\Omega_i\left(q,B,S\right)$$

Each individual sequence needs to be treated anew, but the calculational approach just given should work regardless of the length and complexity.

We will not attempt to reduce this sequence into a set of algebraic equations. Although it is possible to do so for any given sequence, general solutions are not possible.

Final Comments

As was said at the beginning, D/C ratios are not particularly good at predicting realistic delays in the NAS. The dynamic effects of hour-by-hour fluctuations in traffic flow are important factors in generating and augmenting delays. Airports that have relatively low D/C ratios can still suffer substantial delays when and if arrival schedules are dramatically altered because of problems elsewhere in the NAS.

Nevertheless, the general trends derived in this appendix provide some indication of the sensitivity of airports to imbalances in demand and capacity. Airports with reliable schedules will still be in difficulty if their D/C ratio reaches 0.9 or higher. These kinds of insights help inform us that airport demand needs to be significantly less than its capacity if delays are not going to be a routine problem.

APPENDIX E

Evidence That Airport Pricing Works—Reason Foundation Policy Brief No. 67

Introduction

This paper describes the results of research that analyzed mechanisms for reducing congestion and delays at LaGuardia Airport (LGA) in New York. The findings should be equally applicable to any similarly congested airport such as John F Kennedy (JFK), Newark International (EWR) or Chicago O'Hare (ORD).

Slot allocation has historically been limited at LGA by a High Density Rule (HDR) first employed in 1968. Thus, airlines were provided with "slots" (rights to takeoff and land), with a use-it-or-lose it rule that returned slots to a pool for reallocation if the slots were not used 80 percent of the time. Since 1985 operators have been able to trade slots in a secondary market of sorts, but few have been sold other than during bankruptcy proceedings.

In 2004, The NEXTOR universities were requested by the Federal Aviation Administration (FAA) and the U.S. Department of Transportation (DOT) to design and conduct a series of government-industry strategic simulations ("strategic games") to help the government evaluate

The report in this appendix was written by George L. Donohue and Karla Hoffman, with Robert W. Poole, Jr. It was originally published by the Reason Foundation (http://www.reason.org). Printed with permission.

policy options for airport congestion management. We were directed to evaluate alternative allocation approaches for LGA, since the HDR rule was legislated to be removed by January 2007. (In fact, LGA is now operating under an interim continuation of slot controls.) George Mason University (GMU) and the University of Maryland (UMD) undertook the task of leading this research effort. UC Berkeley, MIT, Harvard, and GRA, Inc. played major roles in the design and analysis of the two games. The first took place on November 3–5, 2004 and the second on February 24–25, 2005. The purpose of the games was to test a range of government policy options designed to reduce the expected congestion that was likely to result from the expected expiration of the HDR on January 1, 2007. While a central issue in this research project was the replacement of the slot lottery (the "slottery") and HDR at LGA, it was recognized that the policies being tested could have potential applicability to a number of U.S. airports that are operating at or close to their maximum operating limits.

Conventional economic wisdom suggests that market-based mechanisms such as congestion pricing and auctions are efficient in allocating scarce resources. Both options charge higher fees for peak periods than for off-peak periods, discouraging low-value flights from being scheduled in peak periods. In addition, increasing per-flight cost is expected to encourage airlines to up-gauge (substitute larger-capacity planes for some flights), and therefore increase passenger throughput.

Congestion pricing as applied to runway allocation would result in the price of an arrival or departure time slot varying by time of day and day of week, and the prices would dynamically change as the demand for operations changes over time. Congestion pricing of transport networks has been common in road traffic. Examples include traditional tolling as well as more dynamic electronic-charges to users such as those used in London [4], in Trondheim, Norway [5], Singapore [6], Toronto's Highway 407, and SR 91 and I-15 HOT lanes in California. The airlines would find congestion prices that were set at day-of-operations (as in road pricing) difficult to manage, since their schedules are announced 90 days in advance. Thus, unlike individual drivers, airlines should not be encouraged to cancel flights at the last minute due to high arrival costs. For this reason, we considered a congestion management approach whereby the prices are announced 120 days in advance, and the airlines base their schedules on these announced prices (see Daniel [7], Pels [8], Fan [9], Schank [10], and Berardino [11] for more on runway congestion pricing).

An alternative to congestion pricing is the allocation of slots by auction for a much longer period of time. The buyer has, in essence, leased the right to a given takeoff or landing and can use or re-sell that right for any portion of the lease period. The airlines bid for the right to land and/or depart at a given time. Proposals to allocate airport time slots using market-driven mechanisms such as auctions date back to 1979 with the work of Grether, Issac, and Plot [13] and Rassenti, Smith, and Bulfin [14]. European researchers, DotEcon Ltd [15] and National Economic Research Associates (NERA) [16], conducted macro-economic analysis to conclude that proper implementation of auctions will result in higher passenger volumes, higher load factors, reallocation of flights to off-peak times or to less congested airports, and lower fares on average. Ball, Donohue, and Hoffman [17] put forward the need for three types of market mechanisms: an auction of long-term leases of arrival and/or departure slots, a secondary market that supports inter-airline exchange of long-term leases, and a near-real-time market that allows for the exchange of slots on a particular day of operation.

The Strategic Game

The first simulation was held at GMU in November of 2004. It was principally focused on evaluating and comparing administrative measures and congestion pricing. There were six major game players consisting of teams from four airlines, the federal government and the Port Authority of New York and New Jersey (PANYNJ), which operates LGA. Other participants included representatives of other airlines and airports, the Air Transport Association, and various experts from academia, industry and government. The game projected the participants to a hypothetical setting in November 2007. The baseline scenario was an LGA schedule involving approximately 1,400 total daily operations (arrivals and depar-tures), a number that exceeds recommended operational levels. The airline teams adjusted their schedules in response to various government policies put in place. These policies involved federal regulations, adminis-trative restrictions, and congestion-based fees (substituting for current weight-based landing fees). For each alternative presented in these exer-cises, the resulting aggregated schedule was fed to two independently-developed simulation models to calculate the levels of delay and cancellations that would have resulted from an attempt to operate that schedule (see Lovell et al., 2003 and Donohue and Le, 2004).

The airline teams were asked to make scheduling decisions under dif-ferent hypothetical policy environments. The research goal was to better understand the pros and cons of alternative policy actions. The game details can be found in Ball et al. [19]. The game proceeded through five separate policies: Do nothing, two administrative alternatives, and two

different levels of congestion pricing. Each sequence began with a baseline schedule of operations at LGA, based on the August 2004 Official
Airlines Guide (OAG), with flights added to bring the level of scheduled operations to a hypothetical 1,400 operations per day, similar to the
peak levels expected at the expiration of the HDR. Each airline player
team was responsible for their portion of the schedule.

Included in the rules of the game was a Passenger Bill of Rights
(PBR) that forced the airlines to pay passengers when their flights were
delayed or cancelled. By using the PBR, we could set the metric of
game flight-delay and cancelation in terms of dollars, thereby allowing
a common metric for all analysis.

The simulation proceeded through three sequences consisting of a
total of five moves. Each sequence began with a baseline schedule of
operations at LGA. The first sequence continued by allowing the airline players to make schedule changes in response to the costs imposed
on them by the PBR. The second sequence began again with the baseline, but then proceeded by instructing the government team to use
whatever administrative procedures they felt were appropriate to handle the congestion resulting from the lifting of the HDR. This game
included two rounds of applying alternative administrative actions with
the airlines adjusting their schedules. The final sequence again started
with the baseline, and implemented congestion pricing at LGA in an
effort to reduce the delay costs to passengers. Two rounds of adjusting
congestion prices were executed.

Results of the Game

Table E.1 summarizes the scheduling results and delays for each game
move. As noted above, one tested policy was a Passenger Bill of Rights
(PBR) that forced the airlines to pay passengers when their planes were
delayed or cancelled. The "Pax $" row (near the bottom) shows the PBR
compensation to passengers that would have resulted in each stage of the
game. This value is a proxy for the economic cost to passengers of delays
and cancellations, based on data showing that, on average, a cancellation
cost passengers seven hours of delays (see Wang [3]). The passenger
compensation rate was set at $10 per hour for this exercise and did not
include any other costs such as ticket refunds or hotel costs.

The PBR did not substantially change the delays but did exacerbate
the financial vulnerability of airlines to delays caused by other operators. The penalty fees that would have been paid to passengers amounted
to almost $1.5 million per day (see Table E.1, PBR column, PAX$).
The FAA Cost Guidelines (FAA-ASD 2004) specify that the economic

Table E.1   Summary of LGA Strategic Game

Airline		Baseline	Passenger Bill of Rights move 1	Admin measures		Congestion price	
				Move 1	Move 2	Move 1	Move 2
A	#arr	142	130	131	127	143	133
	arr diff	0	−12	−11	−15	1	−9
	#seats	13,120	12,413	12,125	11,977	13,256	12,590
	seats diff	0	−707	−995	−1,143	136	−530
B	#arr	127	122	119	116	94	94
	arr diff	0	−5	−8	−11	−33	−33
	#seats	14,581	14,037	13,671	13,429	13,834	13,834
	seats diff	0	−544	−910	−1,152	−747	−747
C	#arr	212	208	204	191	174	174
	arr diff	0	−4	−8	−21	−38	−38
	#seats	15,065	15,055	14,282	13,562	13,593	13,593
	seats diff	0	−10	−783	−1,503	−1,472	−1472
D	#arr	22	22	14	13	22	21
	arr diff	0	0	−8	−9	0	−1
	#seats	3,300	3,520	2,228	2,454	3,876	4,098
	seats diff	0	220	−1,072	−846	576	798

(Continued)

Table E.1   Summary of LGA Strategic Game (Continued)

Airline		Baseline	Passenger Bill of Rights move 1	Admin measures		Congestion price	
				Move 1	Move 2	Move 1	Move 2
E	#arr	193	183	124	129	184	186
	arr diff	0	–10	–69	–64	–9	–7
	#seats	23,688	22,769	15,050	16,166	23,015	23,203
	seats diff	0	–919	–8,638	–7,522	–673	–485
Part 135	#arr	18	28	28	28	29	29
	arr diff	0	10	10	10	11	11
	#seats	144	266	266	266	286	304
	seats diff	0	122	122	122	142	160
Total	#arr	714	693	620	604	646	637
	arr diff	0	–21	–94	–110	–68	–77
	#seats	69,898	68,060	57,622	57,854	67,860	67,622
	seats diff	0	(1,838)	(12,276)	(12,044)	(2,038)	(2,276)
Total	Cancel $	$ 784,790	$ 609,498	$ 231,195	$ 207,334	$ 390,206	$ 342,329
UMD	Delay $	$ 837,632	$ 864,716	$ 514,954	$ 461,246	$ 575,135	$ 557,354
Model	Pax $	$ 1,622,422	$ 1,474,214	$ 746,149	$ 668,580	$ 965,341	$ 899,683
	AP $	$ 392,700	$ 381,150	$ 341,000	$ 332,200	$ 866,513	$ 891,688
			$ 1,855,364				$ 1,791,371

cost of passenger time is $28.60 per hour, so the values shown for Cancel $, Delay $, and Pax $ can be multiplied by ($28/$10) to derive an estimate of the full economic cost per day to passengers of congestion at LGA. In the least-delay case (Admin 2), passengers continued to suffer over $668,000 per day as calculated (or nearly $1.9 million if multiplying this number by 2.8) in addition to the $332,000 per day fees incurred by the airlines.

The "AP $" row shows the daily fees paid by airlines, either in landing fees or congestion fees. The second congestion pricing round cost the airlines $891,000 per day in congestion fees, corresponding to an average $19 per passenger (assuming a 70 percent load factor). The passengers still suffered $899,000 per day in lost time (unadjusted) or $2.52 million if adjusted. This adjusted cost translates to $53 per passenger.

We now look more closely at each of the policy alternatives.

Passenger Bill of Rights: Congestion was not significantly reduced by imposing a Passenger Bill of Rights. A possible reason that it had such a small effect on reducing delays may have been the reluctance of any one airline to be the first to make significant reductions in their schedule and loose market share. In game theory, this is known as the "Prisoner's Dilemma."

Administrative Decisions: The administrative decisions did lead to a controlled level of congestion but the delay was still relatively high, and passenger throughput was significantly reduced. Had the government chosen an alternative capacity setting each time period, the delay would have been reduced further. But the government's slot-controlled approach is likely to maintain the relatively inefficient use of LGA's runway, gate, and aircraft resources. Specifically, the Port Authority would like LGA to operate at a 30 million annual passengers (MAP) enplanement capacity (i.e., approximately 68,000 seats per day), a number in line with the estimated land-side capacity of the airport. Under current slot controls and a capacity constraint similar to that imposed by the FAA during the game, the airport is operating at less than 27 MAP (i.e., approximately 58,000 seats per day).

Congestion Pricing: Under congestion pricing, the airlines chose schedules that led to a larger average aircraft size (gauge) when compared to the airline response under the administrative measures. Since under congestion pricing, any airline can use the runway for the stated fee, there is no incentive for an airline to pay for slots and then either not use them or use them inefficiently. In this setting, certain carriers with historically large numbers of slots and operations reduced their operations. At the same time carriers with historically smaller footprints at LGA increased their levels of operations. The increase in average

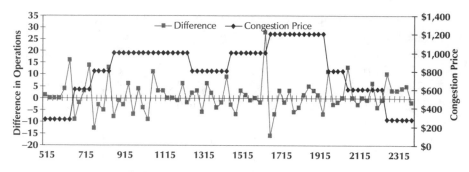

Fig. E.1   LGA flight schedule changes with congestion pricing.

gauge provides some evidence that these changes led to a more efficient use of the slot resources. Congestion pricing increased the passenger capacity of LGA by 9%, compared with administrative measures, achieving the PANYNJ goal of nearly 68,000 daily seats. Figure E.1 shows how the schedule was modified from an administratively dictated schedule (e.g., a schedule very similar to the LGA summer of 2004 schedule). The left axis shows the difference in scheduled flights in 15-minute aggregated time bins. The right axis shows the operational price for each period, set to encourage efficient use of the landing opportunities and to reduce congestion back to 2005 levels. One thing the game highlighted is that the schedules were very sensitive to the times when prices either increased or decreased substantially, i.e., the airlines concentrated flights just prior to price increases or following price decreases. Further pricing changes could mitigate these steep step increases.

Figure E.2 shows the effect of congestion pricing on aggregate airline gauge choice throughout the 24-hour schedule. Overall gauge is

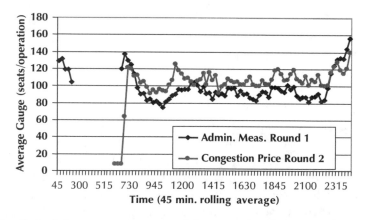

Fig. E.2   Schedule average gauge in Administrative Measures Round 1 and Congestion Price Round 2.

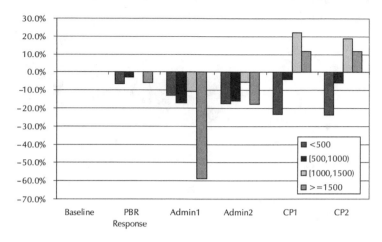

Fig. E.3   Percent change in number of operations by flight distance.

increased significantly at almost all times of the day. Figures E.3 and E.4 show how the schedule was modified by flight distance, aircraft gauge and schedule frequency. Notice that the congestion pricing options produced a complex response by both flight distance and aircraft gauge.

We note that the game invented a hypothetical Pricing Board with authority to set prices dynamically based on schedules submitted (in principle) every 90 to 120 days. The process would work as follows: The airlines submit schedules based on initial announced prices. The Board evaluates the schedules provided, and returns prices to reduce demand in oversubscribed times; the airlines provide new schedules, and the process continues until the capacities and schedules are in balance. This process of determining the congestion prices before schedules are announced to the public results in a pricing approach that is, in essence, a short-term ascending auction for rights to announce schedules at LGA.

More generally the results of this strategic game support economic arguments that market-based allocation mechanisms, e.g., congestion pricing or slot auctions, are likely to lead to better use of the scarce airport resources than the present administrative measures.

We note that the administrative actions could have led to more significant reduction in delays had the administration been willing to set the capacity at a lower level. Thus, one important component to managing delay is the determination of a proper capacity limit. The planned capacity (operations rate) is the most influential control available to determine the level of delays contributed to the NAS by

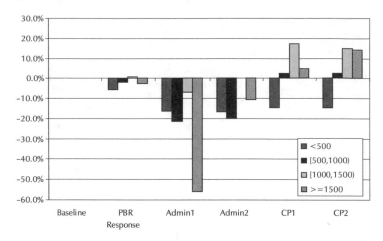

Fig. E.4   Percent change in number of seats by flight distance.

each airport, and the game revealed that there is little policy or consensus providing guidance for trading off delay/unpredictability against unused capacity. The level of schedule predictability is a major public policy issue. Recent over-scheduling at ORD (2005) and JFK (2007) have demonstrated that significant delays at one airport propagate throughout the network. Thus, mis-specification of capacity can lead to significant delays at airports other than the one whose capacity was set incorrectly.

The Second Game

A second strategic exercise took place on February 24–25, 2005 at The University of Maryland. At the end of the first game, the industry indicated that they did not understand auctions and believed them to be too complex. The exercise in February had the industry use combinatorial clock auction software where only price and aggregate demand information was provided to the industry in each round of the auction. Given prices based on time of day, the industry was asked to provide schedules. The industry learned that the auction was not dissimilar from the congestion pricing exercise.

Since the purpose of the game was to illustrate how auctions would work, we only had the industry participate in a few rounds. Therefore, we do not provide any results from this game other than to say that the auction resulted in frequencies and up-gauging similar to those seen in the first game.

Conclusions of the Strategic Exercises

We are not suggesting that the charts and tables provided reflect the final prices or schedules that would occur if these policies were implemented. In each case, only a few rounds were employed. And, as prices got higher, the airlines indicated that they needed more time and their sophisticated scheduling technology to determine their next moves. In addition, they worried that their responses might provide strategic decisions that they were not at liberty to reveal.

One result that we do believe is true: the airlines will be influenced by both the fees they are assessed and by the capacity limitations that the FAA might impose. As the fees increase, the airlines are likely to put slots to their most efficient use, resulting in both up-gauging and frequency reduction. Due to the up-gauging, LGA is likely to find that they handle the same or a greater number of passengers with less congestion of their runways and gate facilities.

It is not clear to us whether a shorter term auction (i.e., congestion pricing as described above) or a longer auction is best for the industry. Shorter term pricing mechanisms require less financing and more ability to move in and out of markets. Longer term auctions provide more stability and thereby more ability to market new locations and services and to invest in infrastructure.

Research to Predict Schedule Changes If Reduced Capacity Were Imposed

A question that came out of these exercises was whether schedules exist that could accommodate actual 2006 passenger throughput at LGA if capacity limits were set at the lower level called for during inclement meteorological conditions (IMC)—a figure determined by the FAA based on the capacity of the runway(s) when instrument landings are required. A second question was: What prices could one expect with such a schedule, given that the congestion price schedules would be at the lowest prices consistent with the airlines maintaining profitability?

In an attempt to determine if such schedules exist, we modeled how a benevolent monopolist airline, representing the best interests of both the PANYNJ and the passengers, might schedule its flights under restricted IMC capacity. The study was undertaken by Loan Le as part of her doctoral studies at GMU. This research project used the same analytical models that the airlines use to generate schedules, determining fleet size based on price elasticities of demand. Two main features characterize the methodology: (a) we model a single benevolent airline instead of individual airlines, and (b) we explicitly account for the inherent demand–supply relation through price. Thus, prices are based on the elasticity of the market based on the competitive environment observed in 2005. In the dissertation [20], Le analyzes multiple scenarios that relax our single benevolent airline concept. The results show that at IMC operating rates, the airline's profit-maximizing responses found scheduling solutions that offer a 70% decrease in flight delays and a 20% reduction in the number of flights—but with almost no loss of the markets served or of passenger throughput. The profitability of the schedule was obtained at prices consistent with the competitive market existing at LGA today. Table E.2 shows the change from the 2005 schedule in terms of aircraft gauge, price, delay, markets served and number of flights. Figure E.5 shows the type of up-gauging that is projected to take place. We find it interesting that the smallest planes remain in the schedule, i.e., those routes are profitable at that size. Where we see the greatest up-gauging is at the 44–50 seat size, and we see the up-gauging taking place at origin-destination pairs that have significant frequency (five or more arrivals per day).

Conclusions

LaGuardia will always be a popular airport with limited capacity. LGA, however, is not the only airport facing congestion caused by scheduling that exceeds runway capacity. There are at least 10 U.S. airports with current schedules greater than their runway capacity, and the number is likely to grow given the costs, long lead-time, and politics involved in airport expansions.

Table E.2   Impact of Simulated Pricing for IMC Operations at LGA

Metrics	Baseline	Flight schedule at 90% maximum profit
Number of markets	67	64 (−4%)
Number of flights	1024	808 (−21%)
Number of seats	96,997	98,100 (+1%)
Average aircraft size	95 seats/AC	121 seats/AC (+27%)
Average fare	$139	$134
Average flight delay	19 minutes	5 minutes (−72%)

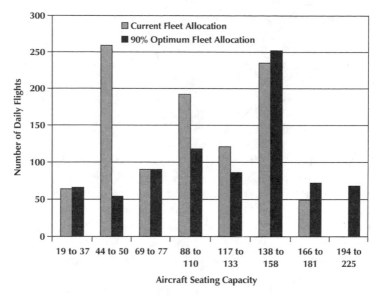

Fig. E.5   Estimated up-gauging for priced IMC operations at LGA estimate of aircraft up-gauging.

To overcome current and future delays, one must address two issues: (a) How should one set the capacity restriction? (b) How should one allocate that capacity? We believe that DOT should consider policy decisions that treat all congested airports uniformly. A workable solution to this problem is to set capacity at each airport to its IMC rate and to use market-clearing mechanisms (congestion pricing or auctions) to allocate the capacity. By so doing, one would provide passengers with predictable travel, reduce airline fuel and repositioning costs, improve the overall safety of the airspace, and improve U.S. economic productivity.

References

[1] Shaver, R. D. and G. Donohue, "Air Travel at the Edge of Chaos: How US Air Travel has Deteriorated and How to Fix It," GMU Center for Air Transportation Systems Research Position Paper, 2008, forthcoming.

[2] Donohue, G. and R. Shaver, *Terminal Chaos: Why U.S. Air Travel is Broken and How to Fix It*, book forthcoming in spring 2008 by American Institute of Aeronautics and Astronautics.

[3] Wang, D. "Methods for Analysis of Passenger Trip Performance in a Complex Networked Transportation System," Ph.D. Dissertation, George Mason University, summer 2007.

[4] T. Litman (2006), "London Congestion Pricing: Implications for Other Cities," Victoria Transport Policy Institute, Tech. Rept., January 10.

[5] T. Tretvik (2003), *Acceptability of Transport Pricing Strategies*. Pergamon, Elsevier Ltd., ch. Urban Road Pricing in Norway: Public Acceptability and Travel Behavior.

[6] C. Keong (2001), "Road Pricing: Singapore's Experience," in 3rd Seminar of the IMPRINT EUROPE Thematic Network: "Implementing Reform on Transport Pricing: Constraints and Solutions: Learning from Best Practice," Brussels, October 23–24.

[7] J. Daniel (1992), "Peak-Load-Congestion Pricing and Optimal Capacity of Large Hub Airports: With Application to the Minneapolis St. Paul Airport," Ph.D. Dissertation, University of Minnesota.

[8] E. Pels and E. Verhoef (2003), "The Economics of Airport Congestion Pricing," Tinbergen Institute Discussion Paper No. 03-083/3, Amsterdam, The Netherlands, Tech. Rept., October 10.

[9] T. P. Fan and A. R. Odoni (2001), "The Potential of Demand Management as a Short-Term Means of Relieving Airport Congestion," in Proceedings of EUROCONTROL-FAA Air Traffic Management R&D Review Seminar, Santa Fe, NM.

[10] J. Schank (2005), "Solving Airside Airport Congestion: Why Peak Runway Pricing is Not Working," *Journal of Air Transport Management*, vol. 11, pp. 417–425.

[11] F. Berardino (2004), "Alternative to the High-Density Rule at LaGuardia," GRA Report.

[12] P. Milgrom (2004), *Putting Auction Theory to Work*. Cambridge University Press.

[13] D. Grether, M. Isaac, and C. Plott (1979), "Alternative Methods of Allocating Airport Slots: Performance and Evaluation," Pasadena: Polynomics Research Laboratories, Inc., Tech. Rept., January.

[14] S. Rassenti, V. Smith, and R. Bulfin (1982), "A Combinatorial Auction Mechanism for Airport Time Slot Allocation," *Bell Journal of Economics*, Vol. 12, No. 2, pp. 402–417.

[15] DotEcon Ltd (2001), "Auctioning Airport Slots: A Report for HM Treasury and the Department of the Environment, Transport and the Regions," London, Tech. Rept., January.

[16] National Economic Research Associates (NERA) (2004), "Study to Assess the Effects of Different Slot Allocation Schemes," London, Tech. Rept., January.

[17] M. O. Ball, G. L. Donohue, and K. Hoffman (2005), "Auctions for the Safe, Efficient and Equitable Allocation of Airspace System Resources," Chapter 17 of *Combinatorial Auctions*. Cramton, P., Y. Shoham, and R. Steinberg (eds.) MIT Press.

[18] D. Lovell, A. Chuchell, A. Odonoi, A. Mukherjee, and M. Ball (2003), "Calibrating Aggregate Models of Flight Delays and Cancellation Probabilities at Individual Airports," Conference on Air Traffic Management, EuroControl.

[19] M. Ball, K. Hoffman, G. Donohue, P. Railsback, D. Wang, L. Le, D. Dovell, and A. Mukherjee (2005), "Interim Report: The Passenger Bill of Rights Game, FAA Congestion Management Game 1 Report," NEXTOR Report, Tech. Rept. NR-2005-01, January.

[20] Le, Loan (2006), "Demand Management at Congested Airports: How Far are We from Utopia?" Ph. D. Dissertation, George Mason University, August. http://catsr.ite.gmu.edu.

APPENDIX F

Regulation (EC) No 261/2004 of the European Parliament and of the Council of 11 February 2004

I

(Acts whose publication is obligatory)

REGULATION (EC) No 261/2004 OF THE EUROPEAN PARLIAMENT AND OF THE COUNCIL
of 11 February 2004
establishing common rules on compensation and assistance to passengers in the event of denied boarding and of cancellation or long delay of flights, and repealing Regulation (EEC) No 295/91 (Text with EEA relevance)

THE EUROPEAN PARLIAMENT AND THE COUNCIL OF THE EUROPEAN UNION,

Having regard to the Treaty establishing the European Community, and in particular Article 80(2) thereof,

Having regard to the proposal from the Commission (¹),

Having regard to the opinion of the European Economic and Social Committee (²),

After consulting the Committee of the Regions,

(¹) OJ C 103 E, 30.4.2002, p. 225 and OJ C 71 E, 25.3.2003, p. 188.
(²) OJ C 241, 7.10.2002, p. 29.

Acting in accordance with the procedure laid down in Article 251 of the Treaty ([3]), in the light of the joint text approved by the Conciliation Committee on 1 December 2003,

Whereas:

(1) Action by the Community in the field of air transport should aim, among other things, at ensuring a high level of protection for passengers. Moreover, full account should be taken of the requirements of consumer protection in general.

(2) Denied boarding and cancellation or long delay of flights cause serious trouble and inconvenience to passengers.

(3) While Council Regulation (EEC) No 295/91 of 4 February 1991 establishing common rules for a denied boarding compensation system in scheduled air transport ([4]) created basic protection for passengers, the number of passengers denied boarding against their will remains too high, as does that affected by cancellations without prior warning and that affected by long delays.

(4) The Community should therefore raise the standards of protection set by that Regulation both to strengthen the rights of passengers and to ensure that air carriers operate under harmonised conditions in a liberalised market.

(5) Since the distinction between scheduled and non-scheduled air services is weakening, such protection should apply to passengers not only on scheduled but also on non-scheduled flights, including those forming part of package tours.

(6) The protection accorded to passengers departing from an airport located in a Member State should be extended to those leaving an airport located in a third country for one situated in a Member State, when a Community carrier operates the flight.

(7) In order to ensure the effective application of this Regulation, the obligations that it creates should rest with the operating air carrier who performs or intends to perform a flight, whether with owned aircraft, under dry or wet lease, or on any other basis.

(8) This Regulation should not restrict the rights of the operating air carrier to seek compensation from any person, including third parties, in accordance with the law applicable.

([3]) Opinion of the European Parliament of 24 October 2002 (OJ C 300 E, 11.12.2003, p. 443), Council Common Position of 18 March 2003 (OJ C 125 E, 27.5.2003, p. 63) and Position of the European Parliament of 3 July 2003. Legislative Resolution of the European Parliament of 18 December 2003 and Council Decision of 26 January 2004.

([4]) OJ L 36, 8.2.1991, p. 5.

(9) The number of passengers denied boarding against their will should be reduced by requiring air carriers to call for volunteers to surrender their reservations, in exchange for benefits, instead of denying passengers boarding, and by fully compensating those finally denied boarding.

(10) Passengers denied boarding against their will should be able either to cancel their flights, with reimbursement of their tickets, or to continue them under satisfactory conditions, and should be adequately cared for while awaiting a later flight.

(11) Volunteers should also be able to cancel their flights, with reimbursement of their tickets, or continue them under satisfactory conditions, since they face difficulties of travel similar to those experienced by passengers denied boarding against their will.

(12) The trouble and inconvenience to passengers caused by cancellation of flights should also be reduced. This should be achieved by inducing carriers to inform passengers of cancellations before the scheduled time of departure and in addition to offer them reasonable rerouting, so that the passengers can make other arrangements. Air carriers should compensate passengers if they fail to do this, except when the cancellation occurs in extraordinary circumstances which could not have been avoided even if all reasonable measures had been taken.

(13) Passengers whose flights are cancelled should be able either to obtain reimbursement of their tickets or to obtain re-routing under satisfactory conditions, and should be adequately cared for while awaiting a later flight.

(14) As under the Montreal Convention, obligations on operating air carriers should be limited or excluded in cases where an event has been caused by extraordinary circumstances which could not have been avoided even if all reasonable measures had been taken. Such circumstances may, in particular, occur in cases of political instability, meteorological conditions incompatible with the operation of the flight concerned, security risks, unexpected flight safety shortcomings and strikes that affect the operation of an operating air carrier.

(15) Extraordinary circumstances should be deemed to exist where the impact of an air traffic management decision in relation to a particular aircraft on a particular day gives rise to a long delay, an overnight delay, or the cancellation of one or more flights by that aircraft, even though all reasonable measures had been taken by the air carrier concerned to avoid the delays or cancellations.

(16) In cases where a package tour is cancelled for reasons other than the flight being cancelled, this Regulation should not apply.

(17) Passengers whose flights are delayed for a specified time should be adequately cared for and should be able to cancel their flights with reimbursement of their tickets or to continue them under satisfactory conditions.

(18) Care for passengers awaiting an alternative or a delayed flight may be limited or declined if the provision of the care would itself cause further delay.

(19) Operating air carriers should meet the special needs of persons with reduced mobility and any persons accompanying them.

(20) Passengers should be fully informed of their rights in the event of denied boarding and of cancellation or long delay of flights, so that they can effectively exercise their rights.

(21) Member States should lay down rules on sanctions applicable to infringements of the provisions of this Regulation and ensure that these sanctions are applied. The sanctions should be effective, proportionate and dissuasive.

(22) Member States should ensure and supervise general compliance by their air carriers with this Regulation and designate an appropriate body to carry out such enforcement tasks. The supervision should not affect the rights of passengers and air carriers to seek legal redress from courts under procedures of national law.

(23) The Commission should analyse the application of this Regulation and should assess in particular the opportunity of extending its scope to all passengers having a contract with a tour operator or with a Community carrier, when departing from a third country airport to an airport in a Member State.

(24) Arrangements for greater cooperation over the use of Gibraltar airport were agreed in London on 2 December 1987 by the Kingdom of Spain and the United Kingdom in a joint declaration by the Ministers of Foreign Affairs of the two countries. Such arrangements have yet to enter into operation.

(25) Regulation (EEC) No 295/91 should accordingly be repealed,

HAVE ADOPTED THIS REGULATION:

Article 1

Subject

1. This Regulation establishes, under the conditions specified herein, minimum rights for passengers when:
   (a) they are denied boarding against their will;
   (b) their flight is cancelled;
   (c) their flight is delayed.

2. Application of this Regulation to Gibraltar airport is understood to be without prejudice to the respective legal positions of the Kingdom of Spain and the United Kingdom with regard to the dispute over sovereignty over the territory in which the airport is situated.
3. Application of this Regulation to Gibraltar airport shall be suspended until the arrangements in the Joint Declaration made by the Foreign Ministers of the Kingdom of Spain and the United Kingdom on 2 December 1987 enter into operation. The Governments of Spain and the United Kingdom will inform the Council of such date of entry into operation.

Article 2

Definitions

For the purposes of this Regulation:
(a) 'air carrier' means an air transport undertaking with a valid operating licence;
(b) 'operating air carrier' means an air carrier that performs or intends to perform a flight under a contract with a passenger or on behalf of another person, legal or natural, having a contract with that passenger;
(c) 'Community carrier' means an air carrier with a valid operating licence granted by a Member State in accordance with the provisions of Council Regulation (EEC) No 2407/92 of 23 July 1992 on licensing of air carriers (¹);
(d) 'tour operator' means, with the exception of an air carrier, an organiser within the meaning of Article 2, point 2, of Council Directive 90/314/EEC of 13 June 1990 on package travel, package holidays and package tours (²);
(e) 'package' means those services defined in Article 2, point 1, of Directive 90/314/EEC;
(f) 'ticket' means a valid document giving entitlement to transport, or something equivalent in paperless form, including electronic form, issued or authorised by the air carrier or its authorised agent;
(g) 'reservation' means the fact that the passenger has a ticket, or other proof, which indicates that the reservation has been accepted and registered by the air carrier or tour operator;
(h) 'final destination' means the destination on the ticket presented at the check-in counter or, in the case of directly connecting flights, the destination of the last flight; alternative connecting flights

---

(¹) OJ L 240, 24.8.1992, p. 1.
(²) OJ L 158, 23.6.1990, p. 59.

available shall not be taken into account if the original planned arrival time is respected;

(i) 'person with reduced mobility' means any person whose mobility is reduced when using transport because of any physical disability (sensory or locomotory, permanent or temporary), intellectual impairment, age or any other cause of disability, and whose situation needs special attention and adaptation to the person's needs of the services made available to all passengers;

(j) 'denied boarding' means a refusal to carry passengers on a flight, although they have presented themselves for boarding under the conditions laid down in Article 3(2), except where there are reasonable grounds to deny them boarding, such as reasons of health, safety or security, or inadequate travel documentation;

(k) 'volunteer' means a person who has presented himself for boarding under the conditions laid down in Article 3(2) and responds positively to the air carrier's call for passengers prepared to surrender their reservation in exchange for benefits.

(l) 'cancellation' means the non-operation of a flight which was previously planned and on which at least one place was reserved.

Article 3

Scope

1. This Regulation shall apply:
   (a) to passengers departing from an airport located in the territory of a Member State to which the Treaty applies;
   (b) to passengers departing from an airport located in a third country to an airport situated in the territory of a Member State to which the Treaty applies, unless they received benefits or compensation and were given assistance in that third country, if the operating air carrier of the flight concerned is a Community carrier.
2. Paragraph 1 shall apply on the condition that passengers:
   (a) have a confirmed reservation on the flight concerned and, except in the case of cancellation referred to in Article 5, present themselves for check-in,
   — as stipulated and at the time indicated in advance and in writing (including by electronic means) by the air carrier, the tour operator or an authorised travel agent,
   or, if no time is indicated,
   — not later than 45 minutes before the published departure time; or

    (b) have been transferred by an air carrier or tour operator from the flight for which they held a reservation to another flight, irrespective of the reason.

3. This Regulation shall not apply to passengers travelling free of charge or at a reduced fare not available directly or indirectly to the public. However, it shall apply to passengers having tickets issued under a frequent flyer programme or other commercial programme by an air carrier or tour operator.

4. This Regulation shall only apply to passengers transported by motorised fixed wing aircraft.

5. This Regulation shall apply to any operating air carrier providing transport to passengers covered by paragraphs 1 and 2. Where an operating air carrier which has no contract with the passenger performs obligations under this Regulation, it shall be regarded as doing so on behalf of the person having a contract with that passenger.

6. This Regulation shall not affect the rights of passengers under Directive 90/314/EEC. This Regulation shall not apply in cases where a package tour is cancelled for reasons other than cancellation of the flight.

Article 4

Denied boarding

1. When an operating air carrier reasonably expects to deny boarding on a flight, it shall first call for volunteers to surrender their reservations in exchange for benefits under conditions to be agreed between the passenger concerned and the operating air carrier. Volunteers shall be assisted in accordance with Article 8, such assistance being additional to the benefits mentioned in this paragraph.

2. If an insufficient number of volunteers comes forward to allow the remaining passengers with reservations to board the flight, the operating air carrier may then deny boarding to passengers against their will.

3. If boarding is denied to passengers against their will, the operating air carrier shall immediately compensate them in accordance with Article 7 and assist them in accordance with Articles 8 and 9.

Article 5

Cancellation

1. In case of cancellation of a flight, the passengers concerned shall:
    (a) be offered assistance by the operating air carrier in accordance with Article 8; and

   (b) be offered assistance by the operating air carrier in accordance with Article 9(1)(a) and 9(2), as well as, in event of re-routing when the reasonably expected time of departure of the new flight is at least the day after the departure as it was planned for the cancelled flight, the assistance specified in Article 9(1)(b) and 9(1)(c); and

   (c) have the right to compensation by the operating air carrier in accordance with Article 7, unless:

     (i) they are informed of the cancellation at least two weeks before the scheduled time of departure; or

    (ii) they are informed of the cancellation between two weeks and seven days before the scheduled time of departure and are offered re-routing, allowing them to depart no more than two hours before the scheduled time of departure and to reach their final destination less than four hours after the scheduled time of arrival; or

   (iii) they are informed of the cancellation less than seven days before the scheduled time of departure and are offered re-routing, allowing them to depart no more than one hour before the scheduled time of departure and to reach their final destination less than two hours after the scheduled time of arrival.

2. When passengers are informed of the cancellation, an explanation shall be given concerning possible alternative transport.

3. An operating air carrier shall not be obliged to pay compensation in accordance with Article 7, if it can prove that the cancellation is caused by extraordinary circumstances which could not have been avoided even if all reasonable measures had been taken.

4. The burden of proof concerning the questions as to whether and when the passenger has been informed of the cancellation of the flight shall rest with the operating air carrier.

Article 6

Delay

1. When an operating air carrier reasonably expects a flight to be delayed beyond its scheduled time of departure:

   (a) for two hours or more in the case of flights of 1,500 kilometres or less; or

   (b) for three hours or more in the case of all intra-Community flights of more than 1,500 kilometres and of all other flights between 1,500 and 3,500 kilometres; or

(c) for four hours or more in the case of all flights not falling under (a) or (b),

passengers shall be offered by the operating air carrier:
   (i) the assistance specified in Article 9(1)(a) and 9(2); and
   (ii) when the reasonably expected time of departure is at least the day after the time of departure previously announced, the assistance specified in Article 9(1)(b) and 9(1)(c); and
   (iii) when the delay is at least five hours, the assistance specified in Article 8(1)(a).
2. In any event, the assistance shall be offered within the time limits set out above with respect to each distance bracket.

Article 7

Right to compensation

1. Where reference is made to this Article, passengers shall receive compensation amounting to:
   (a) EUR 250 for all flights of 1,500 kilometres or less;
   (b) EUR 400 for all intra-Community flights of more than 1,500 kilometres, and for all other flights between 1,500 and 3,500 kilometres;
   (c) EUR 600 for all flights not falling under (a) or (b).
   In determining the distance, the basis shall be the last destination at which the denial of boarding or cancellation will delay the passenger's arrival after the scheduled time.
2. When passengers are offered re-routing to their final destination on an alternative flight pursuant to Article 8, the arrival time of which does not exceed the scheduled arrival time of the flight originally booked
   (a) by two hours, in respect of all flights of 1,500 kilometres or less; or
   (b) by three hours, in respect of all intra-Community flights of more than 1,500 kilometres and for all other flights between 1,500 and 3,500 kilometres; or
   (c) by four hours, in respect of all flights not falling under (a) or (b), the operating air carrier may reduce the compensation provided for in paragraph 1 by 50%.
3. The compensation referred to in paragraph 1 shall be paid in cash, by electronic bank transfer, bank orders or bank cheques or, with the signed agreement of the passenger, in travel vouchers and/or other services.

4. The distances given in paragraphs 1 and 2 shall be measured by the great circle route method.

Article 8

Right to reimbursement or re-routing

1. Where reference is made to this Article, passengers shall be offered the choice between:
   (a) — reimbursement within seven days, by the means provided for in Article 7(3), of the full cost of the ticket at the price at which it was bought, for the part or parts of the journey not made, and for the part or parts already made if the flight is no longer serving any purpose in relation to the passenger's original travel plan, together with, when relevant,
       — a return flight to the first point of departure, at the earliest opportunity;
   (b) re-routing, under comparable transport conditions, to their final destination at the earliest opportunity; or
   (c) re-routing, under comparable transport conditions, to their final destination at a later date at the passenger's convenience, subject to availability of seats.
2. Paragraph 1(a) shall also apply to passengers whose flights form part of a package, except for the right to reimbursement where such right arises under Directive 90/314/EEC.
3. When, in the case where a town, city or region is served by several airports, an operating air carrier offers a passenger a flight to an airport alternative to that for which the booking was made, the operating air carrier shall bear the cost of transferring the passenger from that alternative airport either to that for which the booking was made, or to another close-by destination agreed with the passenger.

Article 9

Right to care

1. Where reference is made to this Article, passengers shall be offered free of charge:
   (a) meals and refreshments in a reasonable relation to the waiting time;
   (b) hotel accommodation in cases
       — where a stay of one or more nights becomes necessary, or

— where a stay additional to that intended by the passenger becomes necessary;

(c) transport between the airport and place of accommodation (hotel or other).

2. In addition, passengers shall be offered free of charge two telephone calls, telex or fax messages, or e-mails.

3. In applying this Article, the operating air carrier shall pay particular attention to the needs of persons with reduced mobility and any persons accompanying them, as well as to the needs of unaccompanied children.

Article 10

Upgrading and downgrading

1. If an operating air carrier places a passenger in a class higher than that for which the ticket was purchased, it may not request any supplementary payment.

2. If an operating air carrier places a passenger in a class lower than that for which the ticket was purchased, it shall within seven days, by the means provided for in Article 7(3), reimburse

    (a) 30% of the price of the ticket for all flights of 1,500 kilometres or less, or

    (b) 50% of the price of the ticket for all intra-Community flights of more than 1,500 kilometres, except flights between the European territory of the Member States and the French overseas departments, and for all other flights between 1,500 and 3,500 kilometres, or

    (c) 75% of the price of the ticket for all flights not falling under (a) or (b), including flights between the European territory of the Member States and the French overseas departments.

Article 11

Persons with reduced mobility or special needs

1. Operating air carriers shall give priority to carrying persons with reduced mobility and any persons or certified service dogs accompanying them, as well as unaccompanied children.

2. In cases of denied boarding, cancellation and delays of any length, persons with reduced mobility and any persons accompanying them, as well as unaccompanied children, shall have the right to care in accordance with Article 9 as soon as possible.

Article 12

Further compensation

1. This Regulation shall apply without prejudice to a passenger's rights to further compensation. The compensation granted under this Regulation may be deducted from such compensation.
2. Without prejudice to relevant principles and rules of national law, including case-law, paragraph 1 shall not apply to passengers who have voluntarily surrendered a reservation under Article 4(1).

Article 13

Right of redress

In cases where an operating air carrier pays compensation or meets the other obligations incumbent on it under this Regulation, no provision of this Regulation may be interpreted as restricting its right to seek compensation from any person, including third parties, in accordance with the law applicable. In particular, this Regulation shall in no way restrict the operating air carrier's right to seek reimbursement from a tour operator or another person with whom the operating air carrier has a contract. Similarly, no provision of this Regulation may be interpreted as restricting the right of a tour operator or a third party, other than a passenger, with whom an operating air carrier has a contract, to seek reimbursement or compensation from the operating air carrier in accordance with applicable relevant laws.

Article 14

Obligation to inform passengers of their rights

1. The operating air carrier shall ensure that at check-in a clearly legible notice containing the following text is displayed in a manner clearly visible to passengers: 'If you are denied boarding or if your flight is cancelled or delayed for at least two hours, ask at the check-in counter or boarding gate for the text stating your rights, particularly with regard to compensation and assistance.'
2. An operating air carrier denying boarding or cancelling a flight shall provide each passenger affected with a written notice setting out the rules for compensation and assistance in line with this Regulation. It shall also provide each passenger affected by a delay of at least two hours with an equivalent notice. The contact details of the national designated body referred to in Article 16 shall also be given to the passenger in written form.

3. In respect of blind and visually impaired persons, the provisions of this Article shall be applied using appropriate alternative means.

Article 15

Exclusion of waiver

1. Obligations vis-à-vis passengers pursuant to this Regulation may not be limited or waived, notably by a derogation or restrictive clause in the contract of carriage.
2. If, nevertheless, such a derogation or restrictive clause is applied in respect of a passenger, or if the passenger is not correctly informed of his rights and for that reason has accepted compensation which is inferior to that provided for in this Regulation, the passenger shall still be entitled to take the necessary proceedings before the competent courts or bodies in order to obtain additional compensation.

Article 16

Infringements

1. Each Member State shall designate a body responsible for the enforcement of this Regulation as regards flights from airports situated on its territory and flights from a third country to such airports. Where appropriate, this body shall take the measures necessary to ensure that the rights of passengers are respected. The Member States shall inform the Commission of the body that has been designated in accordance with this paragraph.
2. Without prejudice to Article 12, each passenger may complain to any body designated under paragraph 1, or to any other competent body designated by a Member State, about an alleged infringement of this Regulation at any airport situated on the territory of a Member State or concerning any flight from a third country to an airport situated on that territory.
3. The sanctions laid down by Member States for infringements of this Regulation shall be effective, proportionate and dissuasive.

Article 17

Report

The Commission shall report to the European Parliament and the Council by 1 January 2007 on the operation and the results of this Regulation, in particular regarding:
— the incidence of denied boarding and of cancellation of flights,

— the possible extension of the scope of this Regulation to passengers having a contract with a Community carrier or holding a flight reservation which forms part of a 'package tour' to which Directive 90/314/EEC applies and who depart from a third-country airport to an airport in a Member State, on flights not operated by Community air carriers,
— the possible revision of the amounts of compensation referred to in Article 7(1).

The report shall be accompanied where necessary by legislative proposals.

Article 18

Repeal

Regulation (EEC) No 295/91 shall be repealed.

Article 19

Entry into force

This Regulation shall enter into force on 17 February 2005.

This Regulation shall be binding in its entirety and directly applicable in all Member States.

Done at Strasbourg, 11 February 2004.

For the European Parliament	*For the Council*
The President	*The President*
P. COX	M. McDOWELL

APPENDIX G

Ten Travel Tips for Road Warriors

It is no surprise to many air travelers: a lot of air trips are not that fast! Figure G.1 tells the story. Counting the time needed to check in and go through security (two to three hours recommended) and the time required to get to and from the airport, air travel of less than 200 to 300 miles simply does not have a measurable speed advantage over land travel in cars or trains. And general-aviation business aircraft now have a speed advantage over the commercial airlines for trips of over 1,000 miles. (The business aircraft used for trips up to 1,100 miles in this analysis was a Cessna 421C eight-passenger turboprop that can cruise at over 220 knots at 25,000 feet. This early 1980s vintage aircraft can be purchased on the used aircraft market, in good condition, for about $400,000. New FAA regulations allow joint ownership of aircraft in 1/16th shares. This is called fractional ownership.) This lack of speed—coupled with the delays, cancellations, and other hassles detailed throughout this book—can make commercial air travel miserable for those who must regularly use it.

Accordingly, the following 10 simple tips and strategies are offered for the "road warriors" to help make their ongoing air travel experiences as painless as possible:

1) For passengers who need to get to their destination on their day of travel, they should not depart after 2:00 p.m. Delays are like dominos and build up throughout the day, turning into flight cancellations in the afternoon and evening. See the temporal trends in Appendix C for evidence of this phenomenon. Check the authors' scheduled flight predictability Web site to see which flight has performed the best. Over 5,000 city pairs are available for review (Fig. G.2).

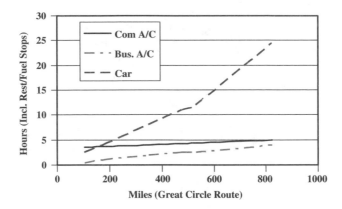

Fig. G.1   Scheduled and calculated trip times (gate to gate) in the U.S. air transportation system, compared to personal car time [authors' calculation].

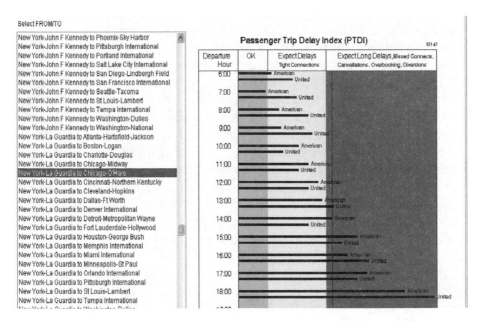

Fig. G.2   CATSR/GMU analysis of previous quarter flight reliability data for New York LGA to Chicago ORD. PTDI for all scheduled flights is shown on the right. See http://www.greenflights.info for over 5,000 flight combinations.

2) Passengers within 300 miles of New York should take the train; it is more predictable most of the time. Passengers who must fly in this area, however, should avoid LGA, and instead use JFK or EWR (but only between 9:00 a.m. and 2:00 p.m.). Islip is a better choice in the evening. Also, passengers should consider using a private aircraft out of Teterboro or White Plains if possible.

3) Passengers should avoid the worst-performing hub connections and the airlines that overschedule them to create the delays (e.g., ATL, BOS, PHL, ORD, EWR, LGA, JFK, MIA). See Table C.1 for airport and airline statistics on the probability of being delayed over 45 minutes, risking a missed hub connection or a cancelled flight.

4) Passengers who must take a connecting flight through a hub should try to fly through Denver, Houston, or Salt Lake City.

5) Instead of always using one of the legacy airlines, passengers should consider using one of the newer low-cost carriers for their next trip. Frontier and Southwest Airlines have the best overall delay and flight cancellation performance in the continental United States.

6) If possible, passengers should schedule flights with a several-day contingency plan, especially in the summer and winter seasons when weather is a known problem. The very high and increasing aircraft load factors are making the system extremely vulnerable to disruption. And cancelled flights, which can lead to a day or more of delay, dump a large number of passengers on an already heavily booked schedule.

7) When not traveling to or from a hub airport and meeting a tight business schedule, passengers should consider chartering an air taxi or having their firm buy into a fractional ownership aircraft.

8) For passengers traveling 400 miles or fewer on a more relaxed time schedule, driving a car will be cheaper and maybe just as fast.

9) Passengers should travel light and never check luggage if possible. This is especially important on the outward leg, where passengers can be stranded for days in strange cities and separated from their luggage. If passengers must check baggage (due to size or weight), they should keep a carry-on with enough clothing and personal grooming supplies to last for several days.

10) Finally, in general, despite what the public might have heard (or read on the Internet), passengers should not schedule their flights more than two weeks in advance. There is usually no price break, and it might even cost more. It used to be common wisdom that scheduling more than three weeks in advance would give a person the best seat selection and the best price, but this is no longer true.

Figure G.3 plots the average fares for all flight options from WAS to BOS (for a booking on 14 August, 2005). Notice that there are no cost

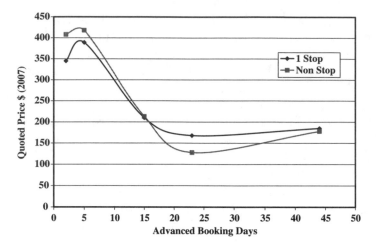

Fig. G.3   Typical price quotes for WAS to BOS, April–May 2007 (346 nautical miles, three block hour trip). Note, no advance booking price advantage beyond 21 days.

savings for flights scheduled more than 14–21 days in advance and that the price can actually increase for +60-day bookings. These advanced bookings are for nonrefundable tickets and decrease a passenger's travel flexibility at no cost advantage. Figures G.4 and G.5 show the same trends for PHL and ORD.

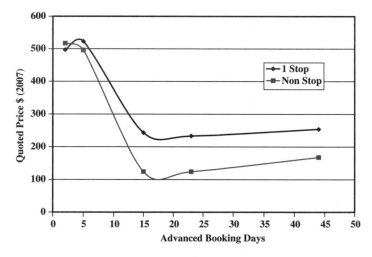

Fig. G.4   Typical price quotes for WAS to PHL, April–May 2007 (103 nautical miles, three block hour trip). Note that most travelers can drive or take the train almost as fast and at much less cost.

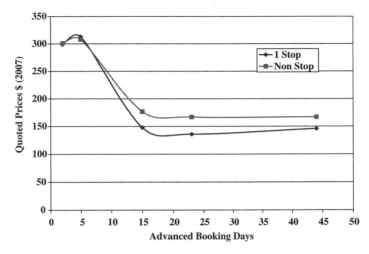

Fig. G.5 Typical price quotes for WAS to ORD, April–May 2007 (530 nautical miles, four block hour trip).

The airline's yield management practices are adjusting ticket prices hourly in the last several weeks before departure, and the advent of the low-cost carrier has made air travel a commodity purchase. The authors thus recommend using www.kayak.com, www.sidestep.com, or www.cheapflights.com booking aggregator search engines to find the best deal on a flight and all of the available combinations. Of course, there are exceptions to this rule. They include advanced booking of 1) flights that are scheduled around typically high-load-factor holidays or special events (e.g., Thanksgiving, Christmas, and the Super Bowl); 2) flights that are part of special promotional sales and have severely discounted fares; and 3) flights that are filling up fast and the passenger cannot risk missing.

APPENDIX H

Why Not 100% Airport Slot Utilization?: Mathematical Justification for Restricting the Number of Allocated Slots at a Congested Airport

It is a good question. If the United States is desperately trying to relieve the growing congestion problem in the air travel industry and there are more landing slots that could be allocated at the most backed-up airports, then why is the air transportation industry not trying to fill them? Is not this kind of like the crew of the *Titanic* not trying to fill up all of the lifeboats when passengers started lining up on the decks (and everyone knows how that travel experience ended)?

This appendix provides the authors' justification for not allocating all of the available slots at a congested airport to airlines seeking access to that airport. There are several obvious reasons for doing so, starting with the observation that some of the aircraft with assigned slots simply will not be able to fill them on a particular day because of excessive delays at their *departure* airport. The most compelling reason for holding some slots open for unscheduled arrivals, however, is to yield the least negative impact on the nation's economy.

For any specific assignment of the airport's available slots, at least four major economic factors come into play: 1) the lost of potential aircraft enplanements that would occur as a result of not allocated all available slots to scheduled arrivals, 2) the number and extent of scheduled aircraft departure delays, 3) the frequency of aircraft flight cancellations, and 4) the average aircraft load factors.

Because the latter three factors have been described in detail in the main text of the book, they are only summarized in this appendix. The focus here is on describing the first factor and providing a crude measurement of the costs associated with it. Interestingly, these costs **increase** monotonically as the number of withheld slots increases, while the costs associated with the other three factors **decrease** monotonically as the number of withheld slots increase.

Costs Associated with Decreasing Enplanements at an Airport

The costs estimated herein are derived from estimates of the benefits that were lost ultimately by the would-be passenger (and more generally to the nation) when he discovers that he could not get onto an airplane at a price he would have been willing to pay when all of the slots were available. The estimate also assumes that the reduction in landing slots reduces the number of airplanes flying to that airport, allowing the airlines to raise their ticket prices and still fill their planes. Situations of this sort are generally clumped together in elementary economic textbooks under the title "Lost Consumer Surplus."

Figure H.1 helps explain to those unfamiliar with consumer surplus why it is a useful tool in assessing costs in this situation and how it is calculated. The curved line—starting at point C at the right-hand side

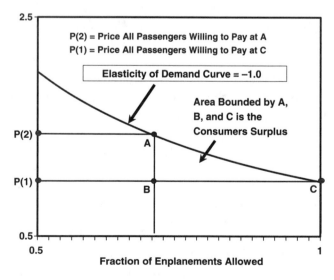

Fig. H.1 Consumer surplus graphic.

of the graph and tilting upward toward the left—is the assumed passengers' cost-indifference curve. The would-be passengers are lined up along the ordinate, with those least able or willing to pay at the right and the most able or willing to pay on the left. Note that (if the airline's ticket price is shown along the abscissa) the higher the ticket price, the lower number of would-be passengers who view flying as worthwhile.

In essence, the cost-indifference curve represents the value to the customer along the ordinate of flying (i.e., it is the maximum price that the passenger is willing to pay). If the airline sets its ticket price lower, this customer would still get the value of being able to fly, but at a price lower than his value. The difference between the two is the "excess" value he gets because of the cheap ticket, and he is now free to take his excess money and buy a fancier dinner at his destination, rent a zippier car, etc.

Still looking at the figure, assume that P1 is the price that the airline will charge when all of the landing slots are available. If the fraction of landings is reduced to a lower number (indicated by line A-B), the airlines will raise the prices to a higher level (as determined by what the competition will allow). That higher level will reduce the implicit consumer surplus that is bounded by the points A-B-C. It represents the difference between line P(1) and the cost-indifference curve, integrated over the distance from the line B to C.

To actually calculate a cost, one needs to know the costs along the indifference curve between points B and C. For simplicity (and this is just a rough example), one can use a curve with an elasticity of -1. In actuality, of course, the elasticizes of flyers vary above and below this figure. It is lower for the typical business traveler (although this might be changing somewhat as business jets become ever more cost-competitive) and larger for the leisure passenger (who, after all, has to take the cost out of his own pocket). Nonetheless, an elasticity of -1 is a reasonable assumption on the whole.

Of course, reductions in enplanements imply negative impacts on those parts of the economy that benefit from the public use of air travel. The authors have not attempted to determine these additional costs but, instead, have simply multiplied the direct consumer surplus lost estimate by a factor of three.

The authors now turn to addressing the issue of 1) emplanements lost and 2) the resulting economic burden on the economy. To start, it is important to understand that cutbacks on operations at busy airports need to be enforced across all congested airports. As reiterated throughout this book, without uniform reductions at the busiest airports, those that are the most congested will simply send more delayed flights into the rest of the airports, causing a degree of chaos if the arriving planes

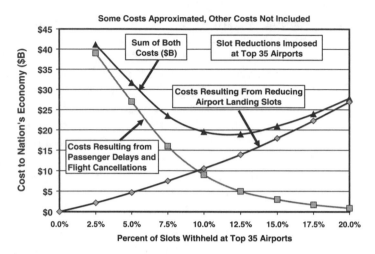

Fig. H.2   Overall cost of congestion as a function of the reduction in the number of available schedule slots at the top 35 airports.

cannot meet their scheduled slot times. So, one has to look at cutbacks at all major airports to **reduce** their operations to levels that were below the airports' stated capacities.

Figure H.2 shows the reduction needed for the top 35 airports as a function that the reduction imposed. (A more detailed study would, no doubt, exempt some of these 35 airports from slot reductions. Hence, the results are slightly pessimistic.) Of particular interest to policy analysts is that the sum of the two prominent costs has a minimum near 90%. In other words, **under optimum circumstances about 10% of the slots at the airports should be set aside to handle unscheduled arrivals**. And, as discussed in Appendix D, these unallocated slots should be scattered more or less uniformly, as is consistent with the scheduled arrival slot times.

Additionally, as more and more airports become crowded, the optimum number of slots withheld will change somewhat. (With few exceptions, projections of U.S. major airports show growth rates in operations and enplanements over the next two decades that exceed expected airport improvements.) Moreover, the optimum shown on Fig. H.2 is a summary of the top 35 airports. It is, of course, likely that the optimum slot allocation percentages will vary from airport to airport, but such specificity is beyond the general nature of this simple calculation.

Finally, note that these "costs" only include a crude estimate of costs related to the aviation industry and its importance to the nation's economy. A broader, more robust assessment of these broader costs could modify the degree to which slots should be withheld.

Author Biographies

George L. Donohue is currently a professor of systems engineering and operations research and director of the Center for Air Transportation Systems Research at George Mason University, Fairfax, Virginia. He is also a codirector of the FAA National Center of Excellence for Operations Research (NEXTOR). Donohue was formerly the associate administrator for research and acquisitions in the Federal Aviation Administration (1994–1998) and has broad experience in managing major research and technology programs in both the public and private sector. Before joining the FAA, Donohue served as vice president of the RAND Corporation, in Santa Monica, California, and was previously director of the Office of Aerospace and Strategic Technology at the Defense Advanced Research Projects Agency. He has also held technical and technical management positions at Dynamics Technology, Inc., the U.S. Navy, and NASA.

Donohue has received numerous awards, such as the Secretary of Defense Meritorious Civilian Service Medal in 1977 and the Air Traffic Control Association Clifford Burton Memorial Award in 1998. He has published over 60 reports and articles and is the principle editor of the only reference book on air transportation systems engineering. He has been listed in Who's Who in America since 1992, was named one of *Federal Computer Week's* top 100 executives in 1997, and was also named one of the top 100 decision makers in Washington, D.C., by the *National Journal* in 1997.

Donohue was chosen to head the United States Delegation to the International Civil Aviation Organization (ICAO) Conference on Air Traffic Management Modernization in Rio de Janeiro, Brazil, in 1998. He was also a director of Radio Technical Commission for Aeronautics (RTCA) and was nominated by President Clinton to become the FAA deputy administrator after demonstrating substantial success in replacing the old FAA technology acquisition process and in pioneering personal reforms at the FAA. He replaced 30-year-old air traffic control computers and radar systems and initiated the new aircraft surveillance system pilot program in Alaska. This Alaska demonstration program, now called the *Capstone* Program, has achieved significant success in demonstrating how the new ADS-B technology can be used to safely separate aircraft with much lower air traffic controller workload. He was awarded the Embry Riddle Aeronautical University Pinnacle Award for Outstanding Individual Contribution to the art and science of air traffic control for this achievement in 2007. He is a Fellow of AIAA and holds Ph.D. and M.S. degrees in mechanical and aerospace engineering from Oklahoma State University and a BSME degree from the University of Houston. Donohue is also a pilot, with a single-engine private pilot's certificate.

Russell Shaver is currently a visiting research fellow in the Center for Air Transportation Systems Research at GMU. He was formerly a senior research analyst at the RAND Corporation. He has held numerous analysis and management positions at RAND for over 35 years with that research organization. From 1994 to 2000, he was the chief scientist for policy analysis at the MITRE Center for Advanced Aviation System Development (CAASD) in McLean, Virginia. He holds a B.S. degree in mechanical engineering from Yale University, a MSME and a Ph.D. in applied mechanics from the University of California at Berkley.

Index

Supporting Materials

A complete list of AIAA publications is available at http://www.aiaa.org.